Experiences of War

The British Soldier

JAMES LUCAS

Experiences of War

The British Soldier

JAMES LUCAS

ARMS AND
ARMOUR

It is with joy that I dedicate this book to my beloved wife, Traude, as the representative of those uncomplaining heroines, the Army wives. To her and to all those who 'followed the drum', goes my love, gratitude and admiration for the sacrifices she and they made, on behalf of us, the men of the British Army.

First published in Great Britain in 1989 by Arms and Armour Press, Artillery House, Artillery Row, London SW1P 1RT.

Distributed in the USA by Sterling Publishing Co. Inc., 387 Park Avenue South, New York, NY 10016-8810.

Distributed in Australia by Capricorn Link (Australia) Pty. Ltd, P.O. Box 665, Lane Cove, New South Wales 2066, Australia.

British Library Cataloguing in Publication Data
Lucas, James, *1923–*
Experiences of war: the British soldier.
1. Army operations by Great Britain. Army. History
I. Title
355.4′0941
ISBN 0-85368-893-1

Designed and edited by DAG Publications Ltd. Designed by David Gibbons; edited by Michael Boxall; typeset by Typesetters (Birmingham) Ltd, Smethwick; illustration & camerawork by M&E Reproductions, North Fambridge, Essex; printed and bound in Great Britain by Richard Clay Ltd, Bungay, Suffolk

Contents

Acknowledgements vii

Introduction 1

'Gone for a Soldier' 3
Voluntary Enlistment and
  Conscription 3
Soldiering in Blighty 11
Soldiering Overseas 18

'Bags of Swank' 23
Regimental Pride 23
Discipline 24

Essentials and Desirables 28
Food 28
Sex 31

'I'll soldier no more' 36
Deserters 36
Self-inflicted Wounds 38
The Black Market 39
'Conchies' 40

Combatants 42
Our Allies 42
The French 42
Americans 45
The Red Army 50
Our Enemies 55
The Germans 56
The Italians 57
The Japanese 58

At War in North West Europe 60
France and Flanders, 1939–40 60
Dunkirk 65
Dieppe, 1942 68
Normandy, 1944 71
The Rhineland Campaign and
  Advance into Germany 78

War in the Deserts of Africa 83
Life in the Eighth Army 84
The Gazala Battles: Summer 1942 88
Tank Attack in the Desert 93
El Alamein: November 1942 95
In the Mountains of Tunisia,
  1942–3 96

War in Sicily and Italy 103
Cassino 105
The Gothic Line 110
The Last Push and into Austria 115

War in the Far East 119
The First Campaign in Burma and
  Malaya 119
The Fighting in Singapore 123
Victory in the Far East 127

The Rewards of Soldiering 130
Death 130
Mutilation 131
Captivity 134

List of Contributors 142

Index 143

Acknowledgements

'Before the War' – that phrase which identifies my generation – I can recall only three anniversaries which were commemorated nationally: Armistice Day, Guy Fawkes' Day and Empire Day. The British people did not celebrate any particular year, although within the folk consciousness there were certain, unforgettable dates as, for example, 1066 and 1745.

Since the war the impact of those commemorative days has been diminished. Empire Day has been abolished; the people's celebration of Guy Fawkes' Day has been channelled into joyless, municipally run firework displays and Armistice Day has been converted to Remembrance Sunday. In place of our national days the United Nations has produced international years and we are encouraged to observe those bland occasions. To the mass of the British people they go uncelebrated because they lack national, emotional appeal.

As substitutes for our national days and, in addition to the UN-designated years, it seems we are now to be given national years to commemorate. In 1988, for example, we were invited to remember the anniversaries of the sinking of the Armada and of the Glorious Revolution. If national years are indeed to be the trend, then a year which deserves to be commemorated is 1989, and the 50th anniversary of that fateful year in which Great Britain went to war with Germany. The Second World War, which began in Europe to combat Nazi aggression, spread to become a world-wide conflict. To win that struggle against the forces of evil demanded the total commitment of the best elements of our nation for almost six years.

Arms and Armour Press, decided to commemorate the watershed year 1939, by producing three volumes of reminiscences. One to cover each of the fighting services. It was my great fortune to be contracted to write the Army volume. The publisher's brief directed me to obtain from ex-soldiers anecdotes and stories connected with their life in the Service. As a first step I contacted regimental comrades and ex-service friends. They, in turn, got into touch with other former soldiers. In the second stage of the operation letters were written to regimental and corps journals asking their readers to help. The excellent response from these sources resulted in an extensive correspondence and that mass of new evidence was added to material already in my possession; the product of research on earlier books. Out of that mass of material this book has been produced.

The greatest number of those who contributed were men who had gained something from their time in the Army; others gave the viewpoint of men who resented the loss of the years they had spent in uniform.

This is a book dealing with the British Army and is confined to the men of these islands who served as Regular, Territorial or conscript soldiers. Consequently, I did not invite contributions from men who had served in the Dominion, Imperial or Colonial Forces. Nor, since the Army is, or was, essentially a male preserve, have I sought any memories from those who were in the Women's Services.

During the preparation of this book I have gained a great number of new friends. To all who contibuted go my most sincere thanks for sharing the memories they have kept, unpublished, for five decades. To one particular comrade go my chief thanks; Roy Cooke, a former Alleyn's schoolboy, who enlisted in November 1939, served in Africa, Sicily and Italy and was twice wounded. Through Roy's active help contributions came in from men in his wide circle of friends and made my work easier. I am grateful also to the officers of the Department of Documents at the Imperial War Museum and to the editors of regimental, corps and ex-service journals for their assistance. Also to the Public Record Office and to the Commonwealth War Graves Commission. Thanks also go to the editorial and lay-out team: David, Beryl and Tony, as well as to Sheila and Mandy, my agents. Nor must I forget to acknowledge the research work carried out by Claire, Victoria and Gary Shaw.

James Lucas, 1989

Introduction

The long history of the British Army and the victories it has gained across the centuries might, one would suppose, have given it in the nation's consciousness a prestige to rank with its sister services. This is not so. Consider how the public sees the three services. The image of the Royal Navy is of jolly Jack Tar, with a parrot on his shoulder, a girl in every port and free and easy with his money. The Royal Air Force image seen by most British people is of a laughing, daredevil fighter pilot, taking off to 'bag' a few Huns before breakfast. The images of McCudden, Ball, Mannock and 'Billy' Bishop of the Great War and of Bader, 'Ginger' Lacey, Stanford-Tuck and Peter Townsend of the Second World War are the enduring ones. The First of the Few is now the folk memory of the Royal Air Force.

And the Army? The thin red line topped with steel is perhaps, the only positive image that the general public has. That memory of the Crimean War is overlaid with less attractive ones including the use of the military in the so-called Peterloo massacre, where cavalry were used to maintain the peace because there was no police force. Political activists relish the myth of troops being sent to shoot down striking Welsh miners in the troubled years before the First World War – even though this did not take place. There is a newspaper reporter's dictum that says: if you can print either the truth or a story, choose the story. Critics apply that dictum as often as possible to the Army. They point to the losses of the Great War as evidence of incompetent generalship or bad strategy, but are unable to suggest alternative ways of conducting a battle or fighting a war. The Army, almost from the date of its establishment, has had a poor reputation, and yet it was for most of its life made up of volunteers; men who did not have to be taken by the 'Press Gang' as many sailors were. Regrettably, Wellington, the great military commander, encouraged civilian misconceptions when he said that the mass of the Army had enlisted for the drink. That slur was accepted and was absorbed into the national consciousness, projecting an image of shiftless, work-shy layabouts who would make pigs of themselves in the drink – the sole reason for their enlistment.

The projected image was cherished while the true picture of devoted service was ignored. The belief that men would join up for adventure, love of country or to better themselves through promotion was not accepted by the civilian masses. The Army was held to be a red-coated drunken rabble, drilled into becoming unthinking robots, incapable of reasoned thought and at best semi-literate. The Army's response to its detractors was unhelpful. Aware of civilian hostility the service grew introspective and self-protective. It was a masculine society where self-praise was considered to be ungentlemanly, where modesty was held to be a virtue and the Army made no effort to publicize its positive features or the deeds it had performed.

Lloyd George vilified the Army by expressing the belief that it was made up of cannon-fodder officered by incompetents. Aneurin Bevan expressed the same sentiments during the Second World War. The distortions which they and their like spread are still not dispelled. Yet millions of men alive today are proud to have served in an army which was led to victory in two world wars against foreign hosts dedicated to the military ethos; enemy armies which had been lavishly equipped and which had been commanded by Generals who had been trained for years. Seen from that fresh perspective, the men of the British Army and their leaders were hardly the lions lead by donkeys of popular, political calumny or the hack newspaper reporter's dictum.

Fifty years ago the then Prime Minister, Neville Chamberlain, announced that Great Britain was at war with Germany. The sons of the men who had held the Ypres salient and who had turned the Somme, in Ludendorff's words, into 'the bloody grave of the German Army', were taking up the new challenge. The scions of the men of Gallipoli, of Passchendaele and of Mons had, in their turn, to face the might of an army which their fathers had thought to be defeated and destroyed two decades earlier. More than that; they also fought and defeated two other enemy hosts; those of Italy and Japan.

The following pages are about the British soldiers who fought in the Second World War. In 1939, before the war began, an Act had been passed authorizing, for the first time in modern British history, the calling up in peacetime of men for the armed forces. Thus, to the traditional two-strata military body of full-time Regular and part-time Territorial soldiers was added a third; conscripts who served in every theatre of operations.

The text is made up chiefly of the stories of those who have much to tell but who have, hitherto, been denied a wider audience than their own immediate circle of family and friends. This is therefore a catalogue of memories; not all of battle and death, although these are the most vivid in the mind of former soldiers. The anecdotes are of other situations; of service conditions, of food and of weapons; what the soldier thought of his enemies and of his allies. It is a frequent complaint that my generation uses the war as its only reference point. This is true but hardly surprising because that conflict wrought the most profound changes in our lives. What happened to us as individuals during the war has to be the stuff of our conversations for, as a result of our years of service, we gathered experiences that could never have been gained in several civilian lifetimes.

This then, is the story of the British Army – our Army – as told by the men who served in it.

James Lucas

'Gone for a soldier'

VOLUNTARY ENLISTMENT AND CONSCRIPTION

During the years before the Second World War those who volunteered for the Army, whether on a Regular engagement or as Territorial soldiers, did not all come from one social class, though it is true that most came from the working class which formed the mass of the population. Neither were they one particular type of man, but ranged intellectually from semi-literates to academics. Nor were the reasons for their enlistment the same. Very few of my correspondents said they joined because they wished to serve King and Country. There must be many who did enlist for just that reason, but who would not admit to it either out of modesty or the fear of ridicule, for flag-waving is no part of the British character. Rather than reveal their true emotion they preferred to advance some other, but less elevating motive. The Newmark brothers, for example, claim they volunteered to pursue a hobby. John Newmark:

'My brother George and I were born in Beckenham and decided that it was only right and proper that we should join a Kentish regiment. The 1st Battalion The Queen's Own Royal West Kent Regiment was stationed in India and not only did my brother and I share the same hobby – bird-watching – but we had a common ambition – to visit India. Neither of us had the money to buy a passage. To join the Army, we decided would provide the solution. We decided that only one of us would enlist and the other would follow if service life was agreeable. We tossed a coin. If it came down heads I would join and if it came down tails George would enlist. It came down tails. George became 6342645 Private Newmark G. and spent six months training at the Depot in Maidstone.'

Trevor Parnacott enlisted in the Artists' Rifles, a crack Territorial Army unit, in order to play football. His enthusiasm was shared, so he later found out, by others who were not in the British Army.

'During the advance to Cap Bon, five years after departing to Vincent Square to join the TA, Harry Peacock and myself had a sudden confrontation with a fair-haired German officer. He was an absolute model of the Aryan Hun. Standing to attention he was crying badly with kit and arms laid out immaculately in front of him. I asked him, at Tommy-gun point, "Are you a Nazi?" "Yes, Sir." I asked him why he had joined the Nazis, to which he replied, "Because I wanted to play football." '

Some men felt so compelling an urge to enlist that they walked miles to the nearest town to find a recruiting office. One of these was Jack Brewin, whose service took him to Dieppe, Algiers, Sicily and the D-Day beaches:

'I joined at the age of 17 years and walked a distance of 10 miles from my Derbyshire village to the recruiting office in the County town. I gave my age as 18 in order to enlist and enraged my father on return home when I told him of my action. However, by the time I received notice to join the Depot, I think both my parents were a little proud of me and gave me their blessing.'

Should anyone think that I exaggerated in claiming that intellectuals also served in the ranks, I can quote Charles Morrison, formerly of the Yeomanry and then of the Intelligence Corps, as one of many University graduates who served in the ranks:

'I had been in OCTU when at school and carried on when I went up to University. Mine was not a family with a great military tradition, but both my mother's and father's sides had lost men in the first German War, all of them serving as volunteers in the Army. I saw my OCTU service as a need to keep faith with my relatives. I graduated late in 1937, and found a job in a small market town in Leicestershire. For social reasons I decided to join the TA. The choice of units was restricted to either a company of the Territorial battalion of the County Regiment or else a squadron in the local yeomanry. I became a trooper and I must say our dress was splendid and we wore it at every social function. There was, at that time, a big recruiting drive under way for the TA and a smart uniform jacket with chain mail shoulder-pieces, overalls with coloured leg stripes and clattering spurs all had a great pulling power. The unit began to train up to war standard, but well before it had reached that standard I had been detached and was posted as a corporal to an Intelligence unit. This came about because I had a Degree in modern foreign languages.'

Donald Featherstone was one of the many who volunteered as soon as possible after the outbreak of war:

'Conditioned throughout boyhood by father and uncle's fearful saga of the horrors of World War One trench-warfare, when World War Two broke out I was determined to avoid the infantry and thus Monday morning (4 September 1939) found me queuing outside a Royal Air Force recruiting office. With little to offer I was inevitably rejected and on the following day the Royal Navy displayed the same good sense by showing me off HMS *President* on London's Embankment. On Wednesday, heart hardened to mother's plea to wait and see if they call you up, my target was the Army Recruiting Office at the Drill Hall in Horn Lane, Acton. Business wasn't good that day and I was the sole recruit to be medically examined, attested, given the Shilling and a railway warrant with directions on getting to the Depot at Bovington in Dorset. The train did not arrive at Wool station until about 0300 hrs on a very dark night and the two odd miles to the camp made it a fearful affair for a Londoner used to streets with lights. I toiled on and was then scared out of my wits by the sentry's challenge at the Cologne Road guardroom. There I met my second sergeant of the day and slept on the floor under a single blanket. The Recruiting Sergeant's promise of a black beret was a "come on" – being RAC we were not entitled to such headgear!'

Thomas Burden, who joined the Territorial Army before the war broke out, had another reason for wanting to join up:

'It was in 1938, that a big drive was made to get men to join the Terriers. None of us was all that keen, but then talk started about joining the ARP and the

AFS. It is funny that there seemed to be a straight choice – either the Army or the Civil Defence. I lived at that time in Hoxton and worked in the Aldgate area. All the Jewish boys seemed to join the Civil Defence or the Auxiliary Fire Service. We said that they only joined those so they could stay at home in their jobs if the war came. The men [the soldiers] would go out to fight. None of us wanted to be thought of as a dodger; so we did not join the Civil Defence or the AFS, but the TA. One of my mates was already in the KRs [the King's Royal Rifle Corps] and he had got some of his friends to join him. To cut the story short I joined because most of my mates had. One of the things that encouraged us was that we got paid for drills, we were taught to drive, we had a canteen with prices cheaper than pub prices, we had a uniform to wear and the Army was becoming popular again so we could always get a girl. I misremember now what we thought about war coming. Well it did and we went overseas to France where I got put in the bag in May 1940. I left home in the summer of 1939 and did not get back again until the summer of 1945. Six years was a long time out of a life and I spent most of that time behind barbed wire.'

Others had compulsions stronger than patriotism, love or sport or the influence of friends. The uniform that Kipling described as 'starvation cheap' was another, but more bitter, inducement to take the King's Shilling in peacetime. There was mass unemployment and an unemployed, single man, living at home was an economic burden on his family. The Army would give him three meals a day, work to do and put money in his pocket at the end of the week. Not a lot of money but, with careful budgeting, the thrifty man could send a little cash home. And once a soldier knew the ropes and was out of barracks in the early afternoon, he could obtain casual labour which would bring him in extra cash. To others, service life offered the chance of adventure, of a life beyond the monotony of 'civvy street'. The chance of foreign travel, at a time when a day trip to Calais was a wild ambition, was another lure. There were some whose ambitions did not aspire to such heights. For them the ideal was to stay in the UK at the Depot and to become a permanent member of Depot Company. Henry Jackson recalls:

'I was called up in the spring of 1942, and went to the regimental Depot for training. What I saw there opened my eyes to the way the Army was run. The Depot Company was typical; they were the biggest rogues unhung. They were nearly all time-serving soldiers with years and years of service. You could tell this by the inverted stripes they wore on the left forearm. One stripe was awarded for three years' service, two for five, three for seven and four for twelve. Included on the strength of Depot Company were the sportsmen; those who were good at boxing or football and who would keep up the regiment's reputation in the Army championships. So if you were a good boxer you were in Depot Company and stayed there, living like a fighting-cock and with only a few duties to do. I never knew a Depot Company man to stand guard or do a picket. If some keen sergeant tried to get them on to fatigues they could produce documentary proof that they were medically unfit, incapable of carrying out the duty. So they never did much.

'Nearly all of them had a regular little job which they did inside barracks and which they had been doing, in some cases, for years. Something light, not too hard; like watering the grass strip in front of the Company office or cutting the grass of that strip. There were some who had been excused wearing boots, some who were not allowed to climb ladders, some who were not allowed to bend down. Complaints!! you name them, they had them or had had them. And yet they were as hard as nails and very fit. Depot Company won nearly every sporting event it went in for in the competitions which were run. Those certified crocks would run like weasels, climb like monkeys and never seemed to be out of breath – and yet they all smoked like chimneys, usually freemans [other people's cigarettes]. Once you were on Depot Company you were made. In peacetime it must have been a doddle – but in wartime with rationing it was a lovely little earner. They flogged the rations and could always find casual labour for their mates who wanted to do it. There was a shortage of men, you see, in wartime. The Depot Company Mafia could get you a cushy number outside the camp, like in a little café making sandwiches; somewhere out of sight of the regimental police or other trouble-makers. They knew every lonely widow who needed a bit of male companionship and if there was a window-cleaning round going spare – they knew someone who could fill it.'

There was one group, however, whose inclusion diminished the military in the eyes of the public. In many English magistrates' courts the prisoner in the dock was offered either the choice of enlistment or a prison sentence. I stressed the word English because from correspondence it is clear that the Army was held in higher esteem in Scotland, Wales and Ulster, and that magistrates in those parts of the Kingdom would not have demeaned the Army in that way. The attitude that the service is the natural repository for the rogues and ne'er-do-wells of society still prevails in England; many people today express the opinion that football hooligans should be put into the Army.

The final path to soldiering was compulsion. The phenomenon of peacetime conscription, if one excepts the Press Gang, was not one familiar to the British people. It had been hard enough to introduce conscription in the middle years of the First World War. In the late 1930s government plans for its introduction in peacetime would be certain to meet with hostility and obstruction. Aware of this opposition the government of the day proceeded with caution. In January 1939, the War Minister, Hore-Belisha, announced a national services appeal, inviting men to enlist. The appeal had the support of the Labour and Liberal parties only because they saw it as an alternative to full conscription. The response to the National Service appeal was poor. Plans were made to double in size the Territorial Army and although this was a popular move what the Army needed was a mass of well-trained men, *before* war broke out. Relying upon appeals would not bring in the numbers needed to fight a major war.

Accordingly, on 26 April 1939, a bill was laid before the House of Commons to provide for a 6-month period of military training for men aged between 20 and 21. After that period there would be a liability for a period of 3½ years in the Territorial Army. As a concession, that period of conscript service with the Territorial Army would be limited to Home Defence of the United Kingdom. The War Minister believed that the scheme would bring in 200,000 men to the services in the first year of operation and more than three-quarters of a million men within three years. In effect, by the end of December 1939, 727,000 men had been registered for the services and 4,320,000 by the end of 1941. That was the peak of British manpower resources and thereafter the numbers already in uniform or available for conscription diminished. Efforts to redress the balance by altering the age limits brought amendments to the National Service (Armed Forces) Acts. The lower age limit had already been reduced to 18, and the upper one raised, first, to 41 years and by an amendment brought in during 1941, to 51. There was strong competition between the armed forces and industry for the available manpower resources. In an effort to resolve the problem there was conscription of women to the services or for war work and of young men of military age to work in the mines, 'Bevin Boys'. More than sixteen million men and women were registered for non-military national service during the Second World War of whom 21,800 were conscripted for work in the pits. Yet, at a time when every person was needed to win the war, the country still allowed thousands of men to evade military service on the unprovable grounds that their conscience would not allow them to fight and could permit other men, eligible for call up, to escape from a beleaguered Britain and to go to America. William Summers:

'I often wonder how those dodgers feel now at having betrayed their country. They were nearly all of them from the so-called intellectual, educated classes. The working-class man stood no chance at all of dodging the column, but those others did and it seems to me that they were helped. How could they live with themselves knowing that in the United Kingdom women were being called up and that women and children were being blown to bits in the air raids baffles me. The worst thing is that when they came back after the war they got the plum jobs, often in entertainment or in the universities because the forces were so slow in releasing the men who should have had those jobs.'

The path of the conscript was a simple one. On attaining the age of 18 every male – eventually every male and female – was required to register at the local Labour Exchange. There were announcements in the newspapers so that nobody could be ignorant of the fact that they were required to register. With registration completed there was a wait of about two to three weeks before notification arrived of the medical examination. If you passed this impersonal examination you received your formal letter of conscription together with a rail warrant from the local station to the assigned barracks.

All new intakes were received on Thursdays. At the barrack gate a regimental policeman would direct the recruits to a blanket-covered table behind which sat several NCOs.

'One of these handed out a strip of paper bearing a number. This was your personal identification number – unique to you. You had to remember it because without it you did not exist. Another corporal told you to which platoon you had been assigned and a lance-corporal escorted you to your new home. The huts were called spiders. A spider consisted of a central section holding the ablutions and lavatories. On either side of the central section, so as to form the letter "H," was a sleeping-hut each holding about 30 men. I think we had a corporal in our barrack-room. The sergeant had a small cubicle of his own in the other sleeping-room. The corporal who was in charge of our room showed each man his bed space, told us to put down our civilian attaché case and to come back to the other hut where the sergeant was waiting. When the whole platoon of the new intake had gathered the sergeant and the NCOs showed us the webbing equipment and how the various pieces fitted together. The most important thing we were told on that first evening was that the colour of the blanco we had to buy to keep the equipment clean, was known as "khaki green No. 3" and that "Soldier's Friend" was the best thing to clean brasses. There was a song which we sang in Depot to the tune of *It's foolish but it's fun*. The words were: "If the Germans should invade this land, our bloody mob will make a stand with a block of blanco in each hand, 'cos bullshit baffles brains." How true it was. All the stories we had heard in civvy street that brasses were to be dulled in this war turned out to be so much eyewash. In our mob we polished all our brasses.

'We were marched down to our first meal. Not in the cookhouse but in the shed that we were later to find out was the 25-yard indoor range. That first meal included tea and doorstep sandwiches as well as bully beef fritters. Cutlery was provided for that meal only. We were later issued with our own knife, fork and spoon. After the meal we were marched back to the spider and then, late in the evening, to the stores where pieces of uniform and equipment were issued at breakneck speed. We just about got back to the spider, loaded down with clothing, webbing, boots and kitbag when we were given half-an-hour to lights out. The Army's day was ending and so was our first day in the Army.'

All intakes reported on Thursday because the TAB and Tet Tox inoculations which were given on Friday morning made the recruits unfit for duty for 48 hours. Thus the Army would lose only a weekend – not that it was empty time:

'We felt like death warmed up for those two days and were given an easy time. That is to say we learned how to put the webbing together, how to make up a bed and had a hut cleaning task apportioned. My task was to keep the window sills free from dust. Others had to blacklead the two stoves in our barrack-room. Some had other dusting tasks and some cleaned windows. Every task had to be done every day and done properly first time round. On that first day we were issued with our rifles. There was a great deal of pointing the rifle and shouting bang, bang you're dead, until the Sergeant shouted at us not to be so adjectively childish. He told us it was a "crime", the army's term that covers everything from dirty buttons to murder, to point a rifle at anyone. We were to learn the bitterness of that lesson when one of our intake was shot dead in just such an accident on the 400-yard range.

'The Commanding Officer gave us a talk in the gymnasium and we were given some sort of intelligence tests by an NCO; I think a sergeant. On the basis of matching what looked like wallpaper patterns we were each selected for special training as transport drivers, Bren Gun carrier drivers, mortarmen, fitters, or radio mechanics. Once we got over the TAB, Tet Tox jabs and I think, vaccination, work began in earnest. About that. For some reason a number of men did not want the vaccination to take and put alcohol on the scratches, but they couldn't say why they didn't want it to take. During the first day we were paraded before our Company Commander and our platoon commanders. We were then "processed". This meant that the Company Commander interviewed each man, with all the others listening to the conversation. What had you done in civilian life, who was your next of kin, had you previous military experience –

Home Guard or Cadet Force? Questions like that, intending to make a preliminary selection of those who had had some sort of discipline and those who had not. We were given our AB 64s, Parts I and 2. [The part one was the soldier's identity document recording among other things courses passed and decorations awarded. Part 2 was the pay book, recording monies received.] The officer then asked each of us how much money from our weekly pay we wished to have sent home to our next of kin as allotment. I think the service paid the equivalent sum so the more you sent home, the more the next of kin received. That first day was filled with talks, lectures, tests and a guided tour round the barracks, including a stop off to hear a bugler sound all the bugle calls. For the first week or two the only ones that concerned us most were Reveille, Lights Out and the Fire Call.'

The transition from recruit to half-trained soldier began and ended on the barrack square. Daily inspections and 'crimings' for seemingly trivial offences were part of each drill parade. The ubiquitous term used in the Brigade of Guards was 'idle'. One could be idle on parade, idle in charge of a Bren gun, idle while riding a bicycle – the permutations were endless. Ex-Sergeant Ramsden:

'I never ceased to be amazed at how many men could not match their foot and arm movements. When a normal person walks his right arm swings forward together with his left leg and vice versa. Those kack-handed ones swung left leg and left arm at the same time. It took a long time for some of them to learn how to march properly. Only one man in my experience never learned. I think he was slightly mental. He also had a bad curvature of the spine. He should not have been in the service at all. As the recruits learned the basic drills it was noticeable how more confident they became, both in themselves and as members of a group. Competition between the huts became very keen.'

At the end of six or eight weeks the recruits were no longer raw. A new batch of rookies had come in and the 6-week 'veterans' could go on to special training. Depending upon the arm of service this might be as little as 12 weeks or as long as twenty. Ex-Lance-Corporal Tony Marshall of the Royal Tank Regiment knew that the training would be intense:

'But then, we had been told it would be. In our training camp we learned to do every job in the tank crew. I do not know if this was something done only in our unit or whether it was usual throughout the RTR. In addition to my basic job as the driver I had to learn gunnery and wireless procedures. The driver's job involved a task system. Every day a special check was made on some different part of the vehicle in addition to the standard checks. One day it would be electrics, then the fuel system, hatches, internal fittings, tracks and pins, and so on. We checked everything. Then the sergeant checked what we had done and then the Squadron Commander. It was drilled into us that in battle our very lives depended upon everything in the vehicle working properly.'

Charles Ridley of the Inniskilling Fusiliers described the transition from recruit to a battalion:

'Late in 1942, I was posted from Depot to our Holding Battalion. This was the last stage as a rookie before going on to an active service battalion. I think that in each [infantry] regiment the 7th or 70th Battalions were holding battalions. While I was with ours a new drill was brought in. This was called battle drill and was supposed to make infantry tactics into a standard drill. If I remember right a

Section would stand in single file and each man would shout out what his task was. It went something like "(I am the) Section Commander, No. 1 on the Bren, No. 2 on the Bren, No. 1 Rifleman, No. 2 Rifleman, No. 1 Bomber, No. 2 Bomber, No. 3 and No. 4 Rifleman, 2 i/c of the Section. At that time the EY rifle was done away with and we used the 2-inch mortar. [The EY rifle projected Mills bombs from a cup discharger. The longer range of the projected grenade meant that the bombs were fitted with longer fuzes than the standard 4-second ones.] I cannot remember whether each section had a 2-inch mortar or whether it was one per platoon. After we had named our duties in the section, the platoon commander would indicate the section's objective – say a blockhouse. He would tell us we were under fire and we would all shout out, "Down, Crawl, Observe, Fire." The section corporal would signal with his arm to tell the Bren gun team to move to one flank. Some of the riflemen would move to the other flank. Then we pretended to give covering fire and the bombers would run and pretend to drop grenades into the firing slits of the enemy blockhouse. The whole time that this little action was taking place each man would shout out what he was doing. "I am firing my rifle," "I am moving to a flank to give covering fire," "I am throwing hand-grenades" and so on. From section drills we did platoon drills and then did them by company. Then there were battalion ones, but I do not think that we shouted out what we were doing on the company or battalion stunts.'

From holding battalion the next step was to an active service one. That unit would be part of a division training for overseas service. At that level the emphasis was on route-marching. Most divisions were moved to Scotland where the low mountainous country gave the commanders experience in solving tactical problems and the empty countryside was excellent for training. In time Commanding Officers would receive orders to line the road for a visit by a 'Mr. Lion'. This was one of the pseudonyms for HM the King who visited each Division before it went overseas. Often Mr. Lion would visit individual battalions in training. Divisional Commanders would visit battalions and give little speeches emphasizing the division's splendid training and its keen cutting-edge. Not many Generals talked about the thrill of battle or knocking the Hun for six, although Montgomery did. A great many divisional commanders had fought as regimental officers in the Great War and in France during the 1940 campaign. They realized that war was not a cricket match.

In a flurry of embarkation leaves and with the departure of the advance parties the units would prepare to march out. Their departure might – or might not – be marked by the local civilian population. The 1st Battalion of the Queen's Own was fortunate:

'We left Hawick in Roxburghshire at about 6.30 in the morning. As the battalion swung out of the park where it had been billeted in huts, we were all surprised to see the pavements crowded with people. The population of Hawick had come to see us off to war. Even now I cannot think of that morning without feeling choked. In addition to the ordinary civilians there was the local British Legion branch with its flag, as well as old soldiers with the medals of the First War on their chests, some medals showed service in South Africa at the turn of the century. The Boy Scouts, Girl Guides, Church Lads Brigade and the Civil

Defence – they were all there on parade on that bitterly cold March morning. I remember Hawick, and this goes for the whole battalion; we remember Hawick with the deepest affection.'

Then it was the special troop train and the vast echoing sheds of the embarkation port, often Liverpool. Inside the cavernous halls there would be a controlled confusion of Staff officers and their inevitable lists. Prowling about would be sinister Red Caps, there to ensure, perhaps, that there were no last-minute desertions. Then followed hours of waiting, sitting on a kitbag until the time came to file up the steep gangplank and burdened with kit to edge along the narrow passageways of a ship that smelt of warm oil, vomit and stale food. Down staircases into the hold. There the hammocks would be slung and kit stowed. Then the sudden throbbing of engines and a slight rocking brought a rush to the decks. The handful of civilians walking their dogs in the twilight did not wave back at us. They were probably blasé – how many troop ships had they seen sail on the tide?

Late in the evening the ship would sail out into open water joining other troop transports and the inevitable destroyer escorts rushing about, fussing and giving out the even more inevitable, mysterious high-pitched, peep, peep, peep signals. Eventually, the engines which had been stilled would begin to throb again and the convoy, only part of a larger one, began its voyage. The group of ships steamed quickly away from land. Soon it was only a dark line on the horizon. Blighty was behind. Ahead lay death or glory. 'The British Army', in Fred Jarvis's words, 'was doing what it had always done. Getting ready to fight in someone else's country.'

SOLDIERING IN BLIGHTY

These days we live in a world of constant, day-long entertainment and it is hard to imagine, and nearly as hard to recall, a Britain where the cinema, the radio and the gramophone and not the televison were the principal vehicles of mass entertainment. There was a greater dependence, then, by the public upon staged events: circuses, Tattoos and parades in which the Army played a significant, sometimes prominent role. The Aldershot Tattoo, the highspot of the summer season, as Bertram Mills Circus was the highspot of the winter, was recalled by one former soldier, A. Withey. He pointed out that in the 1930s an Act of Parliament laid down that Tattoo performers, rehearsing or acting for a period of seven days, should receive the same rate of pay as a professional actor. The Tattoos lasted more than seven days in rehearsal and performance-time, but the thrifty government clerks avoided paying soldiers the amount required by law by making Tuesday a rest day. In lieu of full payment the soldier performers were given a single 1/- (5p) canteen voucher. Withey, who recalled that particular example of service thriftiness, also remembered one Tattoo when:

'We were doing the PT display. Someone at HQ had the bright idea of bringing in the Regimental Employed, i.e., cooks, batmen, horse transport men, storemen, etc. Now training had been going on for about eight weeks and no orders were given on parade, only the beat of the drum. You can imagine the chaos when about sixty of us [new ones] joined the parade on the barrack square. We all got took off the display next day.'

Another Tattoo memory is that of Jacky Allen who saw the display, not as a soldier, but as a child, courtesy of the old London County Council:

'This took place in daylight of course and was very overwhelming to us little kids. I remember the marching and the bands and how we all joined in singing when the tune was familiar. I don't think any of us really understood too much about which battles were being fought, but we were overawed by the number of soldiers dashing about all over the place. The thing I have never forgotten and never will was one soldier lying on the ground pretending to be dead, saying to another squaddie similarly "laid out" – "I didn't join the bleeding army for this." When I got home and told my Mother I had seen the "bleeding Army" I got a whack round the ear. I was only going to say that I couldn't see why they were called that as they weren't bleeding.'

In those days, one-day outings were the only holiday for many people. Not until they joined the Army did they see anything else but pavements and buildings. One of them, Corporal Arthur Pickford was grateful to the service:

'My most enduring memory of soldiering was to be in the countryside. It was only a short route march out of barracks and we were in the open countryside. Before the war, as a child, we had day trips to places like Epping Forest or Theydon Bois. We envied the children who were evacuated at the outbreak of war because they would be out in the country all the time while we had to stay in London. I was not evacuated as I was coming up to school-leaving age when war broke out. We left school at 14 in those days. We marched from the barracks until we reached the Downs and there we did tactical exercises and things that taught us soldiering. One thing I really enjoyed was doing the various crawls; all training for close combat and hand-to-hand fighting. We took haversack lunches with us and the cookhouse would send up big dixies of tea. I don't think I was ever as happy in my life as when I was a young soldier on the hills above Boxley. I was sent on a signaller's course once to Eastbourne and for the first time in my life I saw the sea from the Downs outside Eastbourne. I shall never forget it. In my service I saw lots of sights in foreign countries and had some good times. But nothing was ever as good as the first months after I was called up and was doing my training in Kent and Sussex.'

The Newmark twins, pre-war Regular soldiers, confused their superiors as John's account shows:

'In pre-war days soldiers were not permitted to wear civilian clothes for the first two years of their Army life. When George was posted to Aldershot at the end of his training he naturally wore uniform. Not long afterwards I turned up at the gates of the Depot intending to enlist. I was wearing civilian clothes. As I passed through the gates a regimental policeman on duty stopped me. "Hallo, Newmark," he called out, "What are you doing back here? You were posted to Aldershot, weren't you?" I realized at once that the policeman had mistaken me for George, but I was given no chance to explain. He fired another question in menacing tones, "Why are you wearing civilian clothes?" "Young man," I replied, "do you expect me to come here with nothing on?" The policeman, a lance-corporal, was furious. How dare a private soldier address him as "young man". "Consider yourself a soldier under open arrest, Newmark." "I'll consider it," I replied, enjoying myself enormously. The corporal began to turn purple. "Make that close arrest!" he yelled, moving forward and intending to take me to the guardroom. At this explosive point an officer appeared on the scene. He was clearly expecting me for he shook hands and said, "Ah, you've arrived. My goodness, you really do look like your brother. The War Office told me you were on your way. Are you twins by any chance?" "Yes, Sir, we are identical twins," I told him and glanced at the now very embarrassed policeman. "Lots of people mistake us for one another, but we are quite used to it after twenty years." The policeman withdrew quickly, unaware that he would be the first of a long line of military gentlemen who were to be confused and confounded by the Newmark brothers over a period of several years.

'At the end of my six months' training at Maidstone Depot I was posted to Aldershot and reunited with my brother George. We discussed the prospects of joining 1st Battalion in India and soon discovered that drafts of men were posted overseas at intervals. Volunteers for an overseas posting were always in demand and we had no hesitation in volunteering. Nevertheless, it was the best part of two years before we actually went. In the meantime we played our part in the day to day pursuits of the army. We polished boots, cleaned rifles, went on route marches, practised on the rifle range, stood guard and suffered kit inspections, all for the princely sum of fourteen shillings [70 pence] a week. As in all walks of life, sometimes one or the other of us found himself in trouble. When either of us found himself lining up on parade with the other defaulters it was the Provost Sergeant, poor soul, who suffered. He never knew for sure which twin was which, but he never gave up trying to convince both us and himself that he could tell us apart. It was rumoured that we shared our punishments. If one of us was given seven days' confined to barracks, he would do the first four days and his brother would step in and do the other three. As far as we were concerned it was no rumour; it was the truth. Sometimes we varied our tactics by standing in for each other on alternate days, or two days at a time. There was the occasion when, for example, I was sentenced to seven days' detention and the Provost Sergeant took the bull by the horns. He issued a direct challenge. "Now then, Newmark," he bellowed, "Don't try and fool me because I can tell you two apart even if nobody else can. So just watch your step and don't try swopping over with your brother. If I find you swopping over, you'll find yourself on another charge, so watch it." Poor Provost Sergeant. We had already swopped over. He was talking to the wrong one. What little hair he had soon turned grey – then fell out.'

Bert Stubbings recalled the years immediately preceding the war:

'The bugle call, Retreat, was sounded in the middle of the afternoon, whereupon all parades and fatigues ceased for the day, unless you were on jankers. Puttees and ammo boots could be discarded in favour of plimsolls and after all of four or five hours of light drill, the weary warrior could throw himself into his flea trap and the more hyperactive bods would be exorted to " . . . well get into bed or out of barracks". Would that this were the perpetual life of the peacetime soldier. Chances were that battalion orders that night would order you to parade the next morning in FSMO [Field Service Marching Order], after collecting haversack rations at the 6am breakfast. Thereby, you would know that there was a distinct possibility that you were unlikely to see your bed again for a couple of days. This is why the squaddy is so fond of his kip-machine; there are so many absences – and absence makes the heart . . . During those days away you were either going to chase a fictitious enemy across the Downs or have a nice long route march. The pre-Hore Belisha route march is something that will never be seen again. No slinking along the hedgerows in separate sections. Their Whitehall Lordships, in those days, had not heard of Bleriot or Alcock and Brown, consequently, we marched boldly along the open highway in column of fours, each Company led by its equestrian commander. I remember in my Company, one made a point of not being in leading files of the column. Our Company horse was rather sensitive internally and marching behind a flatulant horse is something to be avoided.'

Recruit training, particularly in the first months of the war, was as rigorous as it had been in peacetime as George Webb found. He came from a family of soldiers; his father and elder brother had all served with the Grenadier Guards. Despite the alternative attractions of driving a railway engine or joining the Ministry, George Webb chose to follow his father and enlisted into the Grenadiers in April 1939.

'The training was so severe I wondered at the time whether or not I would "make it", being a country bumpkin, whereas the majority of my squad mates were nearly all hardened city or town types. Part of the training was more like torture, but I came through well above average. I can well remember our first shooting practice, with a .22 rifle. We all had to contribute a penny, which was almost like gold-dust those days, to a pool and the best shot scooped the pool. Well, when our detail got the order to load, then fire, the next chap let drive almost straightaway and the crack or explosion caused me to lose aim and by the time I regained my aim there was a melodious array of all sorts of noises going on around me. I was certainly relieved to hear the command "Ease springs!" When our targets were checked by the squad instructor, the air was most violently blue. It transpired that the recruit lying next to me had fired on my target. He was immediately disqualified and I was promoted the winner, by virtue of having the highest score. Now whether it was my own shots or those of the other chap, I will never know, but it was the only time I won anything at shooting.'

The multitude of Army rules and regulations guaranteed that a soldier would fall foul of one of them at least once. There was one charge which if all else failed could be used to bring a conviction. This was 'conduct prejudicial to military order and good discipline'. Under that all-embracing charge guilt was almost certain and to be guilty meant days confined to barracks answering the 'Jankers' bugle call, the words of the tune being: 'You can be a defaulter as long as you like, so long as you answer the call.' Immediately after Reveille the 'criminal' would have to parade in front of the Provost Sergeant and would be required to return whenever the bugle blew 'Jankers'. Punishment awarded by the Company Commander might be as severe as extra drills, wearing FSMO, or as light as scrubbing out the officers' mess. This was a doddle and usually brought with it a buckshee supper and beer surreptitiously supplied by sympathetic officers. The Guards regiments, being special, had a more ferocious system than other units of the Army. George Webb recalls:

'When one was on a charge, the charge was read out, usually by the Orderly Sergeant in Waiting. One had to say to the officer, "I thank you, Sir, for leave to speak." When that was granted by the officer hearing the case, you could explain the circumstances. However good your defence was you always came away with some sort of punishment; extra drills, CB or extra fatigues. One very educated Guardsman when on a charge was given permission to speak and said, "I am afraid the Sergeant-Major was suffering from a misapprehension, Sir." The Sergeant-Major, not knowing what misapprehension meant, when asked by the officer hearing the charge if it was correct, said "Sir" [implying consent], and the case was dismissed. There were ways of beating the system, of course. In 1941, at Louth in Lincolnshire, we were billeted in an old house, some of us were upstairs and some downstairs. Well, the officer inspecting always started his kit inspections upstairs. After he had finished in the first bedroom, all manner of things; pull-throughs, knives, forks and spoons came through a hole in the ceiling which enabled the Guardsmen on the ground floor to say, "Laundry at the wash, otherwise kit all present, Sir."

Young recruits were always hungry. Despite the regular and large meals which they received, the open air, physical exercises and their developing muscles demanded even more food than the Army would supply. The low pay made it impossible for the ordinary soldier to eat out regularly. The solution was to get FUT – 'Feet under the Table' was the euphemism given to those lucky enough to have a family whom they could visit in their off-duty hours and from whom a meal could be expected. The farther north one went the greater the hospitality, and in Scotland with fresh salmon, venison and pheasant, the lucky lad with his feet under the table lived well and usually on food he had never eaten before. It was a new experience for young soldiers. Despite the most severe rationing and the fact that FUT seemed not to be found south of Watford, there were still opportunities for free snacks. Sunday evening in Maidstone, and for all I know in other towns, too, it was possible to have three teas. The qualification was to be fleet of foot. At about 5 in the evening there were tea and sandwiches in a small mission hall down near the cinema. To sing a few hymns and to listen to the stories of the Welsh clergyman in charge was a small price to pay for stacks of sandwiches and tea. After the last hymn, there was a sharp trot up the hill and into the main street where tea and sandwiches were to be had in another church hall for another session of hymn singing. The last stop was in the Methodist Hall just off Week Street where there was time to relax and enjoy the singing, the sandwiches and tea, because by now it was too late to get to any other 'free issue'. It was not gluttony, just hunger.

Ex-Gunner Wileman was first sent to No. 1 Holding Unit at Laindon in Essex and after retraining was posted to 387th Heavy Anti-Aircraft Battery near Chatham in Kent.

'To begin with the guns were 3.7in. In a heavy barrage the shells, which stood 5ft long from base to nose, got very heavy. When the gun was being fired in an upright position they had to be punched up by hand on which a leather glove was fitted. Life was not all hard work. One day I was ordered to do stoker's work in the cookhouse and, always eager to please, I warmed up the coal-fired, hot water systems so well that hot water came from cold and hot taps alike. I was picked, together with several other men, to attend a course on the Spigot mortar and the new-type Bakelite grenades. I also learned to drive a Guy 15cwt truck, although I was already a proficient driver in my own right having been continually driving since 1934. The mortar course turned into a hair-raising affair. We picked men were to teach young officers how to use the above-named items although we had a CSM with us. It was his job to inform the officer of the procedure to be followed. One morning I was out with my officer using an old tank as a target [for the Spigot mortar] and all went well at first. I explained that should the mortar bomb fail to explode he was under no circumstances to touch it. He told me quite curtly that he was not taking orders from a bloody Gunner and when one did fail to detonate he kicked it. The explosion blew his foot off. After that incident I was returned to my unit to face a General Court Martial, but was exonerated.

'By this time we had been converted to using 4.5in heavy AA guns, beautiful weapons although, of course, weapons of death. Concrete emplacements were built round them. I was now a Quadrant Elevation layer and a Bearing layer. However, should one get caught late going on duty after the alarm had sounded, one had to act as ammunition runner. This happened to me one night. My bed was next to the alarm bell which was the size of a dinner plate. I never heard the alarm and only woke when the guns opened fire. I hurried into my clothes, rushed up to the gun position and as I entered the emplacement the gun fired. The large cartridge case came out and hit the wall about the thickness of a fag paper from me. If I had been only a few seconds later I would not be writing this now. When I got to the gun, visibly shaking, I found that we had a misfire. The procedure for a misfire was to attempt to fire the shell three more times. Then the order "unload" was given and the unfortunate runner (me) had to catch the 6ft shell as it came out of the breach. It was a fuzed and fixed shell which might explode at any second. My task was to run with that dangerous shell for a distance of 100 yards, lay it on the ground and get back to the gun. I reckon I did a mile a minute sprint. Never again was I late for a shoot out.'

Late for a shoot out, Gunner Wileman, may not have been again, but a disregard of orders brought him detention.

'At the Holding Unit to which I was sent after Dunkirk, I was made the Captain's driver and part of my duties was to go into Laindon village and collect the mail for the unit and also for the ATS who were on our site. One ATS girl, named Olive, pestered me to let her drive the Austin, open-top coupé. One day I let her and that was the day that the Brigadier was walking up the hill for a snap inspection.'

From Close Arrest Wileman passed via a Court-Martial into a Detention Barracks and his description gives an idea of how military prisons were run:

'One day the Staff Sergeant had we prisoners running round the parade ground in Full Fighting Gear in mid-July (in the days when we had good summers). We ran for two hours nonstop and then I flaked out. I was carted off to the camp hospital where the MO asked me how I came to be in the state I was.

I told him and next morning there was a heavy tread of boots coming into the hospital and it was the entire camp staff. They were lined up from one end to the other. The MO came in and stood by my bed. He then addressed them with these words: "Through your stupidity this man is now confined to hospital. If such a thing occurs again while I am MO of this camp I will have all of you from the RSM down demoted and sent to a place that is well known to all of us. He meant Barlinnie, the most dreaded Glasshouse. In Detention breakfast was chunks of bread and butter with bromide-laden tea [mythical] to stop the lads getting sexy. The polishing we had to do was mad. The broomheads and handles, the tables and legs had to be made white like driven snow and all brown lines had to be polished with brown, navy issue soap. All metalwork – dustpans, etc., had to shine like silver, but not with metal polish but with a bathbrick, a soft stone used at that time. I was given a latrine bucket as a punishment because the screw said I had not cleaned the corner of one of my buckles on my small pack. I refused to scour that latrine bucket on health grounds. The cookhouse staff in the detention barracks was made up from inmates and they couldn't cook cold water. Cabbage we called boiled gas-capes, for that is what it looked like. I know one thing. I never made a misdemeanour after that.'

According to Trooper Talbot, detention in the United Kingdom was a fearful thing. Somehow overseas it seemed less terrible, probably because of the sunshine:

'I was in the nick in the UK (at Fort Darland) at the time that two screws there kicked a swaddie to death. It was said that he was suffering from TB and couldn't do the drills they demanded. They were court-martialled and sent out of the UK and to Italy. They didn't go to a glasshouse out there though, but were put in some other unit. I reckon that every solder in Italy was looking for that pair of bastards to fill them in, but they were not found, so far as I know. I also did time in the nick near Naples and by comparison with Fort Darland it was a doddle.'

During the war there were many parades and processions: war weapons week, aid to Russia week, Spitfire week and a great number of similar occasions for which the Army produced marching contingents. One memory of what should have been a solemn event was recalled by John Eardley, who was in the second stage of his recruit training during the winter of 1942:

'In late November our CO died and all normal parades were stopped so that we could prepare for his funeral with full military honours. All the recruit squads were tested by the RSM to find those who were best at slow-marching. That group was given intensive instruction in how to march in slow time carrying their arms reversed. Other recruits who were good at rifle drill, I was one of these, were chosen to line the route in the graveyard between the gate and the grave. We had to rest on our arms reversed, a very imposing drill movement. One thing about that is that the muzzle of the rifle should in fact stick in the ground, but the Army naturally doesn't want its guns dirty, so the muzzle was rested on the left boot. The whole contingent was taken by truck to the village where the CO lived. The parade went off well and then there was food and drink for all. The officers went up to the Colonel's house; the sergeants of the bearer-party and the marching detachment as well as us in the graveyard detail, were entertained in the village hall. There was plenty to eat and lashings of drink. You can guess it was a very merry group which came back from burying the Colonel and we all agreed we had a marvellous time. It made a change from our normal routine.'

SOLDIERING OVERSEAS

The duties of a British soldier in peacetime were chiefly confined to garrison duties and/or minor campaigns in Britain's overseas possessions. Infantry regiments had two battalions, one of which would normally be serving overseas while the other was in the United Kingdom. At the end of a certain number of years the UK-based unit would go out to relieve the overseas battalion which returned to carry out home duties in Britain. It was not unknown, for both Regular battalions of an infantry regiment to be on overseas postings at the same time. The Line cavalry, the Royal Artillery and the Royal Tank Regiment were among the arms of service which had no second Line. A unit from those non-infantry arms would go overseas and when their tour of duty was completed would be replaced in the foreign station by a fresh formation. Although there were small British military garrisons in the Caribbean, it was usually to a station east of Gibraltar that a British unit would be posted. There were Army garrisons in those places which were naval bases or which had once been coaling-stations, including Malta, Cyprus, Egypt, Aden and Somaliland, all stepping-stones on the short sea route to the Far East. There was also a long sea route, round the Cape, whose stations included the Gold Coast, Simonstown in South Africa and Zanzibar. According to J. Rowlands, RA:

'Egypt and the bases in the Med were really glorified transit camps in which the outgoing unit would become acclimatized to the heat and living standards of the East. The home-coming battalions would also acclimatize themselves in the Med to the coolness of that area and would make sort of island-hopping progress towards Gibraltar and finally, Blighty.'

Sam Staples, RTR:

'The recruit in barracks in the UK heard a lot from the old soldiers about life in India and could not get out there fast enough to sample the things he had heard about. For most of the rookies this was their first experience of a foreign country and, really, you either loved India or you hated it. There was no half-measure. Either the East got you or it made you sick with the misery all around you.'

H. Penrose, a Gunner, was one who had heard the East a'calling:

'When I was young I heard a song about the road to Mandalay and wanted to see that road for myself. I saw it and stayed in Burma for years. Looking back it may have been the Burmese women that kept me there after the regiment's first tour of duty was expired. My unit moved on to Hong Kong, I think it was. I asked for a transfer to the new artillery regiment that was going to relieve us and it was granted. I did nearly ten years in Burma, including peacetime and wartime service. I loved the place and the people. Like little flowers they were.'

Another man who when he went East heard the call and stayed for years, was the late 'Nobby' Esplin. He sailed for India in 1904 and returned in 1938. With

34 years of unbroken foreign service, he set a record in the modern British Army which will now never be broken.

There exists among many British people a longing for the romance and the majesty of the East. Jack Kelly of the Royal Fusiliers found that:

'The truth was a world away from that. Of course, as a white man in India you were someone of importance. You were looked upon by the Indians as powerfully rich. The natives were so poor that even a Private's pay was unbelievable wealth to them and they did their best to get some of our wages for themselves. As for the luxury of India – luxury turned out to be a stinking hot, bug-infested barrack-room with only a couple of punkahs which didn't cool the warm air but only stirred it. India was cholera, rabies, the misery of prickly heat, flood, fire and pestilence. India meant double guard on every sentry post north of Peshawar, or in Burma where the dacoits were led by the local Buddhist priests. Sex and drink were available – but you had to be prepared to risk catching the pox from the local girls or else go blind drinking the stuff which the locals produced.'

It was the teeming misery of India that affected Don Harding of the Royal Artillery deeply. He had gone East after the war began with Japan and like all the other new drafts was mentally unprepared for what he found:

'When we first set foot in Bombay, on 10 May 1942, the thing that struck us was the extreme poverty of so many of the people; dressed in rags and begging for a living. Thousands were just living in the streets and others in shelters made of palm fronds, bits of cardboard or wood – anything that would form a cover and sited on any bit of space available. Beggars were everywhere, with the most appalling disabilities, stumps for limbs, twisted bodies, blindness, etc., all displayed with beseeching cries for "baksheesh". Very sickening, especially seeing little children lying there with their begging-bowls – and nobody seemed to care. Sadly we soon got hardened to it all and were indifferent to their plight. There was little else we could do.'

If one saw past the misery at urban street and village level, India could be a romantic place. The late Trevor Marshall was a soldier who served in the pre-war days of the Raj and recalled the glory and the panoply of imperial power:

'The things I remember of India were the parades and the troubles. It goes without saying that India was stifling hot and that there were masses of people, far more than I had ever seen in one place together. The streets were packed with crowds of people by day as well as by night. I was serving with the Dorsets. Our regimental cap badge bore the motto "Primus in Indus", the first into India. When we, the British Army that is, left India it was our regiment, as the last to leave, who slow-marched under the arch at Bombay and on to the troopships. So we were the first and last in India. The British had been in India a long time, but we have never been given the credit for what we did there; irrigating the desert, giving them peace and justice and generally defending the country. I was only out East for a short time, but I remember that the military year in India began with a Proclamation Day Parade on 1 January. This was really what I think soldiering is all about. It was brilliant. The British in white drill and topees with puggarree and regimental flash. I felt sorry for the Jocks with their heavy kilts. The Indian

Army regiments were all in full dress – green tunics, scarlet tunics, blue tunics and turbans of all colours each regiment with its own special way of tying it. We paraded for the Proclamation Day Parade on Poona racecourse and the crowds had to be seen to be believed. The boxes in the grandstand were a mass of colour. Of course, most of the spectators were Whites; civil service wallahs, officers and their wives, I suppose. The rest of the year was marked with parades for almost every type of civilian or military brasshat from the Viceroy down to Provincial Governors. We Trooped our Colour and celebrated things like the King Emperor's Birthday, his accession to the Throne and the anniversary of his Coronation. I think that the parades were meant to keep us busy and to keep the Indians impressed.'

The Newmark brothers, whom we have met, had enlisted in order to go to India. John, the surviving twin, recalls their experiences:

'One day a list was posted on the battalion notice board detailing the men who had been drafted to India. My brother and I were among the first in the mad rush to see if our names had been included this time. Halfway down the list, in alphabetical order, we read, Private Nathan J., followed by Private Newberry S. and then, there it was, Private Newmark J., followed by Private Oldham B. But where was Private Newmark G? Why wasn't George on the list? We read it again and again but Private Newmark G. was missing from that list. There must be some mistake, we decided. How could they send one twin to Indian and not the other? We were both dumbfounded, dismayed beyond belief. Could this be a deliberate ploy to separate us once and for all.'

The two lodged protest after protest to higher authorities, all to no avail. John continues:

'One week before the troopships SS *Nevasa* sailed for India, the thought occurred to us that *King's Rules and Regulations,* which had helped us before, could possibly contain a paragraph, or section or sub-section which might help us again. We borrowed the volume from a friend who worked as a clerk in the Company Office and after much searching among the myriad rules and regulations found one particular sentence. We read it again to make sure we had it correct. This sentence stated quite clearly that an elder brother posted overseas could claim a younger to be posted also. We could not believe our luck. I was older than George, but because he had joined the army first the authorities had assumed that he was the elder twin! No wonder they were sending me to India. They thought me to be the younger. So when I boarded the SS *Nevasa*, together with a few hundred other troops for company, I was in a deeply contented frame of mind. True, George was not with me, but I was confident that we would be re-united before long.

'For the three-week long sea voyage I decided to volunteer to serve as batman to a young lieutenant who was also being posted to the 1st Battalion. In those days officers and other ranks rarely mixed in a social sense, but in the unusual circumstances on board ship *en route* to India, sailing into the unknown as it were, a degree of neighbourliness persuaded me to tell the officer my tale of woe concerning George. I did this just before the ship reached Port Said. "Would you have any idea, Sir", asked I, rounding off my story, "of the correct procedure for me to claim my twin brother and have him posted to India?"

"Leave it to me," replied my young officer. "I understand the position and I understand how you feel about it, so just leave it to me. I'll arrange for him to be on the next draft." 'The SS *Nevasa* docked in Bombay in January 1936. Our draft went by train to Secundarabad in the Deccan, from where we marched to Gough Barracks near Trimulgarry, a small village in the back of beyond, far removed from civilization, but for me it was not too far removed from heaven. I was in India. George arrived exactly one month later. I went to Secunderabad station to meet him, even though the station was out of bound to all troops. Precisely because of that I knew there would be nobody to charge me with breaking bounds and nobody on the new draft would be aware of it either. We fell in at the rear of the column for the march back to the barracks near Trimulgarry and I gave my brother an insight into army life in India.

'It's very much better and far easier than back in England," I explained, "mainly because nothing much happens after about 11 o'clock. By then it is far too hot to go on parade or do any work, so as soon as lunch is over everyone goes to bed!" "Goes to bed?" queried George. "Yes, everyone lies down on their beds under the mosquito nets and we all more or less do nothing. It's an afternoon siesta, really, and then about four o'clock when it begins to get a little cooler anyone who wants to plays football or something. In fact I consider soldiering out here is rather like a long drawn-out holiday. We do have parades and one thing and another in the mornings, of course, before it gets really hot, but in the afternoons it's into bed or out of barracks." "Out of barracks? What do you mean?" asked George. "Well, that's the unwritten rule which stipulates that nobody is allowed to mess around in the barracks when everyone else is resting. They don't want to be disturbed. If you don't want to rest, you have to clear out and disappear. I've been out a few times to look for birds and lizards and any other wildlife, but they also find it too hot so there's not much around in the heat of the day."

After digesting this news, George commented. "Well, I think we might go off occasionally. We've come all this way to India and don't want to waste every afternoon in bed." "Yes," I agreed. "We'll certainly go out occasionally, but I am fairly sure after a time you will be perfectly happy to go to bed like everyone else." As we continued marching I asked George whether he had brought his razor with him. "I've brought two. One for weekdays and one for Sundays," he quipped. "Well, you won't need either. Every morning an Indian comes round and shaves you. Furthermore, he shaves you in bed." "In bed?" asked an astonished George. "In bed," I repeated. "He shaves everybody every morning and you pay him a few annas a week, which is next to nothing. And that's not all. Somebody comes round every day with cha and wads." George interrupted. "What are cha and wads?" "Right. Cha is a cup of tea and wads are cakes. He comes round during break time in between parades or whatever's going on. He is known as the cha wallah." George considered this and began to think that India was a rest cure. "Oh, and there's another Indian who cleans and polishes your boots each morning. He sits on the verandah with about a dozen pairs of boots spread in a half circle around him and then puts a bit of polish on each boot in turn. Then he brushes each one and, finally, polishes them with a bit of cloth. Then he collects another dozen pairs and repeats the performance. Then there's the *durzi*, in other words the tailor and the dhobi who does all your washing; so it's all very pleasant having everyone doing all the chores!"

'We enjoyed service life in India and the months flew by. We were there, at last, proud to be serving with the Royal West Kent Regiment in an outpost of the British Empire. We found it hard to believe that our most cherished ambitions had been realized.'

Bags of Swank

REGIMENTAL PRIDE

The most important lesson in the Army's education of its soldiers was that of unit loyalty. Almost from his first day of service the recruit was told that he was serving in the finest regiment in the Army. In time that direction was even more sharply defined in an endeavour to convince him that he was in the finest company/squadron/battery of that regiment. This stress upon unit loyalty was calculated, unceasing and absolutely necessary. In a fighting unit each man had to know that he could depend upon his comrades doing their duty, just as they, in turn, relied upon him. Each formation had its sacred objects. In the heavy infantry the most important and revered artefacts were the Colours: the Sovereign's, symbolizing the unit's loyalty to the monarch, and the Regimental Colour, the focus of unit allegiance. Units that did not carry Colours had their own sacred objects or traditions which bound their members just as closely. In the Royal Artillery, for example, the guns evoked an emotion as deep as any devotion to a flag, and men sacrificed themselves to save the guns from falling into enemy hands. Such devotion as I have described, is an emotional thing. It cannot be measured, weighed or valued objectively. It is a feeling. The peacetime soldiers, both Regular and Territorial, those willing members of the introspective regimental tribe, felt this emotion and knew with absolute conviction that the things they held to be sacred were outward and visible signs of an inward and spiritual grace – the regimental spirit. Conscripts did not, to begin with, comprehend the mysteries of military honour as expressed in Standards, crests and badges and mocked as mumbo-jumbo or bullshit those things which they did not yet understand. Yet most knew what fervent loyalty meant for most had supported football and cricket teams in civilian life and maintained that support in barracks.

An example of how it is possible for a regimental tradition to be created, almost by accident, is that of a battle-cry first heard in Tunisia. 'During the first days of the Normandy campaign we heard our Airborne men shouting "Whohoa Mahommed", when they were about to attack the enemy. Just after I was wounded, the man in the next bed to me was from the Paras. I mentioned that battle-cry. He told me that it had been first used in North Africa. An airborne battalion in the Tunisian campaign was dug in near an Arab village. At some point during the day one of the Arab locals would have a shouted conversation in another village. The Paras soon noticed that almost all those shouted conversations began with 'Whohoa' and that Mahommed was the most popular name. The battalion took to shouting in that way to one another and eventually it was taken up by the Brigade and then by 1st Airborne Division when it fought in France.'

Roy Cooke, an Englishman serving with the 5th Seaforth Highlanders at El Alamein realized the inspirational nature of the pipes:

'Above all the din the sound of the pipes could clearly be heard and even an Englishman can feel proud to belong to a Scottish regiment when he hears the shrill, warlike sound of a pipe tune above all the racket around him. It sounded so incongruous, yet it was just what was needed to keep up one's spirits for what lay ahead.'

An example of pride of regiment is given by John Newmark:

'When I returned to the United Kingdom in 1940, from Malta, I went to OCTU and was commissioned in the Royal Warwickshire Regiment. I had, of course, applied for the Royal West Kents or the Indian Army, but apparently both were full up, so I had to be content with the Warwicks. At some point during 1943 or 1944, I was transferred to the Shropshire Light Infantry, very much against my will. Most of my platoon were transferred with me and we all refused to "dog trot" on parade. We kept to our regulation pace of 120 to the minute – or whatever it was. Furthermore, I refused to wear an SLI cap badge, keeping my Warwickshire cap badge up, despite my CO telling me to change it. One day Montgomery appeared on the scene and congratulated me on wearing the Warwicks' badge – his old regiment – and my CO avoided me, thereafter.'

A demonstration of unit pride was shown by the paratroops who had been captured at Arnhem. It will be appreciated that hutted prisoner-of-war camps are not the places, nor captivity the time, best suited to maintain the highest standard of turn-out. It must also be realized that men in captivity may degenerate and lose that sense of self-pride, unless the military spirit can be kept alive. The Paratroop RSM kept his camp on its toes and morale was high. In the last weeks of the war the camp was liberated by the Americans who were astonished at what met them. In other camps they had liberated indifferently, even casually dressed troops who had rushed to the gates in welcome. Not at the Para camp. On the gate stood an airborne soldier immaculately turned out – boots gleaming, brasses shining and red beret *comme il faut*. Inside the gate stood a Quarter Guard, just as immaculately turned-out, and waiting to welcome the American Army stood the Para RSM. He handed over the camp as if he were handing over a billet to an incoming unit; everything documented and in good order. It was a demonstration of pride of unit, that factor of morale which cannot be measured or weighed, but which has the power to raise the soldier to deeds he had not though it possible to achieve.

DISCIPLINE

Discipline is a regimen seldom lightly accepted. Those who are incapable of disciplining themselves are reluctant to have others impose it upon them. They resist the compulsion of discipline because its demands are associated with discomfort or inconvenience. Certain disciplines enclosed within the military framework, including cleanliness, punctuality and obedience, contribute to the making of a good soldier.

Sergeant Joseph Ramsden, a Regular with more than two decades as a soldier, recalled the recruits who came in as a result of conscription and those who had enlisted in pre-war days:

'Basically, there was no difference in physique between the two types of soldier, Regular or conscript, when they first joined up. Most were physically unfit, with poor muscle development. Proper feeding and regular exercise soon changed them into fit young men. There were many who had no idea of how to keep their person clean. The Army has one crime which it stamps on very heavily indeed – dirty flesh. I have known recruits who did not wash past their ears so that they had tide-marks on their necks. Others who thought that to have a regular bath would weaken them sexually. About one in four had never used a toothbrush and not a few had head lice. Most settled down and kept themselves clean, but there were always a few who would not wash regularly or thoroughly. They were taught a lesson by a means which although unofficial and frowned upon was still carried out. They were bathed in public on the square. The offender would be stripped and scrubbed using cold water and army issue soap. Once was enough for most, but there were a few persistent offenders thinking, perhaps, that they could gain their discharge using wilful dirtiness as the reason. This had happened in peacetime, when one could pick and choose recruits, but it could not be allowed to happen in wartime, and the conscripts who thought they could "work their ticket", as it was called, soon found that they could not. Punctuality was the most difficult lesson that the conscripts had to learn. It was not that they were wilfully lazy, just that as civilians time-keeping had not been as necessary as the Army insisted it was. One way to overcome persistent idleness was communal punishment. The whole hutful of men would be punished by extra drills or parades – and would be told the reason. The offender soon learned his lesson because his comrades would knock it into him. No soldier wants to be an outsider, to be cast out by his hut mates and eventually the backsliders came round and paraded on time.'

Obedience was the third lesson that the recruits needed to learn. It is a common accusation that barrack square drill was intended to produce automata. Thomas Rodney was called up for service in the Ordnance Corps during 1941:

'I could not understand all the screaming and shouting on the square in the UK. It struck me as absolutely unnecessary. In the middle of the Second World War, halfway through the 20th century, we were being drilled as if we were to take part in 19th-century battles. It was all so archaic and so pointless. As recruits we were taught foot drill, arms drill, musketry and bayonet fighting. Our unit was, in effect, a semi-civilian one and we would never be expected to fight. So all that moving about in double-time and time spent in bayonet drill was a waste. It seemed to me that the incessant shouting was intended to reduce thinking adults to unthinking robots.'

Such an accusation is not borne out by facts. The good soldier is one who by disciplined reaction can adapt to the changing circumstances on a battlefield, who can by thinking evaluate the situation and use his initiative. The unthinking or badly disciplined soldier, generally, soon becomes a casualty. There are known cases where soldiers under fire did not fall quickly to the ground as they had been trained to do, but looked for a dry spot on which to lie. Shrapnel and snipers wait for no man. On the battlefield there are only the quick and the dead and those who are not quick are soon dead. Only on the battlefield can the strength of discipline be proven. If it was lacking the unit crumbled and broke, with men moving to the rear without and, sometimes, against direct orders. There were instances when British soldiers had to be threatened with summary execution in order to keep them fighting. The instance of a battalion of 49th Division in Normandy shows how a unit with poor discipline goes to pieces.

On 30 June 1944, GHQ, acting upon recommendation, withdrew the battalion from the line and broke it up. The men were posted to other regiments of the Division. A confidential report by the battalion's commanding officer, who had been with the unit for only a few days, painted a picture of the neuroses which had infected his unit. He mentioned, in particular, self-inflicted wounds, hysteria, overreaction to shellfire and to casualties. In fairness to the battalion the CO pointed out that there had been 350 other-rank casualties in two weeks and that only twelve of the battalion's original officers were still with it, all of whom were junior. The original commanding officer and all the Company commanders had gone. One Company had lost all its officers. The CO, a Regular officer who realized the gravity of the report he was making, stated that the battalion was not fit to take its place in the line and recommended that it be broken up.

Frederick Jarvis of 46th Division recalls discipline reduced to a nonsense:

'In the Canal Zone there was an IRTD whose commanding officer was said to be raving mad. Annoyed at two hills which he could see from his office window he ordered parties of men to be sent out each day in an attempt to shovel away the offending hills and to reduce them to the level of the desert. Not that he was very pleased with the nature of the desert. Its surface was uneven and he wanted it level. To achieve this he ordered men to drag large, coconut-fibre PT mats across the surface. I was called for a guard at Geneifa camp. We were out in the desert along the shores of Lake Timsah into which the Suez Canal flows. There was nothing around for miles, except native villages and a detention camp. The IRTD mounted a pukka guard twice a week over the jailbirds, a guard as pukka as the ones for Buckingham Palace. It was inspired lunacy. Two days before the guard was to be mounted its members had to hand in one set of their Khaki Drill clothing. This was washed and so stiffly starched that the short trousers stood up by themselves. The KD shirt was less heavily starched but still felt like cardboard. The nick Wallahs scrubbed our webbing equipment with bleach and polished the brasses till they shone like burnished gold. We paraded in the IRTD and then boarded lorries which took us to the detention camp. At the guard tent our parade KD and equipment were laid out. We took off the unstarched KD in which we had arrived and laid it on our bunks. We were then dressed in the starched clothing. Each man had an orderly who helped him to dress and who put on his boots and equipment. One man had two mates on the orderly detail who actually carried him to his position in the ranks. He was after being Stick Man. Every guard detail has one extra man in case of sickness. That supernumerary does not have to mount guard and there is keen competition to become the supernumerary or Stick Man.

'On the parade square outside the detention camp we were inspected by lance-corporals, by full corporals, by lance-sergeants, full sergeants, Warrant Officers of all grades and then by the RSM. Now that we had been checked by the lower orders, it was the turn of the officers to inspect us. We were at attention for all these inspections, of course. Finally, the decision had to be made – who was to be the Stick Man. They actually measured the length of our hair – it had to be the length of a matchstick. Then the guard mounting began. Our first movements produced a series of minor explosions as the KD cracked when we moved. March past in slow and quick time – the whole, full ceremony – and all out in thousands of acres of nothing. This was not discipline. This was bull and totally unnecessary bull at that. All the soldiers in the IRTD – excluding the permanent staff – were veterans of battle. They did not need this sort of discipline. It served no purpose and it was bitterly resented.'

Jarvis, who had been evacuated to Egypt from Italy after being wounded on the River Volturno, also saw the conditions suffered by prisoners under detention:

'Each group had a task. One lot had to scour tin cans. A prisoner would fish rusty tins out of a standing water tank and hand them out as the "screw" directed. The group then sat out on the ground unspeaking and scrubbed the rust away using desert sand. Each prisoner seemed to have a quota of tins to be cleaned. When he had produced shiny tins he had to double over to the "screw" and present them. If "Staff" thought that they were not properly cleaned of rust he would issue extra tins – to prevent frivolous claims – I think it was called. At the end of the day the shiny tins were flung into the water tank and left to become rusty again. Another group, I think they were undergoing special punishment, had to manhandle cannon-balls. These were piled up in the shape of a low pyramid. At the word of command one ball would be carried at the run for about 100 yards and then placed in position. The prisoners spent their time demolishing pyramids of cannon-balls and then erecting them again. As an exercise in stupidity it can have had no equal.'

Many conscientious soldiers were upset at the lack of reason in military thought. One of these was Roy Cooke of the Seaforths, who went into action at El Alamein and served throughout the African, Sicilian and Italian campaigns:

'Talking of the so-called pettiness of British military discipline, I can give you a first-hand account of that. After having survived the Western Desert, Sicily and Italy, I was downgraded and transferred to the Royal Corps of Signals in 1945, Heaven knows why!!! The one and only time I suffered the indignity of "Jankers" was through trying to be conscientious and do my job properly. I had been detailed for fatigues in our billet, a seaside hotel and was trying to sweep a staircase that was in pitch darkness. There was an empty light fitting above and I, temporarily, borrowed a light bulb so as to see what I was doing. Before I knew it I was on a charge for removing (stealing??) government property. When my "case" came up I had to admit the charge, but was never given a chance to explain WHY I had removed the light bulb. So I did seven days' "spud bashing" as a reward.'

Essentials and Desirables

FOOD

Napoleon's statement that 'an Army marches on its stomach' is no empty cliché, for food is important to the soldier and is the subject about which he never ceases to complain. The creation of the Catering Corps early in the Second World War went a long way to ensuring that standards were constant and high, although they could not always be maintained on active service, particularly in the primitive conditions of the jungles of Burma. Of course, even the best cooks in the world have to be taught, and the REME unit with which Harold Field served was one of those selected to test the dishes which the ACC cooks prepared and served:

'The Catering Corps was training recruits to be cooks to send them to various regiments and we were the guinea pigs. In our platoon was a typical Cockney recruit who was forever cracking jokes. His name was Alf Norman and he came from Lambeth. One day a very keen Second Lieutenant was on day duty and came round asking if there were any complaints about the food. Up jumped Alf Norman. "What is it?" asked the officer. Norman replied "I have a mouse's head in my dinner with his ears sticking out." "Good God!" the officer said. "So you have. Bring your dinner, Norman, to the cookhouse." He had the Sergeant Cook and all the recruits lined up and didn't half dress them down. When he had finished he turned to Norman and said, "Would you like another dinner, Norman?" "No fear Sir," was the reply, "I might find his flipping body in it." Everybody burst out laughing and even the officer had to turn away and smile. It was an incident I shall never forget.'

The Army authorities, aware of the failure of the Commissariat in the Crimean campaign, had since that time striven for excellence and for a balanced diet. Before the Second World War nutrition experts tested, sampled, and then retested and resampled until they had produced a very flexible rations system for the British Army. These composite, or 'compo,' rations were of various types. The basic one, contained within a wooden box, held rations for fourteen men for one day, for seven men for a two-day period, or any permutation of seven. Under active service conditions biscuits were issued to replace bread, but these were not the jaw-cracking type of popular fiction. They had to be hard to withstand the handling they would suffer, but they were palatable. They were packed in hermetically sealed tins to protect them from infestation, a common problem on active service. The contents of a box of 'compo' might include tins of oleo margarine, sardines, bacon, jam, meat and vegetable stew, steak and kidney pudding, rice pudding, steamed treacle pudding or tinned fruit. There were tins of boiled sweets, bars of chocolate, small packets of condiments and sheets of toilet paper. From that variety of tins it was possible to produce meals suitable for breakfast, lunch and tea. A variant of the standard box was the high-altitude ration, high in protein, for use by mountain troops, and there were other variants for those fighting in abnormally difficult terrain. Aware of the difficulties of campaigning, the nutritions experts produced light and mobile 'one-man packs' with such exotica as cubes of compressed tea, sugar and milk, porridge in small slabs and dehydrated meat and vegetables.

'After one attack, I found the body of a soldier of the Lincolns or Leicesters, and alongside him two one-man packs. Shrapnel had torn these open and had smashed most of the tea/sugar/milk cubes. My unit had had a bashing and the rifle companies had withdrawn to a vineyard where we had dug in. I got a fire going from the canes holding up the grapes, took a little dixie from an abandoned tank and got a brew on. The tea tasted terrible – as weak as the proverbial gnat's; but it was wet and warm and it steadied us for a bit. Then we went back again into the attack and this time took the farmhouses which we had not been able to capture on the first time. We got them this time and in the courtyard of a farm we found empty champagne bottles with a rubber stamp saying "Reserved for the German Armed Forces". The Jerries did themselves proud. We had weak tea; they had champagne.'

It was perhaps in an endeavour to encomize on shipping space that led to the introduction of dehydrated food which was first seen in the Mediterranean Theatre of Operations during the autumn of 1944. Dehydrated beef mince, which came on to issue at about the same time, was acceptable and some soldiers had tasted dehydrated potatoes before the war. Dehydrated cabbage was terrible both in taste and appearance and dehydrated egg powder when reconstituted could only produce scrambled eggs – never the golden-yolk, fried eggs which accompanied chips – the Army's choicest dish. Another culinary horror appeared at the same time – soya-link sausages. They looked obscene – like grey, triangular, skinless turds – yet, inexplicably, there were some soldiers who relished them. Ron Howard found one such phenomenon:

'I was in a leave camp outside Rome just after the war ended. We had German prisoners as orderlies for lunch and tea but breakfast was a sort of buffet arrangement. To help yourself instead of having food dumped on the plate was a real revolution in catering. On the buffet table there were the usual things, bacon, eggs and fried bread and also soya links. The man in front of me ignored the bacon and eggs and took five soya links which he piled on to his plate and which he then ate with great enjoyment. His only answer, when I asked him why he had taken so many was, "Well I like them and nobody else seems to want them." It was widely rumoured that the staunch defence of the German Army in Italy was due to a belief that if they fell into our hands as prisoners they would be fed soya-links. It was their determination to avoid such a diet that kept them fighting to the very end.'

There was another dish which had been with the Army since the desert days and which was issued throughout the campaign in Italy. This was melon and lemon jam. This surprising combination of tastes produced a jam resembling

Polycell in appearance and flavour. The proportion of fruit used must have been one very large melon to one very small lemon, for there was no tang, no zest, no citric sharpness – just a blank, tasteless sweetness that would have defied identification had it not been for the label on the tin.

'In our unit we called it "Herzog's Revenge" and the story went round that the recipe for the jam had been invented in the last years of the Turkish control of Palestine. The Jews there at the time had made and sold a whole consignment to the Turks. When the Turks went and we came in, the Zionists still had warehouses packed with tins and flogged the lot to the British Army. That was the story. It was tasteless stuff but we didn't complain while the war was being fought in Africa. But when the war moved into Italy, we thought that there might be decent jam coming from the UK. There was not and we had M&L dished up at every tiffin. Of course we sent trucks into Alex to buy some of the luxuries we could not get up in the Blue and these included proper jam. But why should we have had to pay out for good jam? It was up to the QM Department to get it for the troops.'

In addition to dehydrated food and compo rations the Army in north-west Europe was issued with self-heating tins of food, but these were not popular. A far easier method of heating food was to tie tins around a vehicle exhaust. Within minutes the cans were boiling hot – ready to eat. Tank crews who carried luxury items such as primus stoves, in their vehicles could and did produce hot drinks inside the comfortable commodious Shermans. Most Royal Artillery units had similar equipment in their portees. Small wonder then, that to an infantryman a deserted or abandoned tank or portee was looked upon as an Aladdin's cave of goodies. Even the most strictly worded Army Orders could not stop the jackdaw behaviour of infantrymen when they came across such abundance.

When it was not possible to supply the forward troops with compo, or in conditions of siege as at Kohima and Imphal, the beleaguered garrisons fell back on the basic constituents of British Army diet: bully and biscuits. Some of the tins of bully bore a manufacturing date showing the contents to be 30 years old. It was an example of Army thrift. Another example of this was the Carnation milk issued at the end of the war. The cases of tinned milk had formed part of the cargo of a ship which had been sunk in Algiers harbour in 1942–3. The boxes had been recovered and the tins were eventually issued to married families in the army of occupation in Austria.

However much the soldiers of the British Army may have grumbled at the rations they received and the scale of issue, there is no doubt that compared with the other armies the British Service was well fed indeed. Certainly, German reports talk in the most glowing terms of the food supplies which were captured in the desert. In Italy, enemy patrols were often intercepted as they returned from raids on British roadside dumps, carrying on their backs boxes of compo ration. The Germans had taken to heart Rommel's desert directive, 'You want supplies? Go and take them from the British. They have enough.' The Americans, too, shivering in their gaberdine uniforms in the depths of winter in the Apennine mountains, and fed on little tins of corn-beef hash and Spam, would visit neighbouring British units hoping to effect an exchange of food. They, poor devils, did not get meat puddings.

To supply the most advanced units, particularly in Burma, air drops were needed. Aeroplanes, usually the reliable Douglas Dakota, would be loaded with boxes of rations, each fitted with a coloured parachute. The technique of airfreighting supplies was described by T. Payne:

'The air dropping was like the parable of the sower. It was accepted that some rations would be lost completely; either they would be inaccessible or else they would fall on Japanese positions. These were the ones which in the Bible were said to have fallen on stony ground or among thorns. But those which fell on our own men not only gave them the food they needed but assured them they were not forgotten. The aircraft was packed with boxes arranged in the order in which they had to be dispatched. The Dakota would groan as it raced along the runway and literally staggered into the air. I was always afraid it would not make it. The flight over the jungle was always bumpy and when we hit air pockets it was like going down in a very fast lift. We would be told when we were approaching the drop zone and when the lights came on two of us moved to the door of the Dakota. We fitted our harness and then took off the side door. A team of "shovers" pushed the packages towards the open doorway and we, the other dispatcher and I, kicked them out. It sounds easy but we were soon sweating with the strain. One experience that always frightened me was when the plane lurched or banked without warning. When that happened we dispatchers would fly out through the open doorway and into the air. Only the harness kept us safe and when the banking procedure was over the effect of the swing would bring us back inside the machine again, and we would hit all sorts of projecting bits of metal as we swung in. It was frightening, sick-making and painful. And we carried out such a run about every third day, sometimes more frequently, depending upon the situation on the ground.'

John Clark described not the food, but the 'bull' associated with the culinary arrangements in a camp.

'I was in the camp at Capodimonte, outside Naples. Towards the end of the war soldiers went home from this place on demobilization. One day a VIP paid an official visit. He was a Labour MP and was something to do with the War Office. It seems that somebody had written to the *Daily Mirror* complaining about the camp conditions. Well, the VIP came and walked into the first dining-room. There were table-cloths, flowers, cruets and all the sort of unusual things we never ever saw under normal conditions. Of course, he was surprised. No more than we were. Outside the hut he was shown in great detail the washing-up facilities and was introduced to every cook on the camp establishment. This was to give the permanent staff time to whip the cloths and flowers, etc., from the tables in the first dining-hall and to put them on the tables in the second dining-hall. At a given signal the MP was invited to go into the second dining-hall where the tables were now properly laid. It was a lovely exercise in eyewash.'

SEX

In the services there was one aspect of human behaviour to which all discussions turned to as inevitably as night follows day. This was sex, known in the Army as 'subject normal'. Talk could begin on any subject. At some point the argument would change direction and 'subject normal' would have replaced the topic originally under discussion. Of course, everyone is interested in sex, but in the peculiar conditions of service life sex was the inevitable topic. In a situation where men were forced to live for long periods in the closest companionship and with scant opportunity for a social life outside their own circle, sex talk was inescapable. It was more than that. It was all-absorbing and often the only subject which could be discussed without a violent argument ending in an invitation for someone to step outside and settle it. Barrack-room language included sexual words of unusual flexibility, capable of being used as nouns, adjectives and verbs; as punctuation or emphasis, capable of shocking with their brutality or of demonstrating the deepest feelings of comradeship. I remember one of my comrades during the campaign in northern Italy looking down at the dead body of his best mate and asking, 'What the ***** hell, did you ****-well go and get killed for, you ****.' It may not have been Shakespeare, but in those oaths there was as much tragedy and love as anything ever written by a poet.

Even formal instruction in the Army was illustrated with sexual innuendo or description by NCOs who were aware that such words reinforced the message. To explain that a correct map co-ordinate was obtained by first using the latitudinal and then the longitudinal measurements, our instructor said, 'Think of it like a woman. You have to get across her before you can get up her.' The 75 Grenade, an anti-tank device, was an especially good source of innuendo. The two halves of the fuze fitted one within the other and were protected against damp by a small rubber tube. On the grenade-firing range when the sensitive fuzes of the Mills bombs had to be fitted into the body of the bomb, there would always be one recruit who would cry out in anguish. 'I can't find the hole, Sergeant," to which the inevitable response was, 'You would if it had hair round it.'

Postings within the United Kingdom took the soldier to parts of the country where something as normally unremarkable as his accent might be considered by the local girls as sophisticated and he, by association, glamorous. Assisted with the power of the King's uniform and the glamour of the big city, and encouraged by the stories he had heard in the barrack-room the soldier would seek to find some outlet for his desires. He was usually to be frustrated by never achieving the full sexual act. The girl had her reputation to consider and was confined by precisely those restraints and attitudes from which military service had released the soldier. She, too, was the victim of social and family pressures. The great majority of the Army must have been chaste as a result, among other factors, of the social pressures to conform to the the contemporary strict moral code. Ex-Bombardier Millett of an HAA regiment stationed in Scotland wrote that the Army was:

'A fine introduction into monastic life with the emphasis on poverty, chastity and obedience. The soldier's poverty being created by rates of pay kept deliberately low in order to restrict him socially. The demand for total obedience resulted in the issuing of lunatic orders by men who had little idea of the consequences of carrying out those orders. The unnatural demand for chastity was enforced by locating men in wildernesses, deserts and jungles, sometimes for years at a time.'

Not all Bombardier Millet's statements are substantiated. When the British Expeditionary Force went to France at the outbreak of war the soldiers were introduced to continental habits and customs. They found, to their surprise, that there were local, municipally run and licensed brothels. The pay of the British soldiers, although low by British civilian standards, was nevertheless princely by comparison with the pay of the French poilu and brothels were quite cheap. Ladies of the town were also available in very large numbers and were cheaper, but they, being unlicensed and therefore, seldom medically inspected, were often infected with venereal disease. There was an alarming increase in the number of soldiers of the BEF reporting sick with the early symptoms of syphilis and gonorrhoea.

The Army was prepared and its reactions were predictable and understandable. It fought back with a campaign at two levels. The first of those was a combination of blackmail and financial loss. Those who contracted VD were classified as having a self-inflicted wound. There was no court-martial as there would have been in the case of a standard SIW, but all the soldier's pay and family allowances were stopped and the wife who asked why was told that her husband had a sexual disease. The fear of VD in those far-off days was not restricted to only the working class but ran through the whole of British society and manifested itself most publicly when the men of the Desert armies came back to Britain at the end of the campaign in Africa. Lady Astor suggested that those soldiers should be made to wear a yellow disc on their uniforms signifying that they had come from an infected region. Although there was an outcry at her words she was only echoing the sentiments of a great many others who felt themselves at risk from the returning veterans.

The other level at which the Army fought back was education aimed at giving the soldiers information on the diseases as well as inculcating a morbid fear of them. Propaganda campaigns conducted by unit medical officers used luridly coloured oil-cloth charts to show infected organs and the degenerative effect of the diseases upon the sufferers. The temporary result after every lecture was a decline in the number of diseased soldiers. When the rate rose again, the power of the cinema was used by the Army to produce and show films using actual medical case-histories to demonstrate the stages of the terrible diseases. The effect was again a drop in numbers; short term only, chiefly because the films being in black and white lacked psychological impact. They could not be related to one's own body. Not until colour films supplied by the American Army were shown, was the deterrent effect longer lasting although, of course, not permanent.

There came a time during the Second World War when it was accepted that soldiers needed a sexual outlet. The idea of brothels licensed by the Army was unacceptable to the Anglo-Saxon mind and indeed, Montgomery was credited, if that is the right word, with having closed down those in Egypt. If a habit cannot be broken or a desire curbed then every measure must be taken to direct it into safe channels. In that effort the American and British Armies, accepting that their soldiers would seek sex, set up PAC centres, the first of which were opened in Italy. In those cheerless little shacks a soldier about to set out on a sexual encounter signed a book and received a condom. On his return to the PAC centre he signed the book again. His penis was then washed in a mild disinfectant and a cream was squirted down into it. If the soldier contracted VD but could prove that he had visited the PAC, his allowances were not stopped and he was not treated as a case of self-inflicted wound.

So determined were the military authorities to contain promiscuity that the Military Police of the American and British Armies were given the unusual authority to arrest each other's soldiers. If they saw a serviceman whom they suspected of being drunk, it was assumed that he had had sexual intercourse and he would be taken promptly to a PAC centre.

'When I was in Naples in the spring of 1944, one of my mates was a New Zealander with a naturally unhealthy pallor which was accentuated by malaria and jaundice. In the Via Roma one morning he and I were stopped by two US military policemen who took his pallor to be a sign of intoxication. We were taken to the PAC and he was given the full treatment. Back in the street again and pretty soon two more policemen intercepted us and he and I went back under escort to the PAC. The treatment he received made him not only nervous but also unsteady on his feet – there was no tenderness on the part of the medical orderlies – and we were caught again before we had reached the NAAFI down near the San Carlo opera house. Back again to the PAC where the only question which the medical orderly could ask was, "How long have you been up the line then?" We caught a taxi back to our billets in Capodimonte rather than risk walking about in the streets full of suspicious policemen.'

The war-time armies serving in the Near and Middle East found no respectable women readily available for heterosexual exploits. In Egypt and Palestine where virginity was vital to a marriage and loss of it was a ground for divorce, no girl intending to marry would be seen with a soldier. The brothels in Egypt's main cities had been closed and the bulk of the Army was up the Blue.

'It was possible to find some sort of relief from women who hung around the great camps which lay alongside the Sweet Water canal and Lake Timsah. I had finished an early morning swim just near Geneifa and lay down for a rest and a smoke under some stunted palms. I heard the sound of a voice and found it was a shepherd trying to cadge a cigarette. Not until then did I realize that it was a girl, not so young any more, blind in one eye, quite grubby and very smelly. Despite all that when I realized it was a girl I really got in the mood. She was quite willing and I did it to her without any protection. Afterwards I called myself all the fools imaginable and sweated blood until the results of the tests came in and showed that I was not infected.'

There were, of course, British servicewomen and nurses serving in every theatre of war, but these were not generally available to the rank and file. The nurses were commissioned officers and the other-rank WRENS, ATS or WAAFS capitalized upon their scarcity value as white women. They were soon to complain once the war ended and the male soldiers in the armies of occupation found partners in every town or village in Europe or Japan. One of the Sunday newspapers at home carried reports of British girls being lonely in Germany and stuck behind barbed wire because it was not safe for them to be out alone. They were alone because none of the ordinary soldiers wanted them. The Tommies were all busy 'fraternizing' with the local girls.

'Fraternization' had been forbidden by Army Order for British soldiers when they first entered Austria and Germany. Fraternization could be defined as any contact between the locals and the military unless for an official reason. Reduced to its illogical absurdity just to say 'Good morning' might be considered as fraternization. It was ludicrous and the Order being unenforceable, was quickly lifted. Marriage, however, was still forbidden and this the authorities were determined to maintain. In time the demand by soldiers to be allowed to enjoy the comfort of the sacraments of their religion could not be denied and marriage applications were entertained. The Establishment did not give way without a struggle and placed a great many obstacles in the way of those who intended to marry 'foreign'. In Austria the General Officer Commanding, wrote in the soldiers' newspaper *Union Jack,* that 'Austrian girls would make silly wives'. The General did not reply to a letter that I sent to him asking how many Austrian wives he had had that he could make so sweeping a judgement. Unable to stem the flood of marriage applications the Army tried to deter the prospective brides by summoning them to interrogations by NCOs of the Field Security Sections where the girls were humiliated by being asked such questions as 'How many other soldiers did you sleep with before getting this one to propose?'

By 'losing' marriage applications, by posting men away from their units and by any number of other means the Army tried to control the flood. One soldier was posted from Austria to southern Italy. He stole a motor cycle and returned to his intended bride. The sentence at his court-martial for desertion and theft was seven years. He was one of many. Another soldier who fell in love with a girl from a brothel in Algiers was sent to a psychiatrist in a hospital in northern Palestine. The military authorities were nothing if not determined to stop the troops from enjoying the new-found peace. They had a difficult task for they were flying in the face of nature.

'I'll soldier no more!'

The imposition of Army discipline produced in many conscripted soldiers a revulsion which could only find its release in their deserting the service, determined never to return. Other discontented soldiers gave thought how they might capitalize upon the needs of demand and supply by exploiting the shortages which are an inseparable part of a war-time economy. By dealing on the black market they would enrich themselves as a reward for the sacrifices they had made. There were again others who on active service, out of fear, deliberately mutilated themselves or deserted from their units for short periods. In Army parlance there were euphemisms to cover the true nature of these deliberate crimes against KRs; the Army's code of laws. In the Mediterranean theatre of operations the term 'Trotters' Union' was applied to those who deserted and who intended never to return to military service. 'Duckers and weavers' were also deserters, but these intended to be away for only a short period after which they would give themselves up, be court-martialled and spend a period in a detention barracks as an alternative to front-line service. The term 'weaver' also covered those who were guilty of a self-inflicted wound. The euphemism 'colour scheme' was widely used to cover black market activities.

In a very amusing paper, the distinguished naval historian, Martin Brice, expressed the view that only in the service was a soldier considered an important individual:

'If a civilian tires of his job, has a row and walks out, what happens? In some enlightened firms a personnel officer may be sent to interview him. I suppose he could be sued for breach of contract, but nothing else is done to him. Nobody even cares if he deserts his family, and in any case, they may not miss him. But if a serviceman goes absent, deserts or mutinies he will be hunted by police and soldiers for the rest of his life, wherever he goes. If he is caught he will be forcibly dragged back, tried and punished. It will be made perfectly clear to him that because of his one personal transgression the whole fabric of military discipline will crumble and the entire war will be lost.'

DESERTERS

Those who deserted in the United Kingdom did not find it particularly hard to submerge themselves into the civilian world. If they were determined to desert the service forever, they seldom went back to their parents' home. Most parents would have refused to help them or might even have informed the authorities. In addition the civil and military police would be watching out for the deserter. He would not find it hard to buy a forged or stolen identity card and to start life again under a new name in a civilian occupation; there were a great many young male civilians to be seen in the United Kingdom.

Once overseas, to be a permanent deserter was more difficult but not impossible. The greatest difficulty lay with mastering the local language and customs. To procure false papers presented no problem for the bribery of officials was accepted as the norm. Short-term deserters on overseas service followed one of two roads. Most allowed their appearance to deteriorate by not shaving or cleaning their boots. Vigilant Redcaps would soon arrest them. A court-martial was the almost automatic next step followed by detention in a military prison. There was no fear of being condemned to death. Execution by firing-squad as a punishment for desertion had been abolished during the 1930s. The rigours of the 'glasshouse' might be preferred to the dangers of combat. The following accounts are by men who preferred not to be named, for obvious reasons.

'In the glasshouse we got three meals a day, a roof over our heads and safety. Up the line we slept in slits open to the pouring rain which fell most of the time in sunny Italy. Food didn't always get to the forward positions so we often went hungry and then, on top of everything else, there was the danger. Time in the nick was hard, but I had had a hard life in civvy street, so whatever the screws could fling at me was water off a duck's back. Some of the men doing time were well off in the moosh. They had got themselves some right khushti numbers: in the cookhouse as orderlies, in the Sergeant's Mess as waiters – a couple were said to have been bumboys to the screws. What did such nick wallahs want with remission of sentence? This was offered to those who had deserted from front-line units, in order to get them back up the line. After about six weeks the prisoner would be interviewed and told his case was under revision. On a second interview he would be offered remission of sentence if he returned to a front-line unit. At the end of the war in Europe this sort of offer was made in most nicks, in the UK and overseas, to bring the drafts for Burma up to strength. The attitude of most of the blokes doing time was that if we would not fight Jerry in Europe we were certainly not going to fight in a jungle against the Japs.'

As opposed to the deserter who attracted attention to himself by his untidy state, there were those who kept out of trouble in the major cities by having shiny boots, short hair and polished brasses, gambling that no Redcap would check a pukka-looking soldier. To maintain that immaculate military appearance was not easy but it could be done. The easiest way was to find a large transit camp and pretend to be a soldier being posted back to his unit. By this pretence there was food, a bed, a NAAFI whack and washing facilities. There was another sort of transit camp through which, so it was said, all the *serious* Trotters' Union members passed, that is those who were determined to desert the service for good while on active service overseas. R. Fairclough, RAOC:

'I was stationed in a Base Ordnance Depot outside Naples. I think the name of the place was Torre del Greco or Torre Annunziata. Our working day used to finish in good time to get our evening meal, be washed and dressed and in unit transport to the big NAAFI by the side of the Opera House in Naples. Our unit transport would drop us there and pick us up at 23.00 hrs. We would be back in our billet within half an hour, well before midnight. One evening Naples was swarming with Redcaps. I have never seen so many. They checked on every serviceman in the town, not once but all the time. Every military policeman who passed us stopped us and checked us. This kept on occurring for days until finally our unit issued us with a special pass. Apparently, all the permanent base units in Naples issued them. Later I found out what the fuss had been about. It seemed that a couple of sergeants or senior NCOs had joined Trotters' Union and had come into the city. Somehow they had commandeered a billet and got from somewhere proper documentation to make it seem they were officially established as a transit camp for "special units" and there were a great many such units operating in CMF – Popski's Private Army, the LRDG, the SAS, the SS [Special Service] and a great many others. Those NCO deserters knew or learned the ropes very quickly. It takes one to know one and they would chat to soldiers who they suspected to be deserters. It would take some time before the swaddy would admit this; he was afraid that these men might be from the SIB. When he was convinced he would go back to their so-called transit camp. As long as there was a pukka RP guard on the gate it all looked legal from the outside. Inside the Union members would organize thefts from individual soldiers – this used to be called "rolling a guy" – it is called mugging today. Some times a couple of "union members" would pretend to be military police and would flag a truck down which they knew to be carrying NAAFI goods. The union members lived the life of Reilly; high-jacking lorries, mugging. They were up to all sorts of tricks. They were on velvet. One of them, so the story goes, ran a string of girls in Rome. They worked the Colosseum and he used to do a twice weekly journey to collect the money and to dish out rewards and punishments. From what I heard that is how the Trotters' Union transit camp came unstuck. One of the girls became jealous and shopped the ponce. When he was interrogated he spilled the beans but when the SIB got to the Transit Camp only the guard on the gate was there. All the other "union members" were "out working". Very few of them were caught. The local Eytie civvies warned them. But for weeks there was intense pressure in and around Naples. Somehow the city was never the same again. You know how it is if you are pulled up by the police in this country. You sit in your car and wonder what you have done wrong. Going along the Via Roma after that police activity was like that; all the time you were rehearsing what you were going to say when they pulled you up.'

SELF-INFLICTED WOUNDS

To many the thoughts of deserters living in a sort of seedy luxury might be considered humorous. They might be seen as lovable chappies. They were not. Desertion meant abandoning one's comrades in the middle of a fight. Another way of letting down one's comrades was to become a casualty before the battle began. The enemy was seldom so obliging as to give a nice clean wound in a soft, fleshy part of one's anatomy. This had to be organized and the product of this organization was the self-inflicted wound. Such obvious crudities as shooting off the index or trigger finger or a bullet in the foot produced permanent mutilation. A nice clean wound, not too painful and with the minimum of mutilation, was the ideal.

'The only cases of self-inflicted wounds I saw were both in Africa. In one a sergeant loaded a Bren and put the catch to fire single rounds. Presently along came the Bren gunner, saw that the gun was cocked and pulled the trigger – thinking it to be empty and not knowing that the sergeant had put one up the spout. Down went the NCO with a bullet through his calf. I never saw him again. The next SIW was on Tripoli docks where we were waiting to embark for Salerno. One of our draft wrapped a couple of towels round his upper arm and his mate broke it with a blow from his rifle.'

THE BLACK MARKET

Another group of military misfits were those who exploited the shortages brought about by war for their own gain. It may be hard for young readers to understand, but there was a time in Europe when money had little value and the worth of any commodity was expressed in goods – usually in cigarettes, chocolate or soap. Frederick James was in a transit camp at Benevento during Christmas 1944:

'We were under canvas and it was bitterly cold. A gypsy woman came into our tent and told us it was 10 cigarettes, two bars of chocolate or a couple of bars of soap. For a blanket you could have something really special. I didn't fancy her but a lot of the blokes in the tent did. A tent held 22 men. Men from other tents also came in and used her. When the supply of customers ran out, and she had been at it for a couple of hours almost non-stop, she whistled. In came a couple of kids and they piled together God knows how many bars of soap and chocolate. She begged a couple of empty cigarette tins and packed in the fags she had earned.'

That was the bottom end of the scale. At the top end a copious supply of NAAFI goods could purchase the things that would please a hungry Countess or dress an aspiring actress in silks bought up by unit truck from a big city. The black market or 'colour scheme' embraced every social class in the civilian world and every rank in the Army. At the highest level it was rationalized as being a *quid pro quo;* a gesture of thanks for a special favour. At the lowest level it was; 'Do you want, Johnny?' and a negotiated price in Craven A or Players cigarettes.

'I remember Gold Flake were considered too strong for continental tastes – too raw – and Senior Service or any American cigarettes were preferred. I suppose that somebody, somewhere, did smoke the cigarettes that were passed from hand to hand like money. The "colour scheme" died in Austria and Germany during 1948, I think it was, when those countries came off the rationing system. Good old Blighty kept rationing, and the black market that goes with it, until 1953, as evidenced by the Sidney Stanley scandal. We had lectures from unit officers about not dealing on the black market, but we found it hard to take them seriously when they were on the "colour scheme" themselves. About the middle of 1946, there was a move made to replace military officers with civilian officers of the Control Commission. I do not know who recruited that lot or how they came to be selected, but most of them were little short of being racketeers. They seemed to be above military and German civil law. They fiddled on a massive scale – not just fifty free issue cigarettes, but tons of coal taken across frontiers with forged papers, chiefly into Denmark where there was no shortage of food. Out would go the coal – back would come sides of pork, bacon, butter, eggs – all the things you could not get in Hamburg. Some "loot", as they termed it, was converted. Foreign stamps were ideal, being small and valuable; also favoured were small antiques. A lot of antique firearms passed to dealers in the UK. I was told of one British employee of the CCG who bought a castle with his "loot", but I doubt if any of them would have flown that high. A flat, certainly – a villa, perhaps, with the property deeds made out in the name of the harem piece who comforted our hard-working hero. The Yanks, so I heard, were worse than us, in the black market, but then their PXs handed out black-market goodies on a very generous scale. The Americans could buy anything.'

In some perverted way it was not considered really wrong to be a military criminal. And yet desertion from the line meant that those soldiers who stayed and fought had been abandoned. The desertion of every man from a fighting unit meant that his comrades carried an extra burden; each man who mutilated himself by a self-inflicted wound meant that there were fewer proper soldiers to fight the enemy. To be an operator in the black market was not clever and entrepreneurial; it meant the exploitation of the poor – the starving civilians – by the rich, the servicemen with cigarettes and soap. I suppose very few of those who dealt in the 'colour scheme' saw themselves in that light any more than those who deserted felt themselves to have betrayed their mates. It is very easy to be blind to one's own faults.

'CONCHIES'

The final group of dodgers were not military personnel. They had, in fact, never served; had never worn uniform. They were those who for conscientious reasons would not fight for their country. So far as the bulk of the Army was concerned those dodgers were despised because it was thought they concealed cowardice under the term conscience. Roger Cooper, formerly a sergeant in the RAC, was particularly bitter about them:

'Their consciences would not allow them to take part in the war effort. They wouldn't work in the ARP or in the factories producing weapons, for that would be supporting the war. But their consciences didn't stop them eating food which seamen brought in; seamen whose ships had run the gauntlet of U-boats, the Luftwaffe and mines. It didn't stop them, either, from driving cars, using petrol brought in by seamen who risked death or disfigurement on every trip. The worst ones were the dodging bastards who shot off to America as soon as the Blitz started and were looked up to in the States as representatives of the gallant British people. And those cowards bathed in the glory they were too yellow to fight for. There was one bishop who thought that it was wrong for us to bomb the Jerries, in the way that they had bombed the UK, Warsaw and France and all the other cities. It was alright for the Luftwaffe to destroy British cities and to kill British women and children, but it was wrong for us to do the same to them. It was people of that sort who stopped "Bomber" Harris becoming a Lord, like Monty and other commanders. There was an outcry after the abbey at Cassino was bombed. Those who shouted loudest hadn't been in a ruined house in Cassino with that abbey looking right down your throat.'

Combatants

OUR ALLIES

No nation sets out to fight a war unsupported, but seeks to ensure that she has countries which will give her aid. She may require bases or war materials or, perhaps, just the reassurance of offers of assistance. Whatever the reason, a country at war needs allies. In 1939 Great Britain was able to maintain a large navy but only a small land force. Thus, the British Army was placed under foreign leaders. In 1939, the BEF, was commanded by a French General. When France was lost in 1940, the Army was free of foreign influence until December 1941. Within a year our new allies, the Americans, being superior in numbers and more lavishly equipped, demanded and were granted military control, firstly, in the western and then in almost every other theatre of operations. They first exercised this authority when French North Africa was invaded by an Anglo-American force in November 1942. Then, despite his lack of battle experience, Eisenhower was placed above Montgomery and Alexander who had successfully beaten the Axis forces at El Alamein. That battle was the swansong of the British Army fighting in an independent role. Henceforth it would be a junior partner under the overlordship of Americans. By a terrible paradox many British soldiers thought more highly of our enemies than of the Americans, whose aid in the war had sustained us and upon whose support we had depended in the darkest days of the war.

THE FRENCH

At the end of June 1940, France, Britain's last remaining ally in the west, surrendered. As a result of her capitulation Britain stood alone but, paradoxically, this situation produced among the British people, not the fear or despair that might have been expected, but rather a feeling of relief based upon the fact that we had got rid of the foreigners who held us back. Allies, it was felt, were an encumberance, an inhibition to OUR way of doing things. Britain had sent out a fine little Army in 1939, and so far as the man in the street was concerned, because of the incompetence of French generalship our BEF had been shattered. Some of our best infantry divisions had been captured, including the 51st Highland, which had been included in the French surrender at St-Valéry to a German General named Erwin Rommel.

The Allied contingents now in exile in the United Kingdom were welcomed, initially, out of a British sense of compassion for what had happened to their countries. But as the post-Dunkirk euphoria evaporated, resentment of these foreigners grew and with it the prospect of conflict between the British and Allied soldiers. The government, aware of the danger that Allied Servicemen billeted near British Army units might be the unsuspecting agents in a confrontation, sought to avoid such unpleasantness by separating foreign and native detachments The Poles, a major contingent, were eventually sent to Scotland.

Bombardier Millett: 'Almost as soon as the Poles settled in there were stories of their sexual appetites. There were stories that in the grip of sexual passion they had been known to bite off the nipples of their girlfriends. Then, too, it was rumoured that those coming from the primitive areas of eastern Poland, were phenomenally equipped, even by Polish standards. It was rumoured that the Poles had been exiled to Scotland because they had created havoc in the mill towns of Lancashire which led to a very high birth rate among unmarried girls. Sexual jealousy had a bad effect upon our morale and we had lectures from our officers that we should not desert if we were worried about our wives. Compassionate leave would be granted to deserving cases. It seldom was. Such talks did little to reassure the Scottish men in the unit. Those who were married men or were going steady, as I was at the time, were petrified when they heard that foreign units had moved into their home town. We were well aware of the sexual threat; that we would be compared against the foreigners and might be found lacking.'

The armistice of 1940 split the French nation into those who, under the leadership of Charles de Gaulle were prepared to fight on, and those who accepted the terms of the surrender and served the government set up in Vichy. This deep divide was very evident when the Anglo-Americans landed in French North Africa in November 1942. The walls were plastered with posters showing the face of Marshal Pétain.

'It was not until March that I first saw [in Algiers] pro-Allied posters. These did not show de Gaulle but General Giraud who was being groomed by the Americans as a rival in the contest for leadership of Free France against de Gaulle whom the Americans thought to be a British puppet. Those posters that did not show Pétain did not, so far as I recall, show the faces of Roosevelt or Churchill but only quotations from their speeches. Not to put too fine a point on it the French did not like us. A great many of the civvies in Algeria told us we should have surrendered in 1940. Then the war would have been all over and finished.'

Conversely, there were French officers who worked for an Allied victory. One of those who made an outstanding demonstration of loyalty was General Le Clerc who marched his men from equatorial Africa to fight alongside British Eighth Army in the desert. His defence of Bir Hakim in May 1942 was one of the finest examples of courage and devotion to duty by any Allied army during the Second World War. The fighting ability of the French Army in North Africa could not be truly demonstrated because of their poor weapons and equipment, but during the Tunisian campaign the Americans began to re-equip the French and continued the process until the whole Army was completely refitted and supplied with US equipment. Among the many picturesque units of the French

Army in Italy were the mountain warriors known as the Goumiers. These men made a deep impression upon the British soldiers. Ronald Johnston, a driver in an RASC unit which was supplying Eighth Army recalled:

'In many mountain villages it was almost like being back in North Africa. Those places were crammed solid with native soldiers, their families and livestock. They were Goums, who were from North Africa. They were a frightening lot. I was used to the well-disciplined soldiers of the Indian Army. The Goums seemed to have no discipline. They were mostly tall and wiry. Most had fringe beards and stained teeth. It must have been something they ate, something similar to the betel-nut which is widely chewed in the East. They wore a long caftan of rough wool. Basic colour brown with very thin stripes of white or black. Often, but not always, a sort of turban, not like the Sikh one, but more a wide bandage around the head. They wore uniform under this caftan garment. The Jerries hated them. The Goums were quite vicious by our standards although probably not by their own local North African standards. They had no idea of the value of loot. One of my mates asked for a souvenir once. The Goums showed him combs and toothbrushes which they had taken from the enemy. They did not take anything like binoculars or pistols. We could not understand why they wanted combs and toothbrushes – such things had no value to us.'

When the French re-entered the war in 1943, Britain's leadership role had already been usurped by the Americans. It was they who had equipped the resurgent French Army and it was under US command that the French formations fought. In Normandy when Patton's Third Army broke out of the beachhead perimeter, French formations were on its order of battle and it was to Le Clerc and French 2nd Armoured Division that the honour fell of liberating Paris. Since the French fought chiefly with the Americans, the British Army had little experience of their Gallic allies during the campaign in north-west Europe. Relations were chiefly with the French civilians whose attitudes ranged from hostility, through resigned acceptance that the Tommies were back again, to the never to be forgotten joy of liberation. As examples of that first attitude, British troops in Normandy were often asked point-blank why they had brought the war to Normandy? The peasants told them that relations between themselves and the Germans had been good. The Boches had been very correct. They had paid, in cash, for everything they needed and a *modus vivendi* had operated. The British Army had brought artillery and air bombardments which had killed large numbers of cattle, smashed houses, flattened whole cities and brought about destruction on an unbelievable scale. The German occupation had meant a continuation of the normal way of life. Liberation had brought nothing but death and ruin.

The attitude of the French civilians in the cities towards girls who had fraternized with the Germans, disgusted many British soldiers.

'In one little town outside Lille, the locals paraded those poor girls, there were about twelve of them, and publicly humiliated them. A couple of girls were stripped to the waist; another had her skirt held up and her knickers removed so that the townspeople could see what it was the German Army had paid for. All of them had their hair shaved off and swastikas painted on their bald heads. Some of the lads wanted to stop it but our officer wouldn't let us. We didn't understand, he said. All we understood was that these women were being bullied by people who must all have collaborated with the Germans to some extent at some time or another.'

There were other French people who saw the men of British Army in a different light. Some battalions that had fought in the 1940 campaign returned to the same villages and towns during 1944, and were welcomed as heroes; as sons of France. It was to many a most emotional experience to be greeted by civilians who had been abandoned to four years of German occupation, but whose faith had always been that the Tommies would come back again. One citizen of Ypres told me that he regretted that it had not been the British Army, but the Poles, that had driven the Germans from the town in 1944. He thought that as an emotional gesture it ought to have been one of the units that had fought through Ypres in 1940, to whom the honour should have gone to liberate it in 1944.

AMERICANS

A major part of the British Army was already on overseas service before the Americans arrived in the United Kingdom and did not come home again until the bulk of the GIs had themselves been repatriated. The result was that much of what the Tommy knew about his new ally's behaviour in the United Kingdom was hearsay which he had to believe because he lacked personal knowledge. How much of what he learned at second-hand was untrue, ill-founded or just malicious is anybody's conjecture, but what he heard or read made him uneasy. There were stories of the attitude of the Americans towards women in the United Kingdom. Among the German propaganda leaflets fired into the British lines during the fighting in Italy was one which showed on the obverse a British Girl and a GI in what is called, 'a compromising situation'. The Government, deeply aware of the effect on British military morale of the influx of US troops, sought to reassure public opinion at home and the soldiers overseas, that the GIs were warm, generous and friendly. When the soldiers of the two allied armies first met, the Tommy was quick to realize that the GI on active service was often 'a very ordinary bloke.' Not so the ordinary British soldier in the United Kingdom. Try as he would he could not get to like his US ally and the feeling was mutual. This led to hostility and there was at least one murder of a British soldier by a GI in the United Kingdom.

Both at home and overseas it was chiefly the ignorance of the average American soldier which was the chief cause of concern. The GIs knew nothing of Britain or her empire. They were influenced by the fact that their country had once been part of that empire. Theirs was a profound naïvety at every level. A GI once assured one of my correspondents that the Cunard liner *Queen Mary*, on which the Americans had sailed to Europe, was a US ship because 'you Limeys could not build anything as good as that'. Through Hollywood films the citizens of America were, in British eyes, thought to be sophisticated and their conversations filled with quick-fire repartee. From the films it appeared they all lived in luxury houses surrounded by masses of gadgets to make life easy. The British soldier soon found that those people who lived in the big cities were a very small minority. The great mass of Americans were poorly educated peasants whose staple reading matter was children's comics. These hicks knew nothing of the outside world and cared less. Everything they encountered was compared to its US equivalent and found wanting. They firmly believed that America had discovered penicillin, had invented television and radar, had produced the first tanks and had won the Great War. What went on in the United Kingdom between the American soldiers and British women is the stuff of myth and legend. 'Any British girl could be had for a pair of nylons,' was a taunt which would guarantee a fight between American and British soldiers. German propagandists, aware of the potency of sexual jealousy, sought to create hostility between the Americans and the British soldiers overseas, just as they had sought to turn the French *poilu* against the Tommies in France in the first year of the war. The sexual threat was a powerful weapon and one that was exploited by the Germans to the full.

The one area which the German propagandists seem not to have explored in their attempts to undermine the morale of the American soldier was that of race. Yet that was one sector of American life which disquieted the British. There was not at that time the racial awareness in Britain that there is today. The coloured British were few in number and had been either generally accepted or else had learned to ignore bigotted racist remarks. White girls in this country saw all US troops as Americans – their colour was not an issue. What those girls did not realize was that it was deeply offensive to many GIs to see white girls in public with Negro soldiers. The outcome of that tension were race riots in several parts of the United Kingdom.

British military commanders were critical of the way in which American generals planned and executed a campaign. The ordinary British soldiers were scornful of the fighting qualities of their transatlantic allies. The first operation in which the two allies fought side by side was Operation 'Torch', the invasion of French North Africa. Not long after the landings a rumour swept through the British army in Tunisia that the US troops had expected to be greeted as liberators and had carried on their sleeves the Stars and Stripes to distinguish them from the British who were thought to be unpopular with the French. The US invaders were not met with open arms, but by sporadic firing which caused many of them to turn tail and run for the beaches. According to the rumours British infantry units were ordered to dress in American jackets and to make a success of the landing. The men of 78th British Infantry Division to whom the task was given tore off the American insignia before undertaking the assault which captured the area.

'It was naïve of the Americans to expect that they would meet no opposition. They were, after all, invading a neutral country and one which was not occupied by the enemy. Surely, they must have anticipated some hostile response from the local inhabitants.'

The rumours which had circulated after the Algiers landings became a bitter truth at Kasserine Pass in the early months of 1943. US tank forces struck through the mountain pass and were repelled by the Panzers. High ground which US II Corps had occupied without struggle in its advance was given up in a panic retreat and US tankmen abandoned undamaged vehicles. The British Guards

Brigade was sent to capture the mountain peaks from which the American infantry had pulled back. The Guards are particularly bitter about that operation. They had had earlier experiences of American inability to hold ground during December 1942, on Longstop Hill. During Christmas week the Guards had fought their way up the rocky slopes of Longstop. In places their battles against the German defenders had been hand-to-hand. The hill was then entrusted to an American unit which lost it in a matter of hours. The Guards were put back in again and recaptured the feature. Again it was handed over and again the American defenders lost it. Bitter weather prevented the now depleted Guards regiments from undertaking a third capture of the hill and by the time that good weather returned the Germans had turned Longstop into a fortress. It remained in German hands until the final weeks of the campaign when the 78th Division, the men of the Algiers landing, stormed and captured it.

Inexperience, some men of the British Airborne named it cowardice, was given as the reason for the shambles that opened the campaign against Sicily. Americans were piloting the aircraft towing the gliders holding British paratroops. British 1st Airborne Division was to drop over objectives inland from the invasion beaches. While the armada was still flying over the sea, miles away from the landing zone, a German Flak ship opened fire. Unnerved by the explosions many US pilots cast off the gliders leaving them to come down either in the sea or to crash-land on the beaches.

At the Salerno landing, US formations began to retreat back to the landing craft, a movement that was only halted when British units flung back the attacks of a Panzer division. At Salerno, too, the Guards relived the same bitter experience as at Longstop and Kasserine – and so it went on, so far as the British soldiers were concerned, throughout the whole Italian campaign, with them having to take over or recapture positions which the Yanks would not, or could not, hold.

During the campaign in north-west Europe the differences between the Allies resulted in many lost opportunities. British tank experts had produced a number of variants to standard vehicles. These 'funnies', grouped into 79th Armoured Division, included tanks mounting a large-calibred bombard intended to smash the enemy blockhouses and permanent defences on the landing beaches. Squadrons of such 'funnies' were offered to the US units which were to land on Omaha Beach where the principal obstruction was a high sea wall. In the event the US troops who tried to scale it were caught in the fire of German machine-guns and shot down in hundreds. The other US soldiers huddled on the narrow beach were slaughtered by German mortar and artillery fire. It was clear that not until the sea wall was breached could troops escape from the trap which was Omaha. Only the self-sacrifice of some US engineers in blowing a gap allowed other American units to advance off the beach and into open country. The arrogance of their military leaders in rejecting British specialist weapons was responsible for the carpet of American dead on the D-Day beaches and for the hundreds of bodies bobbing in the Channel tide.

And so the dismal story continued. Of the campaign in Italy halted by the deflection of troops and supplies away from a possible victory and into an unnecessary assault landing in southern France. Of the failure of the Allied High

Command to resolve a battle strategy; of the collapse of the Americans in the Ardennes and of the brutalities which accompanied their rapid advance through Germany in the spring of 1945. Of Patton gloating over the towns and villages which his army had destroyed during its drive. Of one US Armoured Division which took no German prisoners for a whole week, but shot, summarily, all those who surrendered. Of post-war court-martials which condemned to imprisonment German children found guilty of 'Wehrwolf' activities.

In Burma the men of the British Fourteenth Army were astonished to learn that an American unit in the jungle had mutinied and demanded to be sent home because it had completed the mission for which it had been recruited. It was certainly a most unusual army. The following compilation of accounts shows them in the way that they were seen by so many British soldiers.

'Their method of service was unusual. A division would enter the line and stay there for months on end. One division, either the 34th or 36th Infantry, spent over one hundred days and nights in action without relief. This must have had a serious effect upon morale. Our method of frequent rotation was much better.'

'As individuals they certainly had greater freedom to move about than we had. They were a highly mobile army; all of them could drive and they had access to transport to a degree which would have been impossible for an ordinary soldier in the British Army. They were also very well equipped and it seemed that they could lose equipment without a court-martial. Once, we relieved a US unit just south of the River Garigliano. Whoever had occupied the slit-trench I got into had left behind a carbine and ammunition, hand-grenades, whole cartons of cigarettes and ration packs. The CO of the outgoing US unit told our CO that it was a real hot spot with frequent and heavy barrages. There was a bit of stonking by Jerry; always punctual and always on the same targets. Unless the enemy had changed his firing pattern because we had come in, this place was an easy sector and not the hell-hole which the Yank made it out to be.'

'One of our armoured car patrols [in Normandy] heard the sound of small-arms fire coming through the bocage. Then we saw, preceded by another fusillade, the strangest of cavalcades. The "enemy" were Americans . . . about a Company strong. In the middle of their column and sitting like Buddha on a mound of kit in the back of a jeep was an officer chewing a large cigar and studying by its glowing ash a crumpled map folded to the size of a small pocket-book . . . casually glancing from his map to the shadowy outline of a tree, as if identifying a landmark he sprayed its topmost branches with a tommy-gun. "Snipers," he grunted. When he ran out of ammunition, someone else took up the running. The amount of ammunition carried by those Americans must have been prodigious, for long after they had scraped by our armoured cars we could still hear them firing at the tree tops.

'They were quite bloody-minded. They opened a super-fast highway for their supply trucks to bring petrol forward. This was called something like the Red Ball Highway. The truck drivers all seemed to be Negroes who drove with one foot out of the cab window. They all smoked fat cigars. God help anyone who got in their way when one of the convoys was moving up. They were just driven off the road.'

'Although we did not mix much with the black GIs we were surprised to learn how much the white Americans hated them. I was on temporary detached duty in Austria and was billeted for a couple of days in Salzburg. One night I saw a Negro soldier walking along arm in arm with a local girl. Suddenly, a jeep-load of US military police roared around the corner and drove up to the soldier. The "Snowdrops" jumped out and started bashing him with their long truncheons. For all I know he may have been a hard case; a wanted criminal. I don't know. As it was all I saw was that one Negro was being bashed into a pulp by six white MPs.'

'In Munich there was an exhibition of US soldiers' paintings and one painting in particular came in for lots of criticism and demands that it be withdrawn. It was labelled, I think, "Munich. Morning. 1945" and showed a blonde German girl lying exhausted on a bed while in the foreground a US Negro soldier was getting dressed.'

'The US Army put a Negro division into the line in northern Italy. As I understood it their senior officers down to battalion level were all white and no attempt was made to form a unit loyalty. The white officers were guilty, according to my informant [a black GI], of blatant racism and of making the most offensive remarks. Most of the white officers had not wanted to serve in the "nigger unit", and had had to be ordered to take up their appointments. They were very upset and felt that their careers had been blighted. So they took it out on the rank and file. This unit with a very low morale was attacked on New Year's Day by a German battle patrol. The Germans penetrated as far as divisional headquarters before they were challenged. It seemed that the soldiers of the Negro units through which the battle patrol had passed had all been drunk on duty.'

'The US attitude towards their coloured troops was shocking and yet their 442nd Regiment, made up of Japanese-Americans' was the best unit they had in Europe. You know the way things spread in the Army? Well, we heard that at least ten of the regiment had been recommended for their equivalent of the Victoria Cross, but that for political reasons it was felt that these should not be awarded. Although I never saw any soldier of the 442nd in action, from reports I heard it must have been a marvellous unit.'

'To me it came as no surprise to learn that so many black GIs deserted. The French, of course, have had black colonies for hundreds of years and treated the coloured GIs just as they would have treated a black Frenchman. This attitude upset a great many white soldiers in France who went about in gangs beating up Negro troops, whether they were with white girls or whether they were alone. It seemed to us that in some way the white soldiers felt that they had to maintain the "white boss – black slave" attitude that seemed still to exist in the States. There were stories that Ku Klux Klan chapters were set up in France.'

A more positive aspect of US/British relations at ordinary soldier level was the extraordinary generosity of the Americans:

'The contrast in attitudes between the American and British peoples towards their servicemen was never shown more clearly to me than in Algiers. The American PX, their equivalent of NAAFI, occupied a very large building about four or five storeys high. On the ground floor they served coffee and doughnuts –

free. At the reception desk they issued free tickets to their shows and these were first class. We had to queue up for our ENSA performances outside the theatre and after the war, certainly in Germany, you had to buy tickets for a performance. Our NAAFI was on the first floor of a house in a side street of Algiers. The only things sold were tea and bread and jam. There were no china cups so that the tea was served in the metal tins that had once contained fifty cigarettes. Handles had been soldered on the tins – these were our tea cups – fag tins.'

'The thing that surprised me most was the casual relationship between the doctors and patients in the hospital. When the MO made his rounds there was none of the bull found in RAMC hospitals. I heard one MO ask a man how he was feeling and when he received the reply that the soldier still didn't think himself fit, the MO told him he'd better stay in hospital for another couple of days. Every day a trolley came round with cigarettes and sweets. The first time it came round I said that I had lost my wallet because I did not want to be embarrassed if I didn't have enough money. I was told that everything was free. So were the coffee and doughnuts that came round twice a day. People came round with newspapers, magazines, reading material – all of it free issue. If you stopped a US unit to ask the way or to fill up with petrol or something, you were always asked in for a meal or given quarters for the night. Whatever time you arrived the cooks would always make some sort of meal – not like the unit cooks in the British Army.'

To many British soldiers the casual attitudes of the Americans was a sign of poor discipline which must lead inevitably to incompetence in battle. Yet this US attitude exactly paralleled the officer/man relationship evident in the British Dominion forces. It was possible in the armies of the younger nations for an officer's commission to be gained by men and women from a wider social circle than in the British Army. The strict, restrictive lines of class and/or education did not apply in the forces of the young nations and this resulted in a more casual relationship. It did not necessarily guarantee a reduction in or a loss of discipline – it was just a different approach to achieving this.

The British soldier envied much of what he saw available to the GI; his uniforms, rations, mobility, pay and opportunities, but considered the American soldier to be pig-ignorant and loudmouthed. Ready to exploit any opportunity to make money he most certainly was, but individually generous in a way that we could not match. And that incredible generosity was demonstrated at national level with the post-war Marshall Plan which did so much to restore war-ravaged Europe. They were a complex lot our American allies.

THE RED ARMY

Very few men of the British Army met the soldiers of our principal European ally, Russia. Those who did were the men who had served with British Ninth Army in Iraq and Iran. They had met the Russians in those Middle Eastern countries when Britain and the USSR occupied them in order to prevent pro-German governments from gaining power. The only other British soldiers to meet the Russians before the end of hostilities were those who had been prisoners-of-war in Poland, East Germany or in Czechoslovakia, and who at the war's end were footmarched westwards by the Germans. Those columns of prisoners were liberated by the speedy advance of the Red Army. The greatest number of men of the British Army who met the Russians did so after the war's end as members of the army of occupation in Germany and Austria, while others, in north-west Europe and in Italy, had actually fought against units of former Russian soldiers who had volunteered to fight with the German Army.

Michael Henshaw, who had been taken prisoner during the fighting on the Anzio beachhead, had good reason to remember his liberation by the Red Army. He had been one of the prisoners marching on a trek from a camp in Saxony and southwards across Czechoslovakia. One night the column halted in an area on the borders of Hungary and Austria.

'One morning in late April we noticed that the guards had left us. We found their uniforms and weapons. They must have changed into civvy clothes and deserted. Our officer told us to stay put. We should not go wandering off. If we left the column and it moved off again we would be without its protection. We all had hard tack saved from the Red Cross parcels and were prepared to wait a day or two. After all, if the guards had deserted then Allied troops must be near. Mid-morning of the second day the Russians arrived. I think our location had been reported by one of their cavalry patrols and the officer of the group which liberated us gave orders for us to remain where we were. It was dangerous to move about, he told us. The war was still on. The Germans were still in the area. So we stayed put. I was sitting down reading late that afternoon. A Red Army soldier, very drunk, came up and offered me a drink. I cannot drink alcohol because during my time as a POW I began to suffer from asthma and found that alcohol affected me. So I refused his offer and kept on refusing. Suddenly he took his rifle off his shoulder and smashed me in the face with the butt end. That blow smashed my jaw, broke my nose and knocked out most of my front teeth. I received no medical treatment from the Russians and our own RAMC men could only patch me up as best they could. I was unable to eat and could only manage things that did not have to be chewed. I lost weight as a result and I was already painfully thin from my time as a POW. I think it took two weeks before we were moved across Germany and into the British Zone and then flown home. Back in the UK there were operations to remove bone splinters and the bones which had begun to knit together had to be rebroken and reset. The doctors were not able to restore my face completely. The pain I felt from the time I was struck until the first treatment in the UK, was terrible although aspirin, the only medicine we had as prisoners, did keep the worst pains down to a dull ache. Bad weather sets off that ache, even now.'

What came across from the Red Army, and this impression is one shared by all who mentioned our Russian allies, was the coldness they displayed. They were frightening in their remoteness. If it was necessary for a Western soldier to enter the Soviet Zone there was always at the back of the mind the feeling that from the barrier pole, in Germany or Austria, with its mandatory red star and red flag and all the way to Vladivostock, it was all *their* territory. There was the worrying knowledge that in that vast area, their silent, grey world, it would be so easy to be lost forever. The feeling of coldness which was so apparent to the British soldiers was translated into feelings of absolute terror for the civilians of the lands through which the Soviet troops had passed or which they still occupied. Three years after the war's end at a performance in the Opera House in Graz in Austria the chatter of the audience before the orchestra tuned up, slowly died away. All eyes were turned towards a box in the dress circle. Three of the four occupants were British Army officers. The fourth was a middle-aged, bald-headed Russian officer whose cold eyes surveyed the audience. Under that impersonal stare the audience stopped talking. Those present were dominated by that one man. By the fear of what he represented, by the memory of what this part of eastern Austria had suffered in the final months of the war. The Red Army had been an instrument of frightening power and its representative was sitting in a box in the Opera House. The civilians were terrified – three years after the war's end.

One phenomenon which surprised the British soldiers was that there were fighting units on the German Army's order of battle composed almost entirely of former Red Army men. These Russians had been prisoners-of-war in Germany and had volunteered to fight in the Wehrmacht as an alternative to starving to death in prison-camps. These men had exchanged the iron discipline of the Red Army for that of the Germans, and had fought for their new masters with undeniable bravery, until their German officers and NCOs had been killed. Most of them then surrendered. They were very pragmatic in their approach. When they had first been taken prisoner they had given away details of their own army's defences and some had even led German patrols through gaps in Red Army minefields to attack their own units. When they fell into British hands in Normandy they were prepared to betray German positions to us and to lead our patrols against their former masters. Loyalty was a very flexible characteristic among the soldiers of our Russian ally.

'Nichevo' (it doesn't matter) was widely used to cover those sort of eventualities over which the ordinary Russian soldier had no control. In their zone of occupation if the Red Army sent out a civilian work detail and a couple of Germans escaped from it, then Nichevo. It was a simple matter to snatch a couple of bypassers from the pavement. The most important thing was that the number of people in the detail had to be correct. The Red Army had an outstanding ability to ignore the feelings of almost everybody. The soldiers had been told that Russia, single-handed, had won the war. Thus, according to Soviet propagandists the world and particularly the nations which had been occupied by the Germans owed the Russians a debt of gratitude. Whatever the Soviets needed, they could have. The world was there to serve them.

Corporal Samuels, formerly of an RASC Company of 46th Division:

'I was in the British Army in Austria and was en route to Vienna in a 15cwt. Also in the van was my driver, a former German soldier and a couple of Austrian people, civilian employees in my unit, who had business in Vienna. They preferred to come with us in our uncomfortable truck rather than go by train with all its dangers and delays. We had crossed the Semmering checkpoint and were approaching Wiener Neustadt. Just outside one village a Russian sentry stepped into the road, cocked his MP and pointed it at us. I told the driver to stop. The sentry walked up and asked; 'Wien?' [Vienna?] "Yes," I replied. He whistled loudly. Two officers came out of a house and without a word climbed into the back of our truck. The sentry waved us on. The Russian attitude was very much that we weren't so much allies who had helped to win the war, but that we were some sort of allied servants, there to do whatever the victors of the Red Army told us to do.'

There were factors which prevented the British soldiers from fully understanding their Red Army allies. The language difficulty was the first and most obvious one. Then, too, the British Army had not seen the Russians in action and could not properly judge them. Corporal Samuels' letter continued:

'There were newsreels showing the "glorious" Red Army in action, but all of us knew that newsreels showing battles and infantry attacks could be faked, so we did not believe camera evidence. Civilians who had experienced the Red Army as conquerors spoke of them as murderers. The soldiers would mutilate people. There were stories of deportation and of the violent rape of any girl over the age of about 11. We found it hard to believe such stories – very few of us at that time realized the degradation that rape means. And, also, we thought that those complaining civilians had been Nazis until the end of the war so they were prejudiced. None of us wanted to believe the stories of concentration camps. We couldn't believe that soldiers, like we were, could act like that or that the Russians could act as brutally as the civvies said they had. Well, we had been wrong about the Germans and the concentration camps. It was very likely that we were wrong about the Soviets and their atrocities.'

In Austria the mass of Eighth Army did not meet the Red Army until after the war's end, but before the two forces met rumours were current among the British divisions in the army of occupation of how in East Prussia the Soviets had taken one man of every rank from the mass of German soldiers who had surrendered. Those representatives were stood in front of the mass of POWs – and were then shot as a warning. Other rumours said that in Königsberg all the Volkssturm men had been slaughtered and in Saxony the atrocities were said to have been unusually brutal. Could such stories be believed of our gallant allies or were they the last efforts of Goebbels' propaganda machine to sow discord between the Soviets and ourselves? And then the British Army met them. Unsmiling, hard, cold men, soldiers of a vicious system that would not scruple to waste thousands of them in senseless attacks. Their discipline was unusual. Within a unit not only officers but also NCOs had to be saluted, but compliments were never – or seldom – paid to officers of other units. So much for the barrack-room lawyers who had said that saluting had been abolished in the Red Army.

There were inevitably confrontations and fights at troop level. One of these, in Vienna involving Red Army men and soldiers of the Argyll and Sutherland Highlanders, resulted in fatal stabbings. The British Army also carried out sweeps against Soviet deserters who, in both Austria and Germany, had turned to crime to support themselves. One of my correspondents, a former military policeman, was on the firing-squad that executed some of those convicted murderers. He has asked not to be named.

'In Hamburg, in those days, there were among the displaced persons going home a lot who decided to stay in Germany. They all lived from the large black market. Others turned to crime and violence. Groups of these would board passenger trains and during the journey would produce firearms and run through the carriages robbing the civilians. This practice is called "steaming" these days. Anyone who did not hand over their valuables was killed without mercy. Multiple rape was not uncommon. One gang was caught and tried for a number of particularly violent murders. Its leaders were sentenced to death by shooting. I was one of the firing-party. It was a very quick operation, done quickly to spare the condemned man's feelings. All they had to do was to walk out of a door in the prison courtyard, turn left and walk for four or five paces, turn and face us. There were other policemen on duty to act as escorts. There was none of the long-drawn-out agony you see in films. Once the men were in position with a circle of white paper over their heart, the squad was given the order, aimed and fired. We had already loaded our rifles, so there was none of the clicking of bolts that you read about. From the time they walked out of the door to the time they fell dead was less than two minutes. I don't believe there were all that many executions in the British Zone and we only shot the most criminal murderers. And remember this was in the first days of the occupation. In Austria, so I believe, the British forces hanged the criminals. I was told that Albert Pierrepoint [the British public hangman] was sent out to show the Austrians the quick British "drop" method. Apparently, the Austrian method of execution had been garrotting.'

Our Yugoslav allies were like the Red Army; a dour and humourless lot who thought that the world owed them honour and glory. Because their Army lacked the proper facilities, Yugoslav wounded were brought into British military hospitals in southern Italy. There they received treatment, food and clothing. According to my correspondents they were an ungracious lot who gave no thanks for anything they received. The fear of the Party informer, the fear of being reported for collaboration with the soldiers of the West, inhibited them from expressing their proper feelings. Ron Johnston, whose account of the Goums has already been given, met the wounded partisans in a hospital in southern Italy:

'There was no distinction between the sexes and that extended even to the ablutions. The first time I came across this was in the latrines dug in the hospital grounds. You know the sort of thing I mean – a wooden box with holes placed over a trench and screened by canvas attached to poles. I was sitting there one day reading some mail from home. Somebody sat down beside me. I turned round and found it was a girl. I tried explaining in Italian that this was a latrine for men but she either wouldn't or couldn't understand me. I was very embarrassed but she wasn't and over the following days I got used to the partisan girls sharing our lats and showers. They were a sad bunch and completely under the control of their commissar. If the *Union Jack* [the British forces newspaper] wanted photographs of partisan and British comradeship, the Jugs would pose and smile to order. Once the pictures had been taken they moved away unsmiling and unspeaking. The impression I got was they resented us.'

The Greeks had become our allies at about the same time as had the Yugoslavs and, like them, had endured years of German occupation. The return of the British Army was welcomed by the great majority of Greeks as liberation, but there were Communist groups determined to seize the country and convert it into a Russian satellite. The Americans saw British attempts to stop that take-

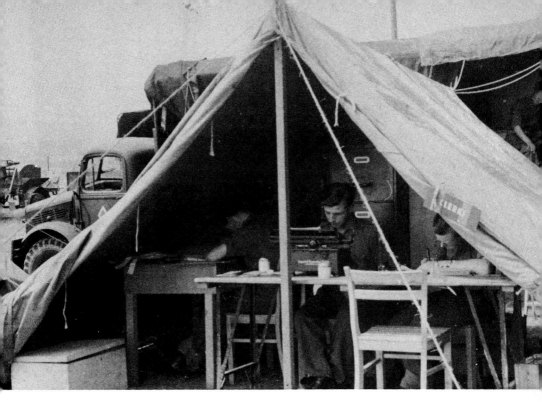

Above: An orderly room in the field somewhere in Germany at the end of the war. (*P. T. Beaton*)

Below: A. G. Bell relaxing, as he says on the back of his picture, 'in Tripoli at last!'. (*A. G. Bell*)

Left: *Danny Exley who fought in Italy and Greece with an infantry battalion of 4th British Division. His account of the battle for Cassino is included in this book. (Mrs Frances Exley)*

Right: *A group of Seaforth Highlanders pictured on the seafront at Port Said, Egypt, while on convalescent leave in May 1943. Roy Cooke is kneeling at the right; Andy Sutherland is kneeling at the left. The names of the other three Seaforths are now forgotten. (R. Cooke)*

Left: *C. W. Carpenter of 2nd Battalion, The Royal Norfolk Regiment. (C. W. Carpenter)*

Right: *Malcolm Armstrong (third left, front row) posing with his comrades in Schilberg Prisoner of War camp in Poland. (M. Armstrong)*

Left: F. Farmborough of No. 4 Commando in 1943. Known as 'Shrapnel' to his comrades because of the number of times he was wounded on manoeuvres, he was wounded on D-Day while serving with the 1st Special Service Brigade. (F. Farmborough)

Left: Harold Field in Paris during December 1944. He enlisted in the RAOC and became one of the first men to be transferred to the newly formed REME. (H. Field)

Right: Men from the 2nd Battalion, The Coldstream Guards, on 'street patrol' in Algiers, November 1942, prior to their unit moving up to Medjez-el-Bab. Pictured with 'Abdul' are, from left to right: Fitness, Craggs, and Smith. (Bill Fitness)

Right: Joe Harris (standing, second from right) in a group pose many modern tourists will recognize. (J. Harris)

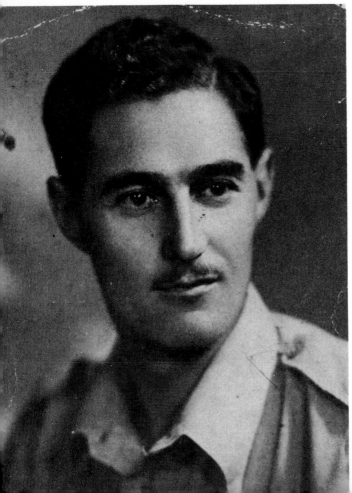

Above: Men from 141 RAC (The Buffs) during a pause in Operation 'Suffolk', 1943. Back row, left to right: Bennett, Bateman, Martin, Bovingdon. Middle row: Cheesman, Underwood, Wood, Moore, and Pearson. Front row: Staples, McColgan and Adams. (D. Hischier)

Left: Joyce, a Regular soldier with 29 years of service in the Royal Engineers, seen here in the Middle East. (Mr. and Mrs. R. A. Joyce)

Above: Baghdad, 1942.
From left to right:
Brockbank, Leacroft,
Morgan, Joyce, Watson and
Outram. (*Mr. and Mrs. R.
A. Joyce*)

Right: The author, James
Lucas, In Austria shortly
after the war.

Left: This photograph was taken in December 1945 after Walter Mole had arrived in Australia for further treatment for some injuries sustained in the Pacific fighting. Taken at Bondi Beach, the back of the snap reads: 'Don't I look happy, so would anybody be, heatwave on and NO BEER – sold out!!' (W. Mole)

Below: A happy group aboard Empress of Canada bound for Singapore in October 1941. Walter Mole is on the far right in the second row from the front. His two comrades on the left of the front row were killed before Singapore fell.

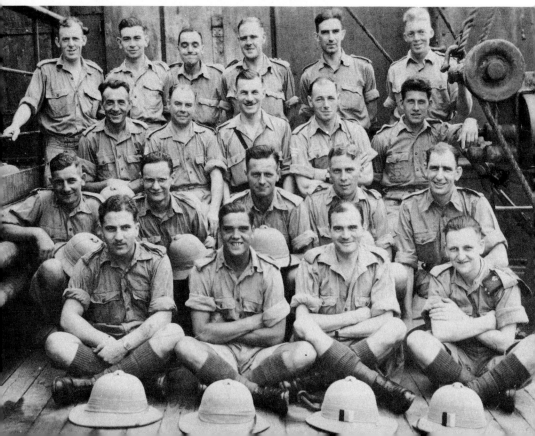

Right: 'Tishy' Parker in France, September 1939. A Regular soldier, 'Tishy' was taken prisoner near Calais in 1940. (T. Parker)

Below: A group of P.O.W.s in a camp in Poland, May 1941. 'Tishy' is shirtless in the front row. (T. Parker)

Left: Parker and others in 1940 at Roggenfeldt working camp in Poland, standing shoulder-to-shoulder with their German guards.

Left: A view of 'Tishy's' first working camp, 'Usch' in Poland, which, he writes, is 'not to be confused with Butlins'. (*T. Parker*)

Right: John Newmark in his tropical gear, Karachi, India. (*J. Newmark*)

Above: *A Standing Patrol in Palestine shortly before the war. Note the cap badges have been removed.*

Left: *Alf Sampson, the soldier-cartoonist. He depicted his record of four years overseas service in the Middle and Far East in his own cartoons. (A. Sampson)*

Top right: *An example of Sampson's cartooning skill reveals some of the humour which existed amongst the ranks despite experiences that might encourage just the opposite. (A. Sampson)*

Right: *'B' Company of The 2nd Queen's Own Royal West Kent Regiment take a well earned tea break during their brigade training. (Bert Stubbings)*

Above: E. W. Stonard, at the front, smiling, with the BEF advance party landing at Cherbourg in January 1940. (E. W. Stonard)

Left: This picture was taken in 1941 on a 'showing the flag' operation in Palestine just before departure to the Western Desert. The NCO is Bombardier E. W. Stonard; the officer is Lieutenant Watson, who was later killed in action at Gazala in 1942. (E. W. Stonard)

Right: Major, later Colonel, G. B. Thatcher, D.S.O, of the Royal Artillery. (G. B. Thatcher)

Above: *A pen and ink sketch depicting life for a 3.7in anti-aircraft gun crew during the war in the desert. This drawing by Fergal Hearns was reproduced in Richard Doherty's excellent book* Wall of Steel. *Grateful acknowledgement is made for permission to use it here. (R. Doherty)*

Left: *Bill Turner of The East Surrey Regiment at Colchester in Essex just prior to the outbreak of war. (W. Turner)*

over as evidence of British 'colonialism' and gave support to the Red guerrilla groups. It was one of the great tragedies of the war that British soldiers who had fought in three campaigns to liberate Europe were murdered by political fanatics of an allied nation in a bloody and bitter civil war. In a number of cases British soldiers who fell into the hands of the Reds were burned alive in a vain attempt to provoke reprisals by the Army.

To summarize the feelings of the British soldier for his allies, in those letters which mention our allies the Belgians are always described as our staunchest friends. This feeling may be a hangover from the First World War, but the Belgians and to only a lesser extent the Dutch, are referred to in glowing terms. The French are held to be a curious lot. The first French that the British met in 1944, when they returned to north-west Europe, were Normandy farmers who made no secret of the fact that they preferred the Germans to us. That feeling was not held by the people of northern France with whom the BEF of 1940, had had time to establish good relations. The pace of operations in 1944 did not allow the troops of the British Liberation Army to establish the same rapport, and although those of 1944 are critical, the men of the old BEF are unstinting in their praise of the friends they made in northern France in the earliest months of the Second World War. The farther east in Europe one went the cooler became the relationship and the tension between Western and Communist ethics made close relationships between the rank and file almost impossible. Language problems merely added to the sum total of barriers.

The Americans as our closest ally were the ones with whom the ordinary soldiers had the most contact. If one discards the envy that most British soldiers felt and which was, perhaps, the background to their accusation that the GI lacked fighting spirit, then what we see of the Americans is a great mass of generous, open-hearted soldiers who, if their attitudes occasionally jarred, illustrated Kipling's cop-out for the British Tommy, ' . . . and if sometimes our conduct isn't what your fancy paints – well single men in barracks, don't grow into plaster saints'. What was surprising about the Americans and ourselves was how much we had in common. Those things which linked us far exceeded in number and importance those which divided us.

OUR ENEMIES

In one of his poems Rudyard Kipling voiced the sentiment of the fighting soldier towards his enemy by asking, 'What is the sense of hating those whom you are paid to kill?' He then went on to declare that he preferred to 'soon as not respect the man I fight'. It was a curious paradox that the British fighting soldier often felt more akin to his battlefield opponents than he did to his own Army or to his allies. The infantryman detested the artillery; the 'long range snipers' and accused them of blunders and incompetence when firing barrages. The gunners of the Royal Artillery countered those accusations and said that the infantry moved either too fast or too slow – charging with berserker ferocity through a carefully co-ordinated fire plan or else advancing so slowly behind the barrage that the enemy had time to emerge from his shattered positions to engage the attackers. Yet the German gunners were praised for their skill and ability even though these resulted in casualties to our own side.

The British infantry hated the armour, especially in those situations where the tanks were used as mobile pillboxes.

'The tanks would roll as far forward as our slit-trench line, fire off a few shots and then pull back. Ted [the enemy] once he recovered from the pot-shots, would open fire on where the tanks had been seen – right on our slit-trench line and we would be deluged in shit. Whenever we needed the tanks they buggered off to refuel or to carry out maintenance or something, and as for the gunners, they refused to believe that their guns fired short.'

The animosity which it might have been thought ought to be directed against the enemy was in fact heaped upon the other arms of service. The enemy was respected – at least the German enemy was. The Italians were considered to have had no chance to demonstrate their military ability for they were equipped with far worse weapons than even the British Army had. It was said that Italian tanks could be opened using the key of a sardine tin. The Japanese soldier was respected for his bravery in battle, his tenacity in attack and his powers of endurance. He was not underestimated by British fighting troops who realized that each Japanese fighting man had to be killed because the warrior code did not allow him to be taken prisoner.

THE GERMANS

The British soldier's respect for the German foe would not have been understood by civilians during the war. Even now, nearly half a century after the end of the conflict, most people still find it strange that British soldiers speak of their former enemies with deep respect. Another paradox is that the farther removed from the battle line a soldier was the more antagonistic he was to the Germans. There were cooks in Allied Forces Headquarters whose hatred of the Germans was pathological – yet they had never ever seen one. Conversely, I have met infantrymen and tankmen who had nothing but praise for the soldierly qualities of our former enemies against whom they had been fighting, in some instances, for many years.

One speaks as one finds. The Nazi fanatics who murdered their prisoners as the SS did in 1940 or in Normandy in 1944, were not considered by many British soldiers to be representative of the German Army. What the British soldier considered to be proper German soldiers were the skilled, hard-fighting, but fair men whom they met on battlefields in Europe and in Africa.

The German soldiers were good fighters who handled their weapons well – and their weapons were first class; many of them superior to those in our own service. Because they had a higher distribution of machine-pistols and faster-firing machine-guns which were capable of being used in a light or medium role, the Germans could put down a volume of fire which we could not match. Their attacks rode in on waves of bullets and the assaults of their enemies died in the criss-cross fire of their fast-firing MGs. Their tanks were better designed than ours and were continually upgunned so that they outranged our vehicles throughout the war. The German artillery had the 88mm gun, which served equally as well in anti-aircraft, anti-tank or field roles. The German Nebelwerfer projectors were frightening in the sound their shells made and in the destruction produced by their detonation. German rations were not to our taste but satisfied them. Like all soldiers the Germans wanted variety of diet and whenever they felt like a change or when supplies had failed to arrive, they penetrated Allied lines and helped themselves to what they wanted. Much of their perishable food came in tubes; butter, cheese and meat paste were the three principal ones. Biscuits (*Knackerbrot*) were foil-wrapped to keep them fresh and they had a lot of sardines. Day-to-day rations were produced in a wood-fired, wheeled, field cooker and man-portered into front-line positions. British Army cookers were fuelled by sump-oil and a forced draught and were more versatile than the high, chimneyed, German version. The German *Landser* had at least two years of disciplined training behind him when he joined the army. Most Germans were at home in the country, whereas most British soldiers were from cities and towns. The German military system was more flexible than the British. The speed with which they could form and deploy a battle group was impressive. In a retreat those who came back would be grouped at a collecting-point and were then sent back into action where they fought well under officers and NCOs whom they did not know. The strength of the British Army lay in the regimental allegiance; that of the German Army was to the nation.

THE ITALIANS

The Italian Army was armed for a war that did not take place. Had there been a major conflict in Europe in the first years of the 1930s, Mussolini's hosts would have been well equipped to fight it. By 1939, all the equipment of the Italian Army was obsolescent. When Italy entered the war in 1940, the infantry arm was being re-equipped and there were five different calibres of rifle in service. Much of the artillery dated from the Great War – some of it was made up of guns surrendered by the Austrians at the end of that war. The tanks were poor; underarmed and lightly armoured. British tankmen felt nothing but pity for their Italian opponents who went out to fight in what were mobile sardine-tins. The Italian soldier was as good a warrior as his poor equipment allowed him to be. When he was well led he was a formidable foe. It was our good fortune that his commanders did not lead him well. The men of the German Afrika Korps in the desert were disgusted to see the vast difference in living standards which existed in the Italian Army. The officers ate first and best. The NCOs ate next and what was left over went to the men. Small wonder that morale was poor among the ordinary troops. It was in the Blackshirt formations that the highest morale was to be found and to only a lesser degree in the *Bersaglieri* and armoured regiments.

During the war it was necessary to show the enemy soldiers in a bad light. Thus the Anglo-Americans nearly always depicted the Italians as heavily bemedalled cowards forever going on about pasta and vino. The image of the German soldiers which was presented to the western public was of blond-haired, sabre-scarred bullies all wearing enormous Iron Crosses. Or they were sadistic psychopaths murdering for the joy of killing or else, comic prison guards forever bamboozled by their quick-witted Anglo-American charges. The German soldier was seldom shown as a normal fighting man, subject to the joys and pressures endured by the ordinary warrior. It was imperative that he be not seen in civilian eyes as having any human virtues. Films and television programmes today project a new image of the German soldier of the Second World War. These productions no longer show the stereotyped and caricatured Nazi of the war and immediate post-war years, but depict German soldiers recognizable as normal human beings, even sympathetic. Very little, however, is known of our other principal enemy – the Japanese soldier. His image is still very much a stereotype.

JAPANESE

He was not, as the films portrayed him, a stunted, bespectacled, sub-human, more at home in the jungle than in an urban environment. The average soldier, 5 feet 3 inches tall and weighing 8½ stones, had as little experience of jungle conditions as had the Allied soldiers. It was his ability to adapt to those primitive conditions which was the key factor. To help him the ordinary Japanese soldier had qualities of stolidity and frugality which were improved by a long and strict military training. As a result he could carry an extraordinary amount of equipment and weapons for distances up to 20 miles each day. On active service his daily 4lb basic ration of food was not always supplied and he was expected to live off the land or from enemy stocks. Because of his natural frugality the Army needed few 'tail' units, allowing its greatest strength to be concentrated in its fighting formations of whom the infantry formed the greatest number. As a result of his training the Japanese soldier on the battlefield would and did attack with a ferocity unmatched by the soldiers of any other nation, advancing stolidly across the bodies of his fallen comrades, enduring wounds and sicknesses in the pursuit of victory. And when victory in attack did not come and he was forced on to the defensive, he was prepared to fight to the death.

Military training began very early, was very thorough and was aided by two factors; an intense loyalty to the Emperor and the literacy of the ordinary Japanese. In that latter respect 96 per cent could read, write and calculate and 50 per cent had learned English. Loyalty to the Emperor was absolute and the soldiers were taught that the disgrace of being defeated could only be atoned for by suicide. The idea of a battle to the last bullet was no empty concept in the Japanese Army. For them, to surrender represented so great a disgrace that a prisoner was considered to be a dead man. Believing that this concept must be accepted by all warriors, the Japanese treated their Allied prisoners-of-war as men who had forfeited their honour and who were, therefore, already dead. The prisoners were men upon whom any and all humiliations could be heaped; who could be worked literally to a physical death because they were already morally dead. The most chilling example of the Japanese code was shown when they executed an Australian serviceman who had been captured after carrying out a daring and successful mission. In the belief that the Australian had achieved the greatest glory in his life by carrying out the operation and that his imprisonment would represent an unbearable humiliation, he was beheaded.

The Japanese, as a race, have always shown themselves prepared to study and to learn from foreign military doctrines. The Army was no exception and its soldiers learned to 'go native'. They learned to live with and in the jungle and not to fight it. It was this ability which gave them the successes they achieved in the first years of the war in the Far East. Once the Allied soldiers had learned the lesson of using the jungle the belief of Japanese invincibility vanished. On active service the Japanese used ruses and strategems, shouting orders in English or calling out the names of soldiers which they had overheard. It was not unknown for individuals to be seen lying by the side of the road, covered with blood and apparently dead, to come suddenly to life and to fire into the backs of advancing Allied soldiers. Seriously wounded Japanese would wait with a grenade in their hands for a chance to kill an Allied stretcher-bearer who went to help them. The use of booby-traps planted under dead or even wounded soldiers was widespread. In the words of an American handbook on the Japanese forces, 'The variety of those devices (booby traps) is limited only by the commanders' or soldiers' imagination.'

Japanese equipment was basic, robust and unsophisticated. The artillery arm was particularly poorly served and it was only from the middle years of the war onwards that new gun types came on to issue. In the matter of tanks there were four principal types; the lightest of 5½ tons to a medium armoured fighting vehicle of 22 tons. Armour was not used in *Blitzkrieg* operations. Tanks had a chiefly infantry support role. The communications systems were poorly equipped with old-fashioned and cumbersome equipment. Of all the support arms of service, the most efficient were the engineers, whose men displayed considerable skill in construction as well as demolition. The ability of the Japanese sappers to construct field defences in the shortest period of time and using local materials was most impressive and their skill at siting and camouflaging those defences was especially high.

It was upon its infantry force that the Japanese Army depended for its victories and to which all other arms were subordinate. The military doctrine demanded sudden and swift offensive action to attack the enemy or to regain from him ground which had been lost. It was obedience to that doctrine which led to the successive waves of attacks which my correspondents recalled, and it was an offensive spirit which was maintained even in the final days of the war. One correspondent who served in a tank unit during the advance to Rangoon wrote of seeing individual Japanese soldiers attacking British vehicles with aircraft bombs clasped in their arms. This was not tank-busting on the German pattern, but self-sacrifice – suicide – the destruction of a tank and a five-man crew for the loss of a single Japanese soldier. Each tank destroyed represented a small victory.

The Japanese soldier was a formidable opponent; courageous in attack, staunch in defence, implacable and cunning – but neither a superman nor invincible. The British soldier beat him as he had beaten those other foes who had stood against him before and after the Second World War.

At War in North-West Europe

FRANCE AND FLANDERS, 1939-40

Following the outbreak of war the first elements of the BEF began their move to France and by 10 September the flow of stores and lines of communication troops was in full swing. Behind those service units came the fighting formations. W. Donovan:

'In my opinion that move was a fine example of British Army organization. It was clear that a great deal of planning had been carried out; routes reconnoitred, meal halts organized and halls for overnight sleeping prepared. Of course, that move by I Corps may have been a "showing the flag" exercise but it succeeded. Even as a soldier you have no idea of the power of the Army, of numbers, of equipment. Our BEF was all mechanized. There was not a single horse on our establishment. This was in contrast to the French Army. Later on, sometime in November 1939, I was on a parade which ended with British and French units marching past the saluting base. The French looked very much as they must have done in the Great War, the same uniforms and horse-drawn artillery. Our men wore the new battledress. As a military policeman on duty I was one of the few still wearing service dress. The only French units which impressed me were the Mountain Troops [Chasseurs Alpins]. They were very smart, very professional with bags of swank.'

The poor impression made by the French upon Bill Donovan was reflected in the opinion of Brooke, commanding British II Corps. He attended a parade to commemorate Armistice Day and wrote in his diary of the French Army:

'Men unshaven, horses ungroomed, clothing and saddlery that did not fit. Vehicles dirty and a complete lack of pride . . . the look in the men's faces, disgruntled and insubordinate . . . '

At 07.00 hrs on 20 May, the battalions of 170th Brigade were resting alongside the Arras–Cambrai road when German armour attacked the Durham Light Infantry. The Tyneside Scottish were at Neuville-Vitasse when news of the attack was received and the battalion was ordered to march to Ficheux. The rear Company was trapped by tanks in Neuville and overrun. At Mercatel other Panzer units struck the marching men and soft-skin vehicles. Despite being in a tactically unfavourable situation it is clear that the Tyneside Scottish put up a desperate resistance. As an example of the spirit of the battalion, it was reported that Provost-Sergeant Chambers was last seen alive trying to prise open the hatch cover of a Panzer with his bayonet. In the unequal battle against overwhelming odds, much of it against Rommel and his 7th Panzer Division, the 1st Battalion lost over a hundred men killed in action; about 1 in 7 of those who fought that day. One of the wounded was Malcolm Armstrong, with HQ Company:

'We marched south of Arras which was in flames at the time. We took to the 15cwt trucks and made our way to Ficheux. I was in the first lorry and we were all standing as we moved. Between Mercatel and Ficheux we had got to a farmhouse when machine-gun fire above our heads halted the lorry. Our truck pulled up suddenly and everyone jumped down on to the ground. In the truck where I had been, Private Todhunter was still sitting in the front. I told him to get out, but he did not do so and then I saw that a single bullet to his head had killed him. Our first casualty. As I turned round I could see a small tank approaching. We fixed bayonets in order to attack. At that moment I noticed that the tank gun was pointing straight at me! I think I escaped being killed then because the gun then swung in a different direction and one of my mates was killed. Together with Private Albert Foster (who was also killed that day) we advanced along the side of a farm as far as the stables. I was about to go inside when a bullet, or something like it, hit my rifle which flew out of my hands. I bent down to pick it up and that movement saved my life for the second time. When I reached a hedge that ran behind this building, I came across about ten of my mates who had been cut down by machine-gun fire. I quickly got down behind them and it was then that I was wounded by a mortar bomb. I immediately applied my first-aid dressing and as the Germans seemed to be everywhere the rest of us surrendered. I remember they led us along a column of tanks but as I was in considerable pain, everything became hazy in my mind. We were all interrogated then. Like most of the other wounded, I was placed on a stretcher. I then fainted through loss of blood and when I came to there were only two of us left. My companion asked for a drink. I was able to get to my feet in order to try to find a tap and I ran into two Germans. One of them put up his rifle to his shoulder and aimed at me. I had quite a job explaining to him that I was only looking for a drink of water. Later I was moved into a hospital at Cambrai and as I was unable to find any other men from my battalion could only presume that many had died of their wounds. I heard a rumour that our French liaison officer collaborated with the Germans. Perhaps he did, because the ambush was so perfect.'

Roy Cooke completes the story:

'There are sixty-two headstones of men from the 1st Battalion, The Tyneside Scottish at Bucaquoy Road, British War Cemetery at Ficheux, all dated 20 May, 1940. Private Albert Foster rests there, aged 21, but Todhunter may be one of the twenty-five unidentified. The name of the farm was "Ferme Fronier" and there is a plaque nearby which commemorates the sad events of that Monday morning in May 1940.'

The Allied armies were soon under such intense pressure from the Germans that withdrawal was the only option if they were to avoid encirclement and destruction. As some of the divisions of the British Expeditionary Force moved back through Belgium they crossed an area which was hallowed in British military history – the Ypres salient. Henri Braem was a young boy living in

Zillebeke, a small village between Ypres and Menin, when the British Army conducted its fighting retreat through Flanders in May 1940. Although this book is restricted to the memories of former soldiers I thought an exception should be made and that the story of Henri Braem should be included because it gives a new dimension: war through the eyes of a young civilian foreigner.

'The year 1940 was a milestone in my life for on 10 May, war broke out. Until that time it had been a strange situation for the British soldiers [in Northern France] as they hadn't had to fight . . . most of them got back to Great Britain during the week-ends and could spend a couple of days with their families at home. For that reason some people translated the initials BEF as BACK EVERY FRIDAY. Although they were at war with the Germans, they hadn't seen a German soldier. Behind our house my father had constructed a shelter of corrugated iron and had reinforced the top and side walls with earth. There were other shelters in the area [British and German ones which had been put up during the Great War]. These were concrete ones because we lived surrounded by WWI battlefields. On Sunday 26 May we went to church as usual and in the afternoon we heard shooting. "German rifle fire," said my father who recognized the dry sound from WWI. My parents decided to leave our village. We would leave as soon as possible and my parents collected some supplies and valuable possessions, locked all the doors and gave a last look at our beloved house. At 5 pm we set out carrying all our luggage and we young people found it really a pleasure because we didn't know the real truth of the danger hanging over our heads. We came across a Belgian armoured train on the Ypres-Roulers track, put there to stop the German advance on that sector. Eventually we reached the village of Poelkapelle which was packed with refugees like ourselves. During the 28th the Belgian Army capitulated. The people were very pleased because if the Germans had bombarded the village there would have been a massacre. On the 29th we saw the first German soldiers in Poelkapelle. We young boys were not accustomed to the grey colour of the tunics and that unusual helmet shape. The soldiers paid no attention to us as we made our way home. We saw lots of discarded equipment. Holes had been dug here and there. There were some trenches, or rather infantry holes [foxholes]. Several houses had been damaged by shellfire, and there were plenty of shellholes. Several cows, pigs and other animals had been killed and some had already begun to give out an awful smell. The front door of our house had been forced and all our food had been stolen. All the pots and pans had been used and food left inside them. An HE shell had destroyed our toilet and all our animals had gone. They had all escaped into the fields, but eventually we got them all back again.

'The first days back it was difficult to get accustomed to the new life; a life of occupation. People began to clear the traces left over from the previous week. We buried the fallen soldiers; British as well as German. One of the British belonged to 6th Battalion Seaforth Highlanders. His name was John MacManus and he was buried by my father and his cousin in the corner of the field along the roadside. John had been hit by a piece of shell and then hit again as he was dressing his wound. Our local carpenter put a wooden cross on his grave with his helmet on top. The cross bore his name and for us his grave symbolized the heavy fighting that had raged in the village. From post-war researches I have discovered that both the British 5th and 50th Divisions had been in our area. They had earlier been involved in the bitter fighting around Arras and began to arrive in the Zillebeke–Hollebecke–Houthem area of Ypres during 25/26 May. They were attacked during the afternoon of the 25th by elements of German Sixth Army, and the rifle fire which we had heard had been the first contact in our area between British recce patrols and the Germans. The British used the natural defence lines in our area. These were Hill 60 and Hill 62, the Ypres–Comines railway line and the canal line alongside it. The Zillebeke sector was defended by: 6th Seaforth Highlanders (17th Infantry Division of 5th Division) and the 4/5th Battalion The Green Howards (15th Brigade, 50th Division) on the left. The 2nd Royal Scots Fusiliers in the centre with 2nd Northamptons in reserve. On the right the 2nd Royal Inniskilling Fusiliers and 2nd Cameronians.

'The main German assault, on Monday 27 May, went in under a heavy barrage. The Germans advanced from Zillebeke village green and Hill 60 against the railway line. The British slaughtered them and each time the German attack was renewed the British shot them down from their good defensive positions. A Mr. Bauwen, who owns the café hardly 30 metres from the railway line, stayed there during the whole battle. From his reports it seemed that the British troops had been ordered to hold the enemy until at least 3 pm on 28 May. Although they were outnumbered, exhausted and without food they held to the last. Meanwhile on the 27th the remnants of 6th Seaforths and 2nd Royal Scots Fusiliers were overwhelmed. The survivors regrouped. The next morning, the 28th, the Germans opened a furious bombardment and attacked with fresh troops. Eventually, the British were forced back to the main road from Ypres to Warneton, and then to Voormezele where a dressing-station had been set up. They continued to withdraw and some may have been lucky enough to re-embark for Great Britain from the area between Dunkirk and La Panne. According to Major-General Franklyn, GOC 5th Division, the Divisions which held firm along the Ypres–Comines canal made it possible for the main body of the BEF to re-embark safely back to Great Britain. The fighting was very heavy and in my village of Zillebeke the 6th Seaforths lost 48 out of a total of 77 killed in action. Inside Zillebeke village the Germans lost 55, who were first buried on the spot, then exhumed and buried in Lommel.'

John Donovan of 2nd Royal Ulster Rifles:

'We were retreating through Belgium and in this town there was a hotel. I remember looking in the door and there was nobody there but a whole collection of musical instruments. Well, me being a musician and all that I dashed in and got a trumpet. I carried that trumpet all the way back to Dunkirk and brought it back with me. I still have it today and if the rightful owner would like it back I'll gladly return it. I suppose we looked on things like that as a soldier's prerogative. I can remember coming across an abandoned train full of NAAFI stores; cigarettes and things like that. A lot of the lads filled their pockets with stuff. Everybody thought that the Germans were going to get it anyway so nobody would worry about us taking it. Well, believe you me, somebody did, for not long after we had reformed in England we were all docked five bob for the stuff we had taken from the train and most of us had thrown the bloody stuff away. We got off the beach at Dunkirk in a small boat which we rowed ourselves. All the lads were shattered; no sleep, no proper food for nearly three weeks and it was all we could do to row the thing. Anyway there was this second lieutenant from some English crowd and he said that we might be at sea for a week or two weeks. I think he had dreams of going to America. Then he promised to take us all to the best hotel in London and stand us all the best meal when we got home. We might have been going round in circles when we heard this boat. It was a Navy patrol boat with a man at the front with a gun aimed at us. We asked where they were going, expecting to be told Dover or Folkestone or somewhere like that and they said "Dunkirk". We couldn't believe it; we had only left the place and here we were going back. I fell into a hazy doze and what woke me up was the boat being hit by shrapnel. We were in Dunkirk. It was awful, like a scene out of Dante's *Inferno.* People screaming in agony and flames. I wouldn't like to go to hell, for that's what that was. And the officer who was going to treat us all to a meal? We never saw him again after we landed in England.'

The Field Regiment with which Gunner Stonard served was part of the 50th Division, which had the dubious distinction of being designated 'motorized':

'Our role was to be a GHQ Reserve, ready to rush to any part of the battle that needed rapid reinforcement. The 50th was to spend the two or three weeks after the German attack, swanning backwards and forwards getting hopelessly enmeshed with the tens of thousands of refugees who blocked most of the route along which the BEF was ordered to move. The Battery arrived at a small village called Bailleul. Immediately in front of the gun position was a large bank of tall fir trees and a German cemetery of the 1914-18 war. On the opposite side of the field was a small British war cemetery. In that cemetery one of the Troop found the grave of a relative. So the first shots that E Troop fired were flanked by the dead of both sides of the last war. We were selected to take part in a counter-attack which was to be launched at Arras by a unit called "Frank Force", after its commander. The Battery came into action during the early hours of the morning of 21 May. Firing began in support of an infantry attack, then at various targets; mainly armoured units. We finally came out of action late in the afternoon and then carried on a long, slow withdrawal during the night. When the Regiment returned to England, exchanges of experiences with the infantry who had also taken part in the counter-attack revealed that the gunfire was quite effective. The German division involved was the 7th Panzer commanded by Rommel. The counter-attack advanced for nearly ten miles and captured four hundred enemy prisoners. General Le Q Martel's 50th Division was considered by the Germans to have been one of the most determined that had been encountered during the campaign. The German High Command gained the impression that the counter-attack had been launched by five divisions and that the BEF was much stronger than had been anticipated.'

The Regiment withdrew via Ypres with 150 Brigade and then to the Dunkirk area where it destroyed its guns.

'The battery withdrew into the corner of a field. All surplus equipment and vehicles were destroyed. The guns fired off the remaining ammunition except for two shells. The Troop decided to destroy their guns by the traditional method of "one down the spout and one in the breech". I volunteered to help destroy my gun, feeling that having spent the greatest part of the last six months polishing and cleaning it I was entitled to the dubious honour of blowing it up. The road to the embarkation port was bordered by fields containing hundreds of lorries, some burning, but most of them with their bonnets raised, the engines having been smashed with a sledge-hammer. The BEF marched in a disciplined order carrying what equipment and weapons they could. Some of the officers and NCOs carried rifles which they had found discarded. Some carried two.'

Stonard was one of several correspondents who recalled that while marching towards Dunkirk they had been sniped at, probably by Fifth Columnists. Bill Priest, who was also in the Dunkirk evacuation and who also recalled that his unit came under sniper fire, wrote that one sentry who complained that he had been shot at was told by an unsympathetic Regimental Sergeant Major, 'Well, you shouldn't have such a bloody ugly face.'

Stonard reached the outskirts of Dunkirk where:

'A sailor directed us towards the docks. There we saw a long queue being formed and joined the men as they shuffled their way along a wooden pier at the end of which was a destroyer. Looking around it was amazing to see that some of the soldiers were in full battle kit, carrying rifles. A closer scrutiny revealed them to be Guardsmen. Although obviously very tired they still managed to have that aloofness that is so distinctive of the Guards. That men should form a mile-long line, three abreast, patiently waiting for their turn to climb aboard a small boat, seemingly oblivious to the constant noise of gunfire and the exploding of bombs and yet maintain a degree of cheerfulness was the true "Dunkirk spirit"; a term now a part of the English vocabulary, often used in the wrong context.'

DUNKIRK

Gunner Evans, a Regular soldier in an AA regiment, was recalled to the Colours shortly before the outbreak of war and served in France during the 1940 campaign. During his time in the Dunkirk perimeter he was asked by his sergeant, 'Tich' Proctor to go with a group that was bringing back one of the guns which the regiment had abandoned near La Panne.

'The French infantry tried to stop our lorry shouting, "Boche", meaning that the Germans were only one and a half miles up the road. We found the gun and firing breechblock. When we got back to the beach out of the blue a young officer came up. He said, "I was on board a boat ready to go to England, but I saw you blokes having a go so I decided to join you." He was calm and cool and one of us. We had no instruments so he used his hands and experience to put us on target. We accounted for seven planes. At night we manned two Bren guns on a bridge up the road. When the beach was nearly clear [of troops waiting to be evacuated] we marched in single file round the back streets. We saw some terrible sights. In front of our eyes were field guns complete with gunner crews, some smiling. I didn't see any blood, but they were all dead. It must have been shell blast. The last couple of days was like hell let loose. On our way along the beach some soldiers were killed or wounded by our own ammo lorries set ablaze by German machine-gun fire or by bombing. We lay on the sand. Near me was a French sailor who was dead. His face was dark-blue. As I went farther along the beach I took cover in a wide tunnel which was filled with wounded. A ginger-headed medical officer was cutting one chap's leg off. Lots of chaps were groaning in pain. It was horrible. We finished up in Liverpool and I heard a man in a civvy suit go on about being dumped at Stoke-on-Trent. He was a soldier who had just picked up his clobber and gone home. I went back to the barracks, dumped all my kit in my valise and thumbed a lift. As I walked through Chatterley valley which led to the bottom of our street, I heard a woman shout to another woman, "That's one of Evans lads isn't it?" So I darted through an entry, up our back-yard, let myself in and sat on the sofa. There was only my dad in. After a bit he said, "OK son?" I said "Yes." He carried on cutting bread and then the penny dropped. He turned round, looked at me and said, "Hast bin in that bit of a do?" He meant Dunkirk.'

The fighting which Bill Priest described so vividly was that in which French and British rearguards held off the attacking Germans, thereby allowing the BEF and other French formations to be taken from the beaches at Dunkirk. One man who was taken off in one of the small boats was R. H. C. Wileman. Ex-Gunner Wileman enlisted into the Territorial Army on a six-year engagement in 1938, and joined a local unit, 57th Field Regiment. This was equipped with 25pdr guns. He recalled that upon being called to the Colours at the outbreak of war, his Brighton-based regiment was billeted in the Dome and the Corn Exchange for three weeks before being moved to Stoke sub Hamdon, in Somerset.

'Soon we were told off to embark for an unknown destination. We sailed from Southampton to Cherbourg, then travelled up country to Ypres in Belgium. A couple of days later we were told to fall back so we retreated to a place called Béthune, only to find that the Luftwaffe had paid a visit and there were many dead or dying people and animals. We moved farther back to Lyons. We used an old coffee warehouse but there were many Fifth Column spies in those days and again the German Air Force were soon dropping their scrap iron on us. We were then ordered to make for the coast and all went well until we reached the La Bassée Canal and it was there I somehow became separated from my regiment. I got mixed up with the Grenadier Guards who had been told to hold a bridge crossing the canal. As I was a Gunner and had no rifle I was speedily transferred to another RA unit. Then we got to Calais only to find that the German Army had encircled the area so we hurriedly moved to the Dunkirk area where we were ordered into a field and told to climb into the surrounding hedge which would act as camouflage. We were there for quite a time and to my horror I found that my Iron Ration had been stolen from me. By the time we were ordered down to the beaches I was feeling weak from lack of food, but still kept moving. I can still remember the Stuka dive-bombers. Even today I can visualize those cannon-shells whipping up the sand. I, for one, used the vehicles bogged down in the soft sand as a cover against them. Soon we were on the move again towards the water's edge to board some of the boats which had come from England to save us. I was one of the fortunate ones and marched along a jetty towards a ship which I boarded with great haste. I quickly went down into the hold not caring what the Germans did and must have fainted from hunger because when I came to, I was in a train which stopped at Salisbury station. I vaguely remember having a bun, an orange and an Army Field Card put into my hand and being told to tick off where necessary and to address it to my family so that they knew I was safe. Eventually, we reached Yeovil town station where we were loaded into ambulances and ferried to Hounstone army camp. I was there for a period of three weeks' convalescence after which I was given a medical examination and found to be unfit for further service overseas. My Regiment, which was part of 44th Division, was sent to Africa. Not many came back.'

Another Gunner who went to France with the first elements of the BEF, was Brian Thatcher, a Regular officer who, by the end of the war, was commanding his Regiment.

'When "in the line' [during the winter of 1939/40] (there was the whole of Belgium between us and the Germans), we found ourselves responsible for observation on I Corps front and were centred round the vicinity of Douai. After we had been "in the line" for some weeks, someone got the idea that we should be withdrawn, so back we went to the little village of Contay, some 10 miles from Amiens. It was a hard winter but we made ourselves pretty comfortable one way and another. We alternated between "the line" and "rest" preferring the latter because the country and surroundings were so much more pleasant. We were very "gas conscious" in those days with our bits of detecting paper – white, yellow and blue, which were alleged to produce pink spots on the approach of anything particularly horrid. When the gas scare was at its height the Colonel was very keen on surprise practices. One day, with a screech of brakes, he drew his staff car up and shouted "gas!" at the sentry outside the headquarters of a certain battery. The chap doubled off smartly as though to give the warning only to return with a 2-gallon tin of petrol. Early in May 1940, I was on leave in England when the Germans started to walk through Belgium. The adjutant was home on leave at the same time so we arranged to meet at Victoria station where, by the use of the loud-speaker, we rounded up a few other members of the regiment who were trying to get back. Against fairish odds we fought our way over to Boulogne and then on to Amiens. We were back with the regiment and involved in battle within 36 hours of having left England. I am afraid that my memories are very vague about the retreat via Dunkirk. We never quite knew in which direction we were fighting and all the time we seemed to be slipping quietly towards the coast. The weather was fine throughout and I remember sleeping the afternoon of my birthday (16 May) quietly in an orchard. Spirits were high and we were never short of anything to eat or drink for by this time we were living largely off the country. Comparatively early on in proceedings the regiment found itself in Dunkirk, the docks of which were still intact. The place was, of course, being bombed from time to time, but there were plenty of cellars in which to take shelter while we waited for some craft to convey us home.

'I wish I could remember the name of the ship in question. I do know that she was one of the little ferries which in peacetime used to function off the west coast of Scotland. Having destroyed everything of value except our instruments, binoculars, etc., which we took with us, we moved aboard in a very orderly manner quite worthy of the Guards, marching in single file up the gangways, later to be battened down below decks. I suppose if one had been less tired and fired with a little more imagination, one could have developed a bit of an anxiety complex shut up down there with the odd bomb falling around, but I know I had only two desires: one was to shave and the other was to sleep. The former I managed with a borrowed razor; the latter I accomplished on the floor, all the way to Dover where we landed. There is no doubt that the regiment enjoyed (hardly an appropriate word but it conveys my meaning) a pretty easy exit via Dunkirk. None of the mud of Flanders or unshaven faces for us. Quite apart from anything else, the Colonel would see to that and he ordered a best clothing parade twenty-four hours after having landed in England. This parade went off well with the exception of one incident. Behind the rear rank of my battery was spotted a tarpaulin lying on the ground, obviously concealing an object of some bulk. The unveiling ceremony revealed one of my ex-trumpeters, now a DR, asleep. Our regiment managed to land home pretty spick and span, but then we had had an easy passage. Even so, in my opinion, there was little excuse for some of the scruffiness we saw. Just about the first sign of demoralization is when a soldier ceases to shave – this I confirmed later on in the war. In any case it was a pity that the expression "Dunkirk Heroes" arose. I know that heroism went on round the perimeter and on the beaches, but the whole thing was a glorious defeat.'

One tragedy at sea, involving a heavy loss of life among British troops, and which is still commemorated annually, was the loss of the *Lancastria* in June 1940. R. A. Joyce, a Sergeant of the Royal Engineers, was on board the ship and his account described the event with characteristic British understatement.

'During the retreat from France, my RE unit, attached to the Advanced Air Striking Force, reached St. Nazaire. We got on board the *Lancastria* at approximately noon on Monday, 17 June, some of the very last to be packed in, so we ended up in the cabins on the boat deck. We managed to get a meal but the ship remained at anchor until about 4.00 pm, when there was the never-to-be-forgotten whine of dive-bombers. Being on the boat deck I quickly realised that there was no point hanging about as the boat was sinking by the bow and was going around and up. I climbed down a rope-ladder and then jumped 40 feet into the water. I swam for about two hours, gradually undressing to make things easier and luckily the water was warm. When I looked back I could see that the *Lancastria* had turned turtle and was covered with little figures singing *Roll out the barrel*, but soon even that stopped and the boat settled. I was picked up, together with hundreds of others, by a tramp steamer which made a dash across the Channel and landed us at Portsmouth where we were concentrated in Devonport Park and held incommunicado. No word of the sinking of the *Lancastria* reached the newspapers until well into July or even later.'

DIEPPE, 1942

On 19 August 1942, British and Canadian forces mounted an assault from England upon the French port of Dieppe. In the years that have passed since then, a great deal has been written about the sacrifice of 2nd Canadian Division and questions asked why the attack had to be made. The town of Dieppe, standing at the mouth of the river Arques, was known to be strongly garrisoned. Cliffs outside the town carried heavy guns to defend the port and to dominate it.

Dieppe's shingle beaches were backed by a high-walled promenade from which there were few exits. As a consequence, soldiers debarking on to the shingle would be held in a killing-ground unless they could force their way over the promenade wall and into the town.

What were the compelling reasons for sending those highly trained but as yet 'unblooded' Canadians into what was so obviously an unequal struggle? It would seem that several factors coincided. The Americans were demanding the opening of a Second Front to take pressure off the Russians, although it was obvious that they had no idea of what such an operation would involve. The British High Command was convinced that the Western Allies were still not strong enough, nor well enough equipped, to undertake a successful full-scale cross-Channel invasion of Hitler's Europe. The impatient Americans must be given a demonstration of just how difficult and bloody an invasion would be. In addition the British had a new tank that had to be tested under battle conditions together with tank landing craft of new patterns. They, too, had to be tested to see whether they would be suitable when the real invasion of France was made. The 2nd Canadian Infantry Division, supported by the new tanks, would prove whether an assault landing and the capture of a strongly defended port was feasible. It proved not to be.

More than 2,000 of the 5,000 Canadians who had set out to test Hitler's Europe were lost. Sixty-five per cent of the assaulting infantry battalions were casualties. Those losses demonstrated two things: *Festung Europa* was too strong to be invaded in 1942 or 1943. More preparation and more assault craft were essential as well as covering fire of fearsome power if the entrenched German defenders were to be destroyed.

Jack Brewin's account is one man's story of the Dieppe operation:

'This account is based on notes which I made about a week after the event when the Special Sea Service squad with which I was serving was given intensive training for a secret operation. At Fort Gomert our NCOs and officers joined us and we then paraded for Lord Louis Mountbatten who startled us with his informal approach, telling us to break ranks and to gather round him. The four special squads were first posted – mine to Sunderland and then ordered to the south coast. During the afternoon of 18 August, things really began to take shape as the jetty crowded with troops, for the most part Canadians, but also men of No. 3 Commando. These were all embarked directly on to landing craft. We left Newhaven about 0100 hours, on a very dark night with a swelling sea. We were under orders not to fire, even at suspicious targets. In the darkness of the night there were several near collisions between craft and we narrowly missed hitting an LCT. I have the impression now of being lonely in my position as gun-layer on No. 2 pompom. I was not afraid of events. I think none of us were, but we had time to think and to contemplate what might be in wait for us. We were all about 19 to 20 years of age and none of us had seen previous active service. About 03.00 hours the sky suddenly filled with tracer and it was obvious that some sort of attack was taking place. I know now that this event was the unfortunate chance meeting with a small German convoy, a meeting which contributed towards the terrible outcome of the operation. As dawn broke we had our first glimpse of a hostile shore, at that stage quite normal with some white cliffs and a town. Apart from some distant thuds there was nothing seemingly other than the common-place. As the morning light grew I could see the magnitude of the operation. The foreshore was obliterated by many craft, the sea around us occupied by many ships. With the coming of full light the scene changed. The air was suddenly filled with aircraft and we fired madly at all of them. At this time we were about half a mile offshore and so occupied with our fire that what was happening on the beach escaped us. There appeared to be hundreds of planes swarming everywhere and identification was so difficult that we fired at everything which came near and when a plane was shot down we cheered and claimed responsibility. The RAF was that day operating Mustang fighters for the first time and resemblance of this aircraft to the German Me 109 was such that we most certainly shot one of these down.

'It was about 0830 hrs when our role changed. We steamed closer inshore and what we had already experienced under air attack was nothing to the holocaust which now presented itself. It is difficult to describe each separate detail of events. I even doubt that I ever could have done so. It now all seems to be one mixed impression of terror and nightmare. I can only try to describe that impression, *en bloc* so to speak. By this time the withdrawal was taking place and landing craft, mostly LCPs, were streaming from the beach filled beyond normal capacity with badly wounded men. My craft lay broadside to the beach and it seemed that every gun, light and heavy, was directed on us from the shore. I seemed rooted to the gun platform, possibly because I imagined the shield would give some protection. Tracer flew in all directions and a great piece of metal from the ship's side landed at my feet. I heard terrible screams all around me, the gun had jammed and wounded were being lifted aboard from the shore. The sights were ghastly. A Canadian minus an arm climbed aboard unaided calmly smoking a cigarette. I could not have believed such courage. Terribly mutilated bodies lay all around; the sea was full of débris and floating dead, tremendous noise and the air full of stinking smoke. The officer's mess-deck was being used as a sick-bay and the orderlies were almost throwing the wounded down to the surgeon. Almost as continuously the dead were being arranged on the deck. One of those Canadians was covered in a Union Jack which had been found inside his jacket. Surely not the reason for which it had been intended. I have no idea how long this terrible episode lasted, but orders were eventually given for our withdrawal and we were among the very last to leave. A heavy cloud of smoke enveloped the town; the beach was filled with immobilized tanks and landing craft. Our journey back was one of utter misery. The mess-deck was crowded with survivors and wounded lay around everywhere. A stench of mutilated humanity prevailed. I myself was in a state of utter shock. I had no knowledge of what our role had been. I knew even less of what, if anything, we had achieved. I suppose someone, somewhere, was able to make a pattern of the day's events. I couldn't. We arrived off Newhaven late at night and as the boom defence nets had been drawn and the harbour entry blocked had to remain outside all night. We entered port next morning and tied to the same jetty as that from which we had left some 30 hours before. Then we had been young and so immature. Now we felt older and full of terrible experience. The wounded were loaded into ambulances and the poor dead were hoisted ashore on large flat boards. A war correspondent came aboard and approached me. "What did you think of Dieppe?" he asked. "So that's where we have been," I replied. How ridiculous that must have sounded to him, but the name meant nothing to me. Hell has many different names.'

NORMANDY, 1944

Four years after it had left France as a result of the catastrophic débâcle of 1940, the British Army returned to north-west Europe via the D-Day landing beaches in June 1944. The personal stories of those who took part in the liberation of Europe begin with Jack Brewin's account of his part in the opening phases of the assault landings.

'On the night of 5 June 1944, we lay off Spithead surrounded by the "vehicles of war", grey battleships, heavy cruisers, sleek destroyers, the heavily laden sea transports and the multitudes of different types of landing craft. The night was cold and wet, the sea was swelly and inclined to be a bit choppy further out. We waited aware that final decisions were being taken, the time of estimation was about to cease and history was about to be made. I was by now accomplished in assault landings having been in on "Torch" [the invasion of French North Africa], in Pantelleria, Syracuse in Sicily and at Salerno in Italy. France was the next target. The LCI on which I served was American-built and designed to carry about 200 troops in three separate apartments. The craft had a speed of about 15 knots, but did not float on the water like the other assault landing craft, which were flat-bottomed, but cut through the water. As a result the ship was almost constantly awash on the upper deck. The troops did not like this type of vessel for they had first to clamber to the top deck and then descend steep narrow ramps on either side of the bows and hope that the water was not too deep from then on. All the previous landings I had taken part in had begun under some secrecy, but in southern England it was obvious that major landings were sure to take place. In fact I think that this tremendous concentration of troops was in itself a great morale builder. The actual victory was 50 per cent won before the first commencement of battle. I understand that as the troop convoys left Portsmouth civilians lined the coast cheering the departure, loud-hailers aboard some of the ships played military music and ships' sirens sounded, almost like the farewell that had been for troops off to fight some colonial war during the previous century. Morale has never been higher amongst troops of any nation. How did I feel as we left Spithead? I don't think that any of us felt fear for we had trained for this great operation and all felt confident that our leadership had been supreme. Then, there was great comfort in the vast numbers and the knowledge that great forces were on our side. The comfort also of one's comrades, although most were new to me. But they looked up to me with some respect due to my previous experience and that fact alone did much for my own morale. How could I disgrace myself when many of those around me looked to me for support. Most of us kept up our good spirits during those early hours. We were spoken to by our Troop Commander and at this point we were told that our destination was to be France; that and nothing more. We knew that 48 Commando was to land with us to perform a pincer movement in order to connect the groups separated by a beach unsuitable for landing on. We were told that ours was to be Sword Beach, Peter Sector, and we were assured that by the time we landed the fortifications would have been softened as a result of heavy air and sea bombardment.

'We were closely packed together, not just because of our numbers. Our equipment weighed individually above 90lb. I also carried a rifle and, as a signaller, had a radio transmitter weighing about 30lb to be shared between me and another of my comrades. Our task was to make contact with 48 Commando and French civilians. To ensure mobility we were to use folding bicycles which were stored in racks in the stern of the craft. I cannot now remember the hour we actually landed but it was certainly after dawn. A tremendous bombardment was taking place almost up to the time we were to land and always it has been a fear of being caught in one's own fire. I could see the sector we were to land on. Later I was to learn that we were far from our allotted place. A tremendous battle taking part on our right flank was, so I learned later, 48 Commando, which lost half its numbers in that fight. By now I was on the deck of the craft with the folded cycle as addition to my load while my signaller comrade was struggling with our transmitter. Then the disembark signal was given – I think it was probably a combination of flashing lights and sirens. The ramps were lowered and we surged towards the beach. We were still a long way from the beach when it finally stopped. I would have felt much better landing from a craft with wider ramps instead of the crazy, steep, ladder-like gangways fitted to our vessel.

'The beach was clearer now, despite the smoke and fog which enveloped it. I saw what appeared to be several large houses on some kind of promenade and then a vivid streak of tracer shell streamed out of the windows towards some object to the left of us. I recall being surprised that anything could have survived the barrage from the sea. This had now stopped. I was first down the portside ramp with my comrade immediately behind me. It was no dash ashore as Hollywood might portray. Instead I remember it as an agonizing stumble down the steep ramp under my heavy load. I jumped into the sea and immediately sank into deep water that came over my head, although thinking about it now it might have been the choppy sea that gave that impression. I scrambled eventually to the beach around the bows of the craft. The bicycle was beneath the waves but I still had all my equipment and rifle as I dashed up the beach to shelter behind some rocks. The rest of the Troop seemed to be some distance from me all lost in the gloom of the morning. The fire from the houses was joined with heavy mortar fire and big bursts which suggested artillery shells. There were a great many bodies strewn around the beach. At that stage they gave the impression of being soldiers other than my comrades. Some Beach Marshals and Redcaps were trying to organize exits from the beach. I looked for my signaller comrade but could see him no more. I found out later that he had been badly wounded on getting ashore. He had had the transmitter so our combined contribution was not to be. A sergeant of our Troop was gathering his men together and I joined him in an attempt to get a foothold to the right of the houses. My mind is very confused from that point. I remember perhaps thirty of us leaving behind a beach of great confusion and gathering in a field behind the houses. I remember also some Canadian soldiers who appeared to be in some confusion and leaderless.

'We were eventually joined by a lieutenant and about twenty Marines. He told us that the remainder of the Troop had now regrouped and had moved to the left against Lion-sur-Mer. We were to attack a large house or château which had been his original objective. The distance seemed a long one and the roads were strewn with German dead. We gained our objective, but the proposed link-up with 48 Commando was never achieved. A big counter-attack was supposed to be prepared by the Germans, but this never took place. In any case there was no strength left in 48 Commando and most never left the beach alive. During the actions of the next three days we took many prisoners. They seemed to be a mixture of asiatic-type Russians who had been recruited from POW camps as well as some young and frightened German boys. Many were suffering from shell-shock following the intense bombardment and I saw little to indicate the fanatical resistance that was to come further inland. It was at this time I was sent back to England with German prisoners and our own wounded, many from 48 Commando. I was treated with great care and consideration on my return to the barracks at Eastney; white bread, well-cooked food and white sheets and, most important of all, leave. I suppose we had achieved something on that day, but success is seldom witnessed by the ordinary soldier. That is for the planners and manipulators of the General Staff to enjoy. Victories are things we are told belong to us long after they have taken place.'

The extreme left of the Allied beachheads in Normandy rested on the River Orne. Airborne troops had landed to capture intact the important bridges across that river and had orders to hold these until relieved by Lord Lovat's Brigade. One of the soldiers taking part in the Commando Brigade's operation was Private Farmborough, who was wounded during the operation.

'We were part of the 1st Special Services Brigade, which comprised four separate Commando units, commanded by Brigadier The Lord Lovat. We were on the extreme left flank of the British Army and landed on Sword Beach at first light on 6 June 1944. The plan was that three of the Commando units went hell for leather to join up with the Airborne troops which had landed around the bridges on the River Orne and the Orne Canal and to hold those bridges at all costs. No. 4 Commando, of which I was a member, had to dash along the coast road, a distance of about a mile, to destroy and blow up a battery of big guns at Ouistreham on the mouth of the River Orne. Then we had to speed with the utmost alacrity to rejoin the brigade at the bridges a few miles inland. We had about 500 men, which included 60 French Commandos attached to us for this little episode. I myself never reached Ouistreham. I was shot on the way, I believe by an automatic weapon. I can't say what type because I never saw it. However, a couple of bullets made a mess of my left arm, shattering the bone in four places. I didn't realize how fortunate I had been until back in England some days later, when they took off my Mae West and found three more bullet lines running along the Mae West and completely missing me. Strange as it may seem, I didn't feel a thing when the bullets hit me and had no pain at all, but I was knocked to the ground. I did feel most annoyed because I was out of action. One of the lads picked up my Bren gun and off he went. You see, in circumstances like those there was no stopping to help the wounded. This we all knew. Luckily,

I was able to get behind a and dune and gradually made my way to the landing area, though not before I had nearly been run over by one of our tanks. The driver didn't see me and I had to roll out of the way a bit sharpish. I must have fainted because when I came to there were a couple of Medics beside me. They helped me back to a dressing-station by a pillbox. They couldn't do much except strap my arm across my body. I had the comfort of a stretcher and was lifted on to a DKW and ferried out to a hospital ship which sailed next day to Tilbury. I had some injections, but no other treatment until reaching England. They soon got me to hospital and started the repair business. Six months later, I left hospital, almost new.'

After the landing British Second Army, in accordance with Montgomery's strategy, attracted to itself the bulk of the German armour in Normandy and the fighting was hard and costly. Against the British perimeters were several SS Panzer Divisions whose staunch defence delayed the capture of Caen – a road communications centre which had been a D-Day objective. Brian Thatcher recalls:

'The month we spent before Caen was a pretty bloody one in more ways than one. Those who had fought in the 1914-18 War told me that the battles before Caen came up to anything they had ever experienced and I know that of the 212 casualties suffered by my regiment in the campaign in north-west Europe, at least seventy-five per cent were incurred during this month in Normandy.'

Among the many attempts which were made to destroy German opposition in the city were massive air raids, but these succeeded only in creating piles of rubble which served the defenders but impeded the attackers. Other ways had to be found if Caen was to fall. It was felt that if the city could be outflanked, the defenders, drawn chiefly from the 12th SS Division 'Hitler Youth', would be compelled to withdraw. In pursuit of his plan to bypass the obstruction, Montgomery ordered 7th Armoured Division, the élite formation which he had brought with him out of the desert, to drive south-east from Bayeux to Villers-Bocage. Once the 7th Armoured had reached and consolidated around that area the German position would be untenable. Albert Kingston served with one of the battalions of the Queen's Brigade which formed part of 7th Armoured.

'The Brigade had served in the African campaign as part of 7th Armoured. I did not get called up until late in 1942, so I didn't serve in the desert. My first action was in Normandy. We landed on 10 June, and I was surprised to see so little destruction. From BBC reports we all expected to see the place [Normandy] looking like the pictures of the Western Front – all mud and tree stumps. They tell me that Caen was a mess, but I never saw it so I cannot say. The countryside was very green with high hedges running along little roads. Some of the roads had hedges which were more than twelve-foot high and so thick you could not see through them. They were good defensive positions and the units that had been fighting in this sort of countryside deserve every credit. It must have been a real hell. There were lots of little cemeteries we passed as we moved up the line. Four or five graves in a group – an infantry Section perhaps, or a Sherman crew, because the place was littered with knocked out Shermans. And some of them stank. There was more than likely bodies still in them. So far as I remember from what we were told in 'O' groups, 7th Armoured was to capture a little town called Villers-Bocage. If it could do this it would have trapped the Jerries in Caen. They would have to pull out or be destroyed and if they pulled back we would have them on the run. Things turned out a bit different from what we were told was going to happen. The Jerry opposition was quite strong and it took us a couple of days to reach the little town which was our objective.'

For there to be an Allied breakout of the confining beachheads the mass of German armour available to OKW had to be prevented from reaching Normandy because each new Panzer Division arriving in the area made the Allied task more difficult. The build-up of German divisions had to be stopped or slowed down. On the German side the Panzer formations which had been fighting since D-Day needed to be relieved and reinforced. The replacement formations struggled to reach the battle line, and as each arrived it was committed immediately to action. The thrust from Bayeux by 7th Armoured was countered along the line Verrières–Tilly, by the newly arrived crack Panzer Lehr Division, whose opposition forced the British formation to seek alternative routes to the objective.

In the fluid situation which existed in the second week of June, possession of Villers-Bocage was vital to both sides. As the most important road centre to the south of Bayeux it was a key point. To ensure that it stayed in German hands OKW had sent forward 2nd Panzer Division, but until it arrived in force a stop-gap unit, 501 SS Heavy Tank Battalion, was put in to hold the ground through which 2nd Panzer would pass to the combat zone. On the British side, 7th Armoured Division, held up in front of Tilly, was probing to locate the left flank of Panzer Lehr Division. Once this had been turned the advance would be resumed towards the high ground which dominated Villers-Bocage. By 13 June, part of 22nd Brigade of 7th Armoured had worked its way round 2nd Panzer flank and begun its move towards Villers-Bocage. Orders were issued that once the little town had been reached, 4th County of London Yeomanry and 'A' Company of 1st Battalion, The Rifle Brigade, were to push on and to take Point 213, the high ground which lay about a mile to the north-east. By 09.00hrs the point unit of 22nd Armoured had reached the little town.

Albert Kingston:

'We were in the town centre, a little square and not much else. There were a few shops open, cafés I think, and we were just standing about waiting for orders when we heard the sound of gunfire coming from the road out of town. There seemed from the noise to be a big battle going on and presently we saw black clouds of smoke in the air. One of our soldiers said they were tanks blowing up. This did not sound so good as we had one of our armoured brigades on the road ahead. Then, all of a sudden our anti-tank platoons were ordered into action – to take post. The ammunition trucks were driven into side streets and all the rifle sections were told to take up positions in windows of houses on the "enemy" side of the village, as it was called. To be honest, I saw nothing of the battle which followed, although I was in it. My memories are of the noise and the solid shot that smashed through the walls of the room in which I and a group of other Queensmen were positioned. I suppose, when you are excited or frightened noise sounds louder in some way. Also the narrow streets seemed to hold the noise in so that it sounded really loud. There were several loud bangs which were our 6pdr anti-tank guns going off and then one very loud explosion. I learned later that this was a Bren-carrier of ammunition that went up. Then we heard tank tracks squeaking and squealing and these must have been Jerry's because the sound seemed to be coming from the "enemy" side. Then there was a whooshing sound and a sort of flashing light behind us in the room. We all turned round and there was a hole in the outside wall and another in the inside one. A solid shot had passed through the whole house – in one side and out the other. It had been an AP round, I suppose, from a Jerry tank. There was a lot of plaster dust in the air, but none of us had been hurt. We didn't think of it at the time, but if that shall had struck a couple of feet from where it did, all of us in that room would have been killed.

'The firing seemed to spread and I believe that Jerry infantry [Panzer Grenadiers] were working their way into the town. Then there was some more tank gun fire, some machine-gun fire and then dead silence. We all waited. Nothing happened for about ten minutes or more. Then an officer came up the stairs and told us to fall in outside. The street was a mess. Bricks and rubble all over the place. A couple of hundred yards up the road there was the biggest tank I had ever seen. It looked undamaged. One of our 6pdrs was lying on its side, just opposite our house. Up came the unit transport and we moved back up the road which we had been along first thing that morning.'

The battle in Villers-Bocage in which Albert Kingston had been engaged was one in which a single Tiger tank crew from the SS Heavy Tank Battalion had created a path of destruction. It had destroyed, according to British official histories, 25 tanks, fourteen half-tracks and fourteen Bren-gun carriers. The SS officer who carried out that destruction was SS Obersturmführer (Lieutenant) Michael Wittman, a veteran of the Eastern Front where his special ability had gained him one hundred and seventeen 'kills'.

From a vantage-point in woodland Wittmann had seen the 22nd Brigade advancing up the narrow road towards the crest of Point 213. Through his binoculars he saw that the British column had halted and that men were jumping down from the vehicles. The commanders of 4th CLY point squadron and the Rifle Brigade trucked infantry were holding an 'O' Group, a final briefing before making the last bound to take the hill. A fresh squadron of the CLY was ordered to take over duty as point unit. To make room for that squadron to pass, the tanks and half-tracks already on the narrow road were ordered to 'close up' and move tight against the bocage hedge at the side of the road. It was a tactical blunder. The road was not wide and with the vehicles closed up, nose to tail, they were immobile until the new point detachment had passed them. It was a tactical blunder which Wittmann was quick to appreciate and to exploit. Moving downhill out of the woods in which he had been concealed, he smashed the leading Cromwell with a single shot. Now that he had knocked out the lead tank the British were bottled-up. They could not advance, neither could they pull back except by reversing, nor could they fire at the Tiger as it cruised down the road firing round after round into the column. A succession of shots from his massive 88mm gun destroyed the vehicles of CLY and of the 8th Hussars which came up the road to challenge him and now, reinforced by the other tanks of his

Command and the Tigers of another SS Company, he drove towards Villers-Bocage.

In the narrow streets of that place, the 6pdr anti-tank guns of the Queens went into action. A shot fired by one of them blew off the track of Wittmann's Tiger and he and his crew were forced to abandon the vehicle. In the centre of the town the other Tigers came under such fire that they were forced to pull back. This was a retreat of short duration for the Panzer Lehr Division's units soon entered the battle and launched a pincer attack upon Villers-Bocage. The 7th Armoured Division withdrew out of the town and towards Tilly from which its formations had advanced that morning. Raymond Rolls is critical of the whole operation and of the weapons with which the units were issued:

'I was in the 7th Armoured Division, but not at Villers-Bocage. I heard about what had occurred there some time later and it only confirmed what many of us thought about the division's leadership. It must have been obvious to those in command that the 22nd Brigade was in enemy territory. We had been fighting for days and regimental histories make it clear we had got round the flank and were behind the German Panzer Lehr Division. Behind the enemy line implies that you are in his territory. Yet on a narrow road in enemy territory the CLY stop and then close up their vehicles nose to tail. Why didn't they do that in the main square of the town, where there would have been more room for one unit to pass the other. Some of the histories mention the PIAT mortar as if it had been the best anti-tank weapon in the world and not, as it really was, the worst. The German anti-tank projectiles were rocket-propelled. One, which was a single shot weapon, was called the *Panzerfaust*. One man operated that. Then there was the two-man weapon, the *Panzerschreck*. One man loaded the rocket and the second man fired it. Our PIAT was spring-loaded. It had to be cocked before firing the first round and the easiest way to cock it was standing upright with both feet fixed firmly on the shoulder piece. The spring's recoil, so it was said, would recock the weapon. If the PIAT misfired, it had to be recocked again. Imagine it! Standing up in view of the enemy to pull on a strong spring. The shell it fired was shaped like a turnip. It was fitted into a cutout section on the top side of the PIAT. The sights were primitive and the range was short; effectively, about 50 yards. When the turnip flew through the air it had to strike its target squarely. If the nose did not hit point on the target the bomb did not explode. I understand a graze fuze was fitted some time later, which meant in theory that the projectile should explode so long as any part of the fuze hit the target. I must admit that when a Piat grenade did explode a lot of damage was caused. I do not think it could penetrate the front armour of a Tiger tank, but it could smash through the side and rear armour. That stupid weapon, which had to be cocked while standing up; which had only a short range and was fitted with a useless fuze, was lauded as if it were the most brilliant anti-tank device in use in any army. I know that Fusilier Jefferson of the Lancashire Fusiliers of 78th Division won the Victoria Cross at Cassino for knocking out two enemy tanks. Being a cynic, I think it was the fact that he survived that particular engagement that earned him the Cross he so richly deserved. We had PIATs in use in north-west Europe, but the number of Panzers which were knocked out were very, very few indeed when one considers how many PIATs were in use.'

THE RHINELAND CAMPAIGN AND ADVANCE INTO GERMANY

Montgomery wanted to press on into Germany without delay. He planned to establish a bridgehead and outflank the Siegfried Line with an ambitious airborne drop combined with a rapid thrust by Second Army. The 1st Airborne Division (British) and 82nd and 101st Airborne Divisions (US) would seize bridges and strategic points, hold them until reinforced and thereby assist in forming a corridor which would end in a bridgehead on the Rhine from which Second Army could sweep on to the North German Plain. The subsequent Operation 'Market Garden' in mid-September 1944 failed badly but it did not deter Montgomery from persisting with his efforts to cross the great river barrier.

The planners at Supreme Headquarters chose to make the point of maximum effort on the sector held by Montgomery's 21st Army Group. In preparation for the crossing of the Rhine the most intensive geological research was undertaken and such details obtained as the speed of the river's current, the tidal movement and the height of the river's bank. For Operation 'Plunder', the code-name for the offensive, 21st Army Group would deploy three armies: First Canadian (eight divisions) on the left, Second British (eleven divisions including three armoured) in the centre and Ninth US (eleven divisions including three armoured) on the right flank. More than one and a quarter million men would be involved in the operation, of whom a quarter of a million would be in the first assault. For Second Army alone, the logistics problem was enormous and included the movement and storage of more than 30,000 tons of Engineer equipment, 28,000 tons of supplies and 60,000 tons of ammunition. The barrage on Second Army's assault sector, between Xanten and Rees, would fire 1,000 shells each minute for four hours.

Efforts to conceal the preparations reached a climax on 19 March, when an artificial smoke-screen was laid. A press report on this 60-mile long opaque curtain reads, in part:

'The greatest artificial wall of smoke, the longest and thickest in the history of warfare has been laid across the western bank of the Rhine to hide [our preparations] from German eyes. A mixture of oil and water is passed through a heated boiler and is pumped out through small exit holes. A white steam is produced. The smoke-screen is laid from an hour before first light to an hour after last light. As a further camouflage measure, dummy vehicles and guns were set up in the American Army's sectors and smoke-screens of lesser density laid. The local civilian population in those sectors were moved away, which seemed to confirm that the main assault would be made by the US Army.' Much of the preparations to 'lift' British Second Army men across the River Rhine suddenly became academic. The Americans had found and had crossed the Rhine on an unblown bridge at Remagen early in March and had gained another bridge south of Mainz later in that month. Montgomery continued to press ahead with his own plans which included not just crossing in boats but also an airborne drop behind the 'Berlin' bank of the river. Among the letters received which describe the crossing of the Rhine, were ones from T. Bridges, in an RASC unit, R. Maloney and A. Jenkins, both members of the Royal Artillery and extracts from them are reproduced below:

'We were told that the AGRA, which had the task of firing the barrage on our sector, had nearly a thousand targets on which there would be the heaviest concentrations of fire. There were, so far as I remember the figures, 54 confirmed and 70 possible German gun positions; over 40 observation posts, 50 or more headquarters areas, 36 depots, a number of enemy concentration areas and forward routes. All those thousand targets would be bombarded from 01.00hrs until 10.00hrs, according to a precise fire plan. At 21.00hrs the first waves of 51st Highland Division began to cross. The searchlight batteries behind our gun positions shone their beams on to the low cloud so as to produce a pale sort of glow that we called "Monty's Moonlight". We were given an almost continuous running commentary on what was happening. The German artillery fire was heavy but patchy, and there was little counter-battery fire by them. They concentrated more on the boats making the crossing and on the 51st Division's bridgeheads. There was a massive air raid on Wesel. A couple of hundred bombers went in. I read later in *Union Jack*, I think, that the RAF had dropped 1,100 tons of bombs in a couple of minutes, some of them being over 5 tons in weight. Wesel was flattened. In the words of a newspaper report, "The RAF gave a perfect demonstration of night-time, precision bombing." As a Gunner [LAA] I must say how proud I was of being in the Royal Artillery, particularly for the Rhine crossing. As you will know the Luftwaffe, the German Air Force, had not worried us much. From the first days of Normandy we had hardly seen them. By the time we had reached the Meuse [Maas] it was a rare thing to see them. They were said to have attacked and sunk ferries crossing to the far bank of the Rhine during the first crossings, and although we were on full alert at the time we did not go into action at all. When the airborne drop was made there were so many of our fighter planes in the sky escorting the Dakotas and the gliders that it would have been suicide for any German aircraft to attack them. So the LAA and the HAA had little to do. The thing that made me most proud was to see our 5.5s lined up. You must have read of guns standing wheel to wheel. Near us there was a whole regiment of 5.5s lined up just like that. There is a picture of it in the War Museum. That picture says it all. We did not have to worry about German air raids or their artillery fire so the guns are standing in the open and not a camouflage net in sight. No slit-trenches either and the guns are not dug in or have sandbag sangar walls. It is a picture of near victory; of our superiority. No wonder I am proud.'

An account of the Rhine crossing and the fighting on the 'Berlin' bank has been supplied by Lance-Corporal Bagshaw who was a Section commander in an infantry battalion of the 51st Higland Division:

'At the end of March 1945, 5th Battalion, The Seaforth Highlanders, with which I was serving, crossed the River Rhine. The enemy put down a very heavy barrage to try to prevent our crossing, but like all well-trained and seasoned veterans we carried on regardless of all his efforts to try and halt our advance. We were all determined to try to end the war as quickly as we could. I was a veteran of the battle of El Alamein and the Sicilian campaign, like so many men from the famous reformed 51st Highland Division, under Major-General Douglas (Big

Tam) Wimberley. One of the assault boats I was in reached the far side of the Rhine. We marched inland ready to meet enemy attacks, but all was clear. As we approached the town of Isselburg at night, it was alight like something from Dante's *Inferno*. I shall always remember that town as there was no sign of life and we ran quickly to reach the narrow bridge which was minus its wooden flooring. We clambered along the sides with enemy shells coming in close. It felt as if the shells were crawling along the ground toward us, such is one's imagination at night in a battle area. Incidentally, many of the assault boats were lost during the Rhine crossing. We finally formed up under our Company Commander who detailed his platoon commanders to do likewise to our Infantry Section commanders, of which I was one. In the far distance at night I could see a large house alight, with groups of our infantry crossing in front of it and the enemy in the basement of the house busily firing at them. Whilst we were advancing a German plane dropped several butterfly bombs on us. I spotted a shellhole and dived into it. Later on each Section formed up at its prospective defensive position. My Section had the task of holding the bridge that was nearest to my Company HQ. The unfortunate Section on the opposite bridge of the Astrang Canal embankment was in the pillbox nearest to Battalion HQ. We consolidated at approximately 12.30 am and on checking my Section, found that during the enemy shelling of our position, four of my Section had deserted into the night.

'At 2.30 am approx. some 200-odd Germans started to attack towards my Section on the far end of the two bridges, having succeeded in wiping out the other Section – minus the Section commander, who, I later heard had been out on the scrounge at the time. It was a pity that the other unfortunate lads were not out on the scrounge likewise, but such is war. One slip and we pay the extreme penalty for being caught off guard, as they did. My Bren-gunner, Pte Kavanagh, stood up in the middle of the canal bridge road and was firing at the enemy as they tried to rush us. His gun stopped, either due to an empty magazine or to a stoppage. I can't say which it was, and as he tried to remedy matters Jerry fired in his direction and he fell down, mortally wounded in the head. From where I was in my slit-trench opposite him I could see he was dead on hitting at the ground and at the time I was thankful that he wasn't lying down badly wounded yet still alive. I had seen this in many other cases during my various actions in the war. My aim was to make up for the loss of so reliable a comrade as he was to me in my role of Section leader. I had with me a German Schmeisser machine-pistol with two full magazines, which was much better than my Lee Enfield rifle. I discarded this minus its bolt, which I flung in another direction. I waited my time for the enemy to make another dash towards us and I told the last remaining member of my Section to be sure to keep his head down. At last they came towards us in the early dawn light. I fired a whole magazine into them and could hear their screams of pain. Just as I was getting my head down to reload the Schmeisser a machine-gun burst hit me in my left arm, right in the muscle, severing the bone and the radial nerve (as I learned later in hospital in England). I held on to my left wrist to try to ease the fracture and luckily it was all numb. At the same time I told my only companion, Pte George 'Boy' White, who was aged 18 then, to get out and over to Coy HQ which was behind us on the left of a field. He helped me to get out and said "Shall we go by the bridge road?" To this I replied, "No, into the water as the enemy will only shoot us in the back." I was glad to know that my mind was at the top of its form as I needed it badly to try and save both our lives. I didn't even consider how deep was the canal and if it had been too deep I would have drowned. Thank God, it was OK.

'We walked across a field towards a house which was surrounded with barbed wire that was too high for us to get over. This was our Coy HQ and I remember a stretcher-bearer there who was full of the German civilian's wine with the owner looking on dismally as he was drinking the place dry. On reaching this house I must have collapsed, due to loss of blood. I woke up to find myself lying on a double tier bunk. The stretcher-bearer, whose name I didn't know, had tied string or something similar around my arm as a makeshift tourniquet. He asked me about my Bren-gunner, who had been a friend of his. I told him the sad news and he wanted to go out and shoot every bloody Jerry on sight, until I told him I had made them pay for the death of my Bren-gunner. Later on I was taken out to a Bren carrier on a stretcher and our wireless set contacted the artillery to give us covering fire as Jerry was advancing into our area, having now crossed the empty bridges. We had tried so hard to defend those bridges to the last man, with the exception of the cowards of my Section who had deserted us in our hour of need, leaving us to die. On reaching the carrier our mortars were coming too close to where I was lying on my stretcher. With me was that wonderful Padre, Captain J. I. Simpson, MC, who was nicknamed "Ironside" by the men of the 5th Seaforths. He saw to it that I was moved back into the house, having covered me with his own body while the heavy mortaring lasted. I shall always be grateful to so fine and fearless a man. After some delay I was then taken out to an amphibious vehicle known as a "Duck". I was strapped down on top minus the tin hat that I had worn ever since Alamein and right through Sicily, Normandy and so to Germany. Up the road we went at about 60 mph, to the nearest Casualty Clearing Station where I found to my horror that I was the only British wounded. All the rest were Jerries lined up along the pathway and chock-a-block inside with a German Corporal medical orderly busily looking after his own wounded. Coming towards me was an RAMC doctor whom I recognized as being my old TA Medical Officer from when I served with the 2/7th Middlesex Regiment. The MO told me that he would give me some morphia to ease the pain and that I would be flown home after an operation at the main hospital.'

That operation was the first of six which H. J. Bagshaw underwent to save his shattered arm. As was usual in the Service, Lance-Corporal Bagshaw was reduced to the ranks due to his wounds. It was a strange reward to be penalized financially for having been wounded in the service of one's country.

Resistance stiffened along the front of 51st Highland Division as its battalions moved deeper into Germany. The Highlanders were up against the paratroopers of Schlemm's First Airborne Army, many of whom were veterans with years of battle experience. The Scottish infantry battalions were not supported by armour at that time because the ferries bringing the tanks across had been attacked by German aircraft and some had been sunk. The 51st came under fire from SPs firing from the centre of Rees. That town, unlike Wesel, had not been bombed and was a centre of fierce resistance until it was captured.

Winston Churchill reached the Rhine and witnessed the British Army's crossing. One contributor wrote that he had been told that the Prime Minister had urinated in the German river. "He had come a long way, had Churchill. In 1940, he had been made PM at the time of Dunkirk. It was our worst time. Now Britain was on the last lap. Germany would soon be defeated."

Field Marshal Brooke wrote in his memoirs; 'We found a very proud Montgomery, proud because he had set up his TAC HQ for the first time in Germany.' On the following day Churchill witnessed Operation 'Varsity', the air drop on the Berlin side of the Rhine. Brooke records that it was a glorious day and that they had a good view of the crossing between Xanten and Wesel: 'At about 10 am the skies filled with aircraft . . . which disappeared into fog on the eastern side . . . Then the first aircraft came back from the para drop with open doors and trailing ripcord lines . . . About an hour later wave after wave of gliders passed over our heads . . . Then we [now on the Berlin bank] went in two armoured vehicles via Xanten, Marienbaum and Hochwald to a small ridge to the south of Kalkar. Here we had a very good view of where the 51st Division had crossed.'

The *Sunday Express* reporter sent a dispatch on Operation 'Varsity' which included the words: 'It is 1 o'clock German Summer Time. We are flying at just over 1,000 feet. Looking eastwards so far as the eye can see Germany is shrouded in smoke and flames. What is happening all around us in the air, on the ground and on the water is like a futuristic painting of the Day of Judgement. And, indeed, for the Germans on the east bank of the Rhine this is the decisive battle, then this is a day in which every type of invasion is rolled into one. The sky is filled with transport machines, two-engined Dakotas, four-engined Halifaxes which stream across the sky in two columns. I saw the first wave of this aerial armada go in. A row of little dots left each aircraft. They suddenly became larger and then parachute canopies unfolded. In a moment a thousand soldiers were falling to earth . . . The flight in continues as the second wave approaches. Through the window of my observation plane I see the huge machines each towing two gliders on nylon ropes. These are the small American Waco gliders . . . Then follow the large British Horsa machines towed by Halifax bombers . . . They come in hundreds. Their tow ropes are cast off. They begin to descend circling and diving to find a landing place. To the North the next wave of gliders is landing. For miles the fields are covered with red and orange parachutes . . . The gliders carrying men or supplies take risks when they land. I see how some crash into hedges and fences, how some dive into the ground and others run into trees. Men leap from them and run into action.'

The *Daily Telegraph* reported: 'Within four hours we had gained all our objectives and had formed a bridgehead. There were camouflaged 88s in the fields loaded with incendiary shells. There were [German] machine-gun nests and infantry positions in the hedges, but the sight of our assault caused a panic flight.'

With the Allied armies now firmly established on the 'Berlin' bank of the Rhine, the advances began which would end the war in Europe. Churchill, and the British Army had, indeed, come a long way.

War in the Deserts of Africa

On 14 June 1940 Mussolini, the dictator of Fascist Italy, declared war on Great Britain. He gave his Generals in Africa orders to invade Egypt and to seize the Suez Canal. The first advance of the Italian Army, on 13 September, was brought to a halt by his hesitant commanders, after only 60 miles and there was little further action until 6 December, when Archibald Wavell launched a counter-blow. His offensive had been planned to be only a short, sharp jab for it seemed unlikely that a major assault could succeed by a British force which was outnumbered by ten to one. Boldness in war is often rewarded and Wavell's offensive flung back the Italian Army in total disorder. By early February 1941, it seemed likely that the thrusting drives by the British Army of the Nile would destroy the Fascist empire in Libya and Tripolitania. In an effort to bolster his flagging Italian ally, Hitler sent a German force to Tripoli and the arrival of Erwin Rommel and the Afrika Korps changed the situation dramatically. Rommel was able to halt Wavell's understrength and overstretched force. A German offensive during March 1941, drove back the British and fighting in the desert then swung backwards and forwards, one time in favour of the Germans and then to the advantage of the Eighth Army, as the British force was now named.

At the end of May 1942, Rommel resolved to pre-empt a new British offensive by launching an attack of his own. His plan would avoid a direct, frontal assault against the 'Gazala Line' as the British positions were called. That line was a series of 'boxes', each defended in Brigade strength by an all-arms group, and protected by extensive minefields. They were, in effect, con-temporary versions of the British Square. Rommel's plan was for his German/Italian army to drive southwards, deep into the desert, to turn the landward flank of the Gazala Line and then strike northwards so as to come up behind the 'boxes'. Each of these would be attacked and destroyed in turn and then through the gaps which had been made his Panzers would drive towards Cairo and the Canal. His plan nearly succeeded and Eighth Army retreated in an undignified scramble towards Cairo and Alexandria in a flight that was thereafter known as 'The Gazala Gallop'. The Axis thrust towards the principal cities of Egypt failed to smash through British prepared positions at El Alamein for now it was the Axis forces that were overstretched and tired. Certainly, they were not strong enough to force the Alamein defences, only 60 miles or so from the Canal. There was then a lull in operations as both sides built up their strength for the decisive battle. In September there was an unsuccessful Axis attempt at Alam Halfa to repeat the success of the Gazala operation. When that offensive was destroyed Rommel strengthened his defences to meet the British assault which he knew would come in against him.

On 23 October, the guns of Eighth Army opened a barrage of First World War intensity. There were tank and infantry battles climaxing in a charge by 9th Armoured Brigade to crush an Axis gun line. This succeeded and by 5 November, the German and Italian forces were in full retreat. Three days later Anglo-American divisions landed in Algeria and had soon marched into Tunisia. Between Eighth Army in Libya and the Anglo-American forces in Tunisia the Axis armies were certain to be trapped. The end was never in doubt and although there was to be hard fighting before the campaign in Africa ended, end it did in an Allied victory on 13 May 1943. The entire German/Italian host passed into captivity. The Fascist empire in Africa was destroyed and the campaign had demonstrated that the Anglo-American Allies could plan together and fight together.

LIFE IN THE EIGHTH ARMY

Many of those who served in the 'old' Eighth Army in the desert recall with pleasure the time they spent there. They wrote of open skies, beautiful dawns, spectacular sunsets and the peace that was to be found up in the 'Blue'. Life was uncomplicated and basic – there was little that war could destroy nor too many people in danger of being killed – always excepting the enemy, who was looked upon almost with affection. Rommel was so popular with Eighth Army that an Order was issued, which in effect, forbade British soldiers to think kindly of him and the Afrika Korps. Roy Cooke served as an infantryman in 5th Battalion, 51st Highland Division, and his recollections of life in the desert are representative of most of the men who served in the old Eighth Army:

'What was day-to-day life like in the desert? Despite the ever-present possibility of hostile enemy action, on the whole life was a very healthy one. There was plenty of fresh air and sunshine and there were miles of absolutely nothing in every direction. If you were lucky enough to be stationed within sight of the Mediterranean you occasionally were able to go for a dip in the deep blue sea. Before the battle of El Alamein it was quite common for British troops to swim naked in the Med and to see a mile or two further to the west, men of Rommel's Afrika Korps doing exactly the same. At Alamein we had the single line Alexandria–Mersa Matruh railway which was later pushed on almost to Tobruk. From June to October 1942, Rommel made good use of this as far as he was able, despite constant RAF interference. About a mile nearer the coast there was the famous desert road, known in Libya as the Via Balbia. The Italians had been working on this in 1940, from the frontier at Capuzzo/Sollum towards Sidi Barrani via Buq-Buq. Then, between the coast road and the sea there were dazzling white sand dunes, whereas further inland the sand was more yellowish in colour. Before the battle of Alamein we lived in what were known as "boxes". These were areas that were surrounded by several coils of Dannert wire for all-round defence. Once inside these "boxes" our life was fairly uneventful, apart from the occasional unexpected Stuka raid. In fact, one of our locations was simply known as "Stuka valley". We slept in holes in the ground for protection against the shellfire, etc., and every morning and evening there was "stand-to" for a certain period. The nights were bitterly cold and if on the move Reveille was before dawn. We had to wash and shave in ice-cold water with our frozen fingers trying to hold an often blunt razor. Our food was very basic. Plenty of bully and hardtack Army biscuits and, of course, during the daytime it became extremely hot so that if a tin of bully were opened, the contents dried up very quickly. Nearly all our food was in tins; butter, bacon, sausages, cheese, potatoes, rice pudding and Australian tinned fruit. Rommel's men enjoyed this whenever they happened to capture one of our supply dumps. At times water was severely rationed and was often less than a gallon per day per man, for all purposes. On a very cold morning it was not unknown for men to drink half a mug of tea and to save the rest for hot shaving water. Further up in the desert the water was often brackish or very salt, with the result that a mug of tea with milk in it just curdled.

'There is a very famous photograph in the Imperial War Museum's photographic archives of two Eighth Army men standing beside a 3-tonner lorry which has a teapot painted on the door with the message, "When in doubt. Brew-up." Now the expression "brew-up" could have two meanings. One was when a tank caught fire, but it usually meant the time-honoured Eighth Army "tea ceremony". When on the move no self-respecting 3-tonner or 15cwt truck would think of setting off without its "brew can" dangling at the rear. Perhaps I ought to go into more detail. Jerry (our affectionate ?? name for our enemy), as always, was much better equipped than ourselves for war. We in Eighth Army had what were commonly known as "flimsies" to carry petrol. These were made at the Base in Egypt and as the word "flimsy" implies, the tins were made of very thin metal with a flimsy handle on top. The result was that more petrol was lost on the way than ever was poured into any petrol tank. Jerry, on the other hand, was superbly equipped with extremely robust large cans which have ever since been known by British and US troops simply as Jerricans. There were two distinct types: the most common ones being painted green and marked "Kraftstoff" and "Feuergefaehrlich" (Fuel; Inflammable). The other type had a big white cross painted on the side with the one word "Wasser" or "Trinkwasser". Needless to say, these Jerricans were much sought after by the Eighth Army. They each held about 5 gallons and it wasn't long before the Allies were making their own Jerricans, though needless to say, the German pattern was far superior to our imitation model. The German one had an ingenious catch which locked the can and allowed air to enter the can whilst it was being poured. The Allied model just had a round cap which was not nearly as efficient as the German one.

'To revert to the "tea making ceremony". When in convoy, whether on the coastal road or far out in the desert – commonly known as the Blue – there came a time when a halt was called and the cry "brew-up" was given. Previously a good fairly robust empty "flimsy" would have been selected and cut in half. One half would then be almost filled with sand and petrol was poured on top. The mixture was then stirred with a bayonet as if stirring up cement. Another flimsy half would be ready filled with water. A match would then be thrown into the sand-cum-petrol mixture and this would blaze merrily away. The other half, containing water, would then be placed sideways on top and as the water came to the boil, a handful of tea-leaves would be added. As soon as it was strong enough, mugs would be produced together with tinned milk and some sugar. Tea was the common Eighth Army "brew". Coffee was unheard of.

'Although day-to-day life "up the Blue" was on the whole very healthy, there were problems such as Gyppo Tummy, desert sores and, of course, the fly menace. Gyppo Tummy was quite common; a form of diarrhoea which often turned into dysentery. Desert sores were quite a problem, If you had a graze on an arm, finger, knee, etc., it was almost impossible to keep the sand out of it and in consequence it festered and became filled with pus. Flies were an absolute menace, especially before the El Alamein battle. The problem became absolutely impossible when trying to eat, for example, a piece of hardtack biscuit with jam or marmalade on it. It was almost as bad trying to drink a mug of tea. However many flies you killed or swatted, reinforcements would be on their way. I believe that Rommel's men in particular, suffered very badly from both Gyppo Tummy and flies. Also a flesh wound would soon become infested and swell up. I myself was slightly wounded at Alamein but carried on, only to be evacuated for that very reason. Hygiene was of the utmost importance in the desert, especially when we were static. Fresh latrines had to be dug and old ones filled in. Out in the Blue, when Mother Nature called, you just borrowed a shovel and went for a walk well away from the others. The Western Desert has often been compared with the sea, as far as navigation was concerned. When off the coastal road we always travelled in convoy, as at sea, with a navigating officer in the lead. At night it was very easy to become lost, even over a distance of 50 yards or so. Major-General Wimberley, GOC, 51st Highland Division, once spent hours in the dark trying to walk from one place to another. A compass bearing was essential.

'During Alamein and afterwards the British infantrymen often tried to capture a German MG 34 or 42, their quick-firing machine-gun, commonly known to us as Spandaus, so as to add considerably to our fire power. Sunsets and sunrises were spectacular in the Western Desert. One moment the sun was there and the very next moment it had sunk below the horizon. The opposite happened in the morning. You could literally see the sun shoot up from below the horizon. This had certain advantages and disadvantages, as in the early morning Rommel's men were dazzled by the early sunlight and in the evening it was the Eighth Army who had the sun in their eyes.'

Roy Cooke considered that the worst day of the Battle of El Alamein was 2 November:

'Having gained our objectives during Operation "Supercharge", [the second stage of the El Alamein offensive] we were forced to lie out in the open desert, unable to dig down more than a couple of inches as the ground was rock-hard. At dawn a mass of our Sherman tanks came through and over us – we had to watch it or we'd all be crushed alive – and the whole of that day was spent in the midst of a terrific tank battle at Tel el Aqqaqir. Rommel's Panzer Armee still had quite a few tanks available. I think that the greatest menace was his 88s and other anti-tank guns, as by the time sunset arrived you saw nothing but brewed-up tanks as far as one could see; both his and ours. Rommel was later to forecast that D-Day

Right: This photograph of Arnold Watson, RASC, was taken in Alor Star, Malaya 1941, before the Japanese invasion. (J. Wyatt)

Below: A unit of Royal Artillery from Singapore, pictured in Ceylon. (A. Watson)

Left: G. Webb, a Regular soldier in the Grenadier Guards, saw service in Tunisia and Italy. He was wounded on Monte Battaglia. (G. Webb)

Below: The ruins atop Monte Battaglia following the fierce combat to capture the heights. (G. Webb)

Right: The Monte Battaglia area in 1988. The ridge to the right (not in picture) extended north-west from the castle and was occupied by Nos. 1 and 2 Companies. The building on the partly wooden hill in the centre was the tactical H.Q.; the one in the valley was where 75 P.O.W.s were taken after the attack. The ridge on the left was the causeway from Castel del Rio and was occupied by Welsh Guards.

Below right: This hymn sheet was expected to serve, and did for many, as an inspiration shortly before going into battle. (G. Webb)

FIRST ARMY SIGN

THE SHIELD Representing our country – our home set in the midst of the sea, a sure and a safe refuge – a land, shaped like a shield, which has stood us in good stead all through the long pages of our history. The base of our strength to-day. "Breathes there a man with soul so dead, who never to himself hath said, 'This is my own, my native land'?"

THE CRUSADERS CROSS The symbol by which all men shall know the ideals and principles for which we stand. No sacrifice being too great in the cause of freedom. For nothing can be higher than the hope expressed by that symbol – persecution, oppression and terror banished, and replaced by christian peace and toleration. No one can doubt the intention of those who serve and follow The Cross.

THE DRAWN SWORD Long ago a Christian soldier gave us an example of the cause for which the sword should be drawn. This example we of First Army endeavour to follow. St George drew his sword and destroyed a dragon which had enslaved a nation. We endeavour to destroy a dragon which has arisen in Europe which would enslave the whole world. We cannot sheath our sword until our task be thoroughly finished.

A prayer for final victory

Almighty God, Who art set in the throne that judgest right judge our cause we beseech Thee, and if we seek only that which is agreeable to Thy will, grant to us both victory in this war and grace, in the day of victory, to seek no selfish ends, but only the advancement of Thy kingdom among men; through Jesus Christ our Lord. Amen.

A dedication of ourselves to the tasks that still lie ahead.

Teach us, good Lord, to serve Thee as Thou deservest; to give and not to count the cost; to fight and not to heed the wounds; to toil and not to seek for rest; to labour and not to ask for any reward, save that of knowing that we do Thy will; through Jesus Christ our Lord. Amen.

HYMN

Lord of our life, and God of our salvation,
Star of our night, and Hope of every nation,
Hear and receive Thy Church's supplication,
Lord God Almighty.

See round Thine ark the hungry billows curling;
See how Thy foes their banners are unfurling;
Lord, while their darts envenom'd they are hurling,
Thou canst preserve us.

Lord, Thou canst help when earthly armour faileth,
Lord, Thou canst save when deadly sin assaileth,
Lord, o'er Thy Church nor death nor hell prevaileth;
Grant us Thy peace Lord.

Grant us Thy help till foes are backward driven,
Grant them Thy truth, that they may be forgiven,
Grant peace on earth, and, after we have striven,
Peace in Thy heaven.

(Sung to the tune of A & M 214)

ADDRESS

Left: *Bert Stubbings relaxing on his cot at St Andrews Barracks, Malta. (Bert Stubbings)*

Below: *Two British soldiers who have just escaped from the enemy share a cigarette with men of The 16/5 Lancers as the Eigth Army advance continues. The two escapees are Lance-Corporal George Dobson of The Durham Light Infantry and Hector Bowman of The Scots Guards.*

Right: *'When in doubt, brew up.' This was the Army's solution to every problem.*

Below right: *In the absence of actual battle shots, Army photographers often posed their subjects. This picture purports to show Germans surrending at the Fuka Pass in the Western Desert in 1942.*

Above: *Lieutenant-Colonel R. Dawson of No. 4 Commando gives a last-minute briefing to some of his men as they prepare for the D-Day landings on 6 June 1944.*

Top right: *An '88' and its half-track, knocked out during the German retreat from El Alamein.*

Right: *Vessels packed with men of the BEF who had been evacuated from France and Flanders arrive at a port on the southern coast of England in 1940.*

Above: *The aftermath of the battle of El Alamein, November 1942. The wounded of 51st (Highland) Division lie in the open air awaiting treatment.*

Left: *A piper of the Highland Division plays-in the crew of a Bren gun carrier as they return from patrol in the Western Desert.*

Top right: *Winston Churchill inspecting the mortar platoon of battalion headquarters, Seaforth Highlanders (Caithness and Sutherland) in Egypt, 1942.*

Right: *A platoon of Royal West Kent Regiment, 132 Brigade, 44th Infantry Division, moving forward to the start line for an attack in the desert, September 1942.*

Left: *There may have been a war on, but it did not stand in the way of a Derby Day sweepstake. The board shown here was at TAC H.Q. of 2nd Armoured Brigade, Creully, Normandy, in June 1944.*

Below left: *Another posed picture for home consumption. This shot taken near Roubaix, northern France, in the late autumn of 1939, is intended to show a group of Royal West Kents happily making music while one of their number keeps watch on a trench parapet.*

Above: *The Welsh Guards march past at the conclusion of a ceremony held in northern France at which General Gamelin (second from the left) awarded the Legion of Honour to Lord Gort (right) and General Ironside (far left).*

Below: *A group of men belonging to the 4th Lincolns who were cut of by the Germans at Steinkjer during the invasion of Norway in 1940. The troops marched 56 miles across snow-covered mountains in order to reach British lines.*

Left: A Priest gun crew preparing to attack Ngazun village en route to Meiktila, Burma.

Bottom left: A 3in mortar crew in action during the fierce battle near Singu on the Irrawaddy bridgehead, one of the toughest contests in the Burma war.

Below: A patrol of The Buffs of 26th Brigade advance cautiously through Burmese jungle country on the northern approaches to the Japanese-held town of Myitson.

*Left: Fusilier Jefferson of The Lancashire
Fusiliers, 78th Division, was awarded the
Victoria Cross for destroying a German tank
with the short-range PIAT mortar, thereby
breaking up an enemy tank attack at Cassino in
Italy 1944.*

*Above: One of the features of the fighting in
Cassino was the use of snipers. This picture
shows a Grenadier Guards sniper in the ruins of
a house in the town.*

*Below: British troops coming ashore in Sicily,
July 1943.*

Above: *Scottish troops, led by their piper, march inland from the beaches of Sicily.*

Left: *George Newmark was wounded during the fighting in France, May 1940. A bullet passed through his AB 64 and penetrated deep into his chest. This photograph shows the bullet-torn document, the bullet which was removed from George's chest and a letter sent by him from the prisoner of war camp. (Courtesy of V. Moss, Curator of the Redoubt Museum, Eastbourne)*

Sergeant George Newmark's army pay book which he was carrying in his breast pocket when he was shot by a German sniper. The bullet (above) went straight through the pay book and into his chest. He was captured and taken to hospital where the bullet was removed by a vet. After its removal he demanded it back, insisting it was his own property.

RIGHT: Some of the letters Sergeant Newmark wrote home from a prisoner-of-war camp in Germany. When addressing these letters he used a code: the initials in the address spell the name of the town (FREUDENTHAL) where he was held captive. He used this method each time he was moved to a different camp, and it was never discovered despite all letters being censored by the German authorities.

in Normandy would be the "longest day", but 2 November 1942 was without doubt MY longest day. I was expecting that fatal shell or mortar bomb at any second and was never so thankful in my life as when nightfall finally came.'

Another soldier of the 5th Seaforths who remembered that day was R. Stuart Wilson:

'I remember seeing Captain Farquhar Macrae, MC, our battalion medical officer, in a captured Jerry truck picking up both British and enemy wounded in the midst of a very heavy shelling and surrounded by 88mm air bursts. An ambulance he was driving was knocked out previously and it had wounded men on board. During the last big attack which resulted in our breakthrough, we were the most forward platoon in the entire battalion and when we were digging in after taking our objectives an Aussie soldier from 9th Division wandered into our positions and proceeded to dig-in with one of our lads. In the afternoon of that day (2 November) Jerry put down a number of very heavy "stonks" on top of us. One shell landed almost in the slit-trench dug by the Seaforth and the Aussie. One of them was killed outright and the other had some dreadful wounds and died soon afterwards. I shall always remember his awful screams. The strange thing about this was that both the Seaforth and the Aussie had the same name. Later on our Platoon Sergeant was killed, just behind me.'

Roy Cooke remembers how well dug-in were Rommel's Panzers:

'We saw several sloping holes which had previously held hull-down Panzers. When his army finally withdrew we stayed behind for a day or two then followed up the famous desert highway, the Via Balbia, in three-tonner trucks passing other three-tonners coming back the other way, crammed with Rommel's men who had surrendered. They all wore the Afrika Korps long-peaked caps and tropical uniforms with lace-up boots. Then on past the famous white mosque at Sidi abd el Rahman, which was reputed to have been Rommel's HQ during the battle of Alamein, and on to Fuka with masses of smashed Luftwaffe fighter planes on the airfield. We bypassed Mersa Matruh and all along the highway were many burnt-out Italian trucks, both Army and Italian Air Force, also some Italian tanks which were sometimes referred to as "mobile coffins" as they were pretty well useless. We finally halted at Mersa Brega, as Rommel had decided to make a stand at El Agheila.'

It was at Mersa Brega that Roy, who had served with 'I' Section of his Battalion, was posted to 'B' Company to bring it up to strength:

'One night I was selected to join a recce patrol and we emptied our pockets beforehand so as not to help Jerry in the event of capture or death. We set out as it was getting dark under a platoon officer who was a very keen type. He detailed me to be the "Get-away man", which meant that should we run into trouble, an ambush, etc., my job was to try to get back in order to say what had happened. It was a very still night and as we were quite close to the sea we would clearly hear the waves breaking on the shore. It was quite dark and we could barely see anything. Suddenly we came across a steep slope and our platoon commander motioned for us to stay at the bottom of the slope while he silently crept up to the top. This we did and he very soon came down again. He made it clear that we were to withdraw without delay. Later on he was able to tell us that he had peeped over the top of the slope only to see that Jerry was just a few yards on the other side. We had been very lucky not to have been spotted. Later we found somewhere to spend the rest of the night as our officer decided to await daybreak before attempting to re-enter our lines, just in case we happened to be mistaken for the enemy. Later on we were badly held up just beyond Homs, at a place called Corradini. Here the 90th Light Division ambushed us. We called it "The battle of the Hills" and our ultimate objective was nicknamed "Edinburgh Castle", as it looked just like it in the darkness. We put in a pre-dawn attack and had many casualties. I was one of them and was evacuated down the line from one CCS to another before being taken out by tender to a hospital ship at Benghazi and finishing up at Alexandria in a very comfortable hospital.'

A. G. Bell was with an artillery regiment and recalled the winter campaign of 1941 as seen by a gunner:

'This was the start of what was called the "Second Push". We set off up the desert road as far as Mersah Matruh and then turned south on to the track which led eventually 200 miles away to the oasis of Siwa. As soon as we got on to the Siwa track we fanned out into what was called "Desert Formation", several columns wide and with about 100 yards between vehicles in all directions. After three days we joined 1st South African Division which we were to support. We took our positions in this formation and the entire division moved forward in desert formation, a most fantastic sight. Thousands of vehicles as far as the eye could see in every direction, and disappearing into the heat haze and looking as though they were driving in the sky, all keeping their station 100 yards apart, all travelling on the same compass bearing, each with its little plume of dust behind it. The guns were in the centre, Bren-carriers in front, the soft vehicles further back and all around the outside the OPs and the armoured scout cars. And so we travelled first south then eventually west, through the wire and finally turned north in what was to become the classical desert manoeuvre of a hook round the lightly held southern enemy flank. During the afternoon the guns dropped into action. The sun had already set and the light was fading fast, but the OP ACK of the other Troop went forward with his Troop Commander to make contact with a squadron of tanks. They got to what they thought was the correct map reference and dismounted to check, spreading the map out on the bonnet. The squadron of tanks was there alright, but the voices calling "come here" didn't sound very English and the Troop Commander ordered the driver to keep the engine running as he didn't like the situation. Eventually one of the soldiers in the tanks gave the game away by shouting "Avanti". Immediately, everybody leapt on board and the truck belted away taking slit-trenches and other obstacles in its stride and came racing back to the guns which then fired their first rounds, hopefully, at the Itie tanks. This was the kind of confusion which was to become the regular pattern for the whole of the rest of that part of the campaign.'

THE GAZALA BATTLES: SUMMER 1942

By the summer of 1942, the Germans had taken over the direction of the war in Africa. There was, nominally, an Italian Commander-in-Chief, but the *de facto* leader was Erwin Rommel, the Desert Fox, who had arrived in the Italian colonies during February 1941, and who had stamped his image immediately on the fighting. Aware that the Eighth Army was about to launch an offensive against him, he pre-empted that assault by an offensive against what was known as the Gazala position. Rommel's plan was to turn Eighth Army's flank, come up behind the main body and strike it in the back. Rommel made his move on 26 May 1942. There followed days of hard and wasteful fighting for both sides, but then on 12 June, Eighth Army suffered a disaster. Rommel's two Panzer Divisions acting in concert, smashed the British armoured reserve in what became known as the "Battle of the Cauldron". When that day of combat ended Eighth Army's strength had been reduced to just 70 'runners'. The Cauldron was not only a disaster for the British armour; both the infantry and the artillery also suffered grievously. The destruction of 3rd battery of 28th Field Regiment is described by Captain R. A. Doyle, in a piece he wrote for his unit publication, *This was your Regiment*:

'I remember that day as clearly as if it were yesterday. A Sunday paper of 7 June was headlined "Fury rages in Devil's cauldron", but this fell short of reality. I was there with the 3rd Field Battery, RA and it was the last day there was a 3rd Field Battery for us. Clearest of all I recollect the sound of German solid shot, whirring through the air in their strange throbbing ricochets, perhaps because these signalled the new day's coming and portended its finale. We huddled behind the guns, half a mile east of the Tamar Ridge where, yesterday, the attacking armoured brigades and our infantry had been hardly dealt with by Panzers and 88s. At nightfall the weary Crusader tanks clattered their way rearwards through our defensive positions. The guns of D Troop fanned out in an arc facing west and by each gun and in the Command Post, artillerymen crouched in shallow rocky trenches at best only a few feet deep in this iron rock, where tools and hands were battered and bruised in wresting a few inches extra from mother earth; to whom many of us were soon to return. High-explosives we were accustomed to, both in giving and receiving, but there was something uncanny about these heavy bolts of steel flashing down on us from a crest, hazy and laden with dust and smoke so that we could not see to retaliate. We sat in our holes. For an hour death thudded among us. One [shell] crunched down in front of me and came jerking, trundling and rolling up to where I sat by the gun position signaller. I put out my cautious hand and the burning warmth of the still hot metal seared my finger. A solid shot would thrash in one's face like a burst tomato.

'But it was fire and high-explosive which drew first blood. Shells dropped to burst graciously and harmlessly with their bright flash, spume of sulphurous smoke and lively crack, but they drew nearer and became dangerous. One of our ammunition trucks was hit and the energy of a hundred shells was dissipated in brilliant pyrotechnics. To the south and south-east many vehicles were now on fire, fingers and pillars of blue-black smoke eddying upwards in a motionless air, a familiar sight to desert soldiers. And still the shellfire increased. I walked over to No. 1 gun to have a chat to the sergeant for a few minutes. A yard or so in front of me the Troop Commander returned from a useless observation post and scanned the crest with binoculars from a meagre slit-trench. Over at No. 4 gun some of the detachment were starting to disperse the long, brass, cordite-filled cartridge cases so that all could not be hit together. The Battery Commander and two other officers were nearby. The Major stood on top of the limber amongst the flying metal in an effort to pierce the haze; then the blow fell. There was no gradual merging of life with death; they coincided instantaneously. A snapping roar and a huge sheet of flame pulled all eyes to No. 4 gun. An enemy shell had dropped right on the cartridges of cordite and had exploded. The ferocious heat of the flame instantly roasted to death the gunner bending over them and his comrade was pierced through the neck by a sliver of steel. I rushed across to meet a young soldier still brave and cheerful, reeling away with gory wounds in his head and body and half-helped, half-carried him to an RHQ truck, just in the rear. I can still see now the bloody knots of flesh and steel driven into his skull. As I returned to the scene the two officers were being loaded into a truck, the one pale and unconscious beneath a blanket, the other with thighs smashed to pulp. The Major, wounded, having been taken off, was hit again before he reached the Aid Post. Of these none lived. A signaller had a hunk of flesh knocked out of his back and the gun's bombardier, his officers and comrades decimated in a second, was dazed. A few paces to the right the driver of our Bren-Carrier was wounded in the foot so we placed him for safety inside a knocked-out tank. The day was not a few hours old and so far we had not fired a single round, yet death was already whittling deep.

'Hardly had the wounded left when a senior officer drove into our position and barked an order, "Pull out immediately to your old position and engage tanks." Within seconds the tractors were up from the nearby wagon lines and as I hung on to the door and framework of the first to move off, I experienced a strange mixture of exhilaration, excitement and calmness as the roaring tractor raced the few hundred yards to action. Within seconds we had unhooked the gun, swung it around on its metal firing platform and, as the other guns came in on the left, our first shot, fired over open sights, crashed out. About half a mile away lay a small group of Rommel's tanks, two Mk IIs and a Mk IV. At that range the odds were on the side of the Panzers as they lay at the extreme range of effective field gun range and presenting the smallest and thickest part of their epidermis; the front. They fired back with their 75mm guns at men protected intermittently only by the thin steel of the gun shield. When we had fired three rounds there was a deafening explosion and I felt my face blasted and riddled. For a fraction of a second I thought I was shattered. I clapped both hands to my skin and brought them away again stained with blood and grit. I worked the muscles of my face but miraculously felt unhurt. A German shell had burst directly under the shield, puncturing the nearside tyre and slicing steel rashers from the firing platform. The layer collapsed in his seat with a faint groan, the base of his spine and the top of his buttocks a bloody exposed mass of red flesh slashed raw. My face had been splattered by gobbets of pulverized tissue. Two minutes earlier he had rubbed his hands with glee at the prospect of action; now he was dead and in an amazing way had shielded me from the blast as I stood on the left of the trail a couple of feet behind him. Beside him the ammunition gunner dropped lifeless. I don't know what killed him as I could see no mark. The loader was hit in the wrist and a little Scotsman, the last gunner, went deaf as a door post. With a lance-bombardier I dragged the two bodies clear of the gun. As I bent over to grip the layer's ankles he gave a death grunt. As the body slid backwards over the sand it left behind a large shining slice of liver glistening with drops of blood. I kicked sand over it so that the others would not see. These happenings all occurred within seconds and in a fraction of the time it takes to tell. The Panzers were still firing.

'A signaller leapt forward and with the lance-bombardier we got the gun firing again. One laying, one loading and myself ramming the shells into the breech and slipping outside the shield to observe the shots. Then we changed and I layed and fired. We were all quite mad, swearing and cursing the Germans for what they had done to our comrades. One gun versus one tank and we were all oblivious to all else; E Troop was pulling in on our right, more tanks and enemy guns on the ridge. All we saw was the front of one stationary tank. I let the air out of the other tyre to level the gun and its movements on the wheels became sluggish. To make matters worse the extractors, which are used to expel the hot and expanded cartridge cases from the breach, cracked and slid over the lips of the case. Each time this happened the signaller had to rush round me to the front of the gun and throw the rammer down the muzzle to knock the case out of the breech. The ground was hard and dusty and the teeth of the firing platform failed to bite the earth. Each time we fired, a cloud of sand was raised and the whole gun slithered back about six inches. Once or twice the trail was brought up against the layer's body and I had to drag it clear. Suddenly, the firing died down. The action seemed to have lasted hours but it was probably more like ten minutes. Our adversaries still squatted quiet and motionless in the same position, damaged, out of ammunition or just not wanting to come in any nearer. There was a long lull after the storm during which we licked our wounds. Half a mile to the north lay a crest of German tanks. We had no tanks and hardly any infantry left. Our casualties in gunners was already high. We scraped away at the ground trying to protect ourselves, but digging was impossibly hard. At the best we got down six inches so we placed the broken body of the layer in the rude and shallow grave and scraped back the earth over him. His best friend, the signaller, made a rough cross from a piece of wood and pencilled on his name. The other body, lying motionless nearby, was covered with a blanket. We said no prayers and removed no identity discs; we ourselves were still too close to death. The Germans were masters of the high ground and had perfect observation on us. More and more tanks assembled in that threatening arc. Through binoculars I could see a few of the crews come out of the tanks for a smoke and a breather. All we could do was to sit and wait for them to come in. None of us expected to see the day out but nobody seemed unduly worried.

'A few Bofors guns pulled in to our right rear. Away to the left were a couple of anti-tank two-pounders. Here and there were Indians in weapon pits; Brens against 75mm guns in armour. On rising ground to the east our other Troop had come into action. Solitary vehicles moved around on the flanks, probing for a getaway. The Germans scorned to fire a shot. The Troop Commander, observing from a point just behind me, shouted "Tank Alert". As the Panzers moved in we leaped to the guns and opened fire. Within seconds a hellish battle developed. A quick side glance showed E Troop shooting it out with tanks closing in on them. Those advancing on my Troop eased into a fold of ground and, halting, poured in a hail of shells and bullets. At the same time the German artillery opened up and they had our range to a yard. At intervals of a few seconds there was a rushing roar, followed by a black smoking crash as the shells burst in the air about thirty feet above our heads. These were quite terrifying and distracted our attention from the bullets hissing past the gun shield. At each crash we crouched down and then went on firing. It was indeed a devil's cauldron of flame, explosion, heat, cordite, fumes, fire and death. We had fired a dozen rounds when there was a wild crashing rush over the gun and with dazed shock I saw a stream of blood pouring from a channel gouged across my wrist, soaking shirt and shorts and spattering on to my boots. I thought a main artery was severed and turned to the Troop Commander for a field dressing. Even today I can still hear myself saying queerly, "They got me, Joe." As I walked towards him another rush of blood came from my thigh where a jagged piece of metal, ricocheting upwards from the trail drove itself into my flesh above the knee. I felt no real pain, just shocked a bit and thought I was bleeding to death. The little Scotsman was hit in the arm. There were no bandages left so Joe tied my wrist up in a brown silk handkerchief. The Panzers at last crushed the guns and the few survivors were defenceless. As I was helped towards the collecting post for wounded, I passed a tragic sight. A troop of four guns laid out in action, breeches still open, trails littered about with cartridge cases, silent as a grave. At No. 2 gun a corpse, white and naked save for a pair of boots, was draped like a gruesome pinwheel over the right gun wheel, head and arms hanging to the ground. This was the symbol of our defeat. Four regiments of field artillery were decimated on this day. My Troop was one of the many which died thus; without fame or mention, but simply in the line of duty.'

Another soldier of the 28th was Bombardier J. P. Blackmore, who served with E Sub Section of 1st (Blazers) Battery of that Regiment:

'My story begins on the night of 5 June 1942. We were artillery support to 5th Indian Division forming the Knightsbridge Box, and for six days we had fought and held the box. We had now been told to expect strong tank attacks from first light. We stood-to an hour before dawn, this being the normal practice through the whole Army. At about 10 o'clock when we were trying to make a brew of tea, what remained of some of the tank crews and anti-tank gunners came through our position, most of them on foot and all looking rather grim. At about midday what remained of the infantry withdrew through our position. The order came "Tank alert" and with it the order to destroy all sights on the gun, less the telescopes. All personal documents, letters, photographs and pay books were to be immediately burned. We laid our gun roughly in the centre of our allotted anti-tank zone. It was now a matter of team work if we were to fight and survive. I set a thousand yards on the telescope and laid on the far escarpment. We waited and weren't kept waiting long. The first enemy tanks nosed their way slowly over the escarpment, paused and then seemed to slide down the other side one by one. I laid on as many as three tanks at once through my telescope and it was agony to keep my hand from the firing lever. Before we fired one round we had a direct hit on the limber. We were hit again, this time on the front of the recuperator, followed by another hit on the axle which blew the gun wheel off. This was rather surprising because that was where the Major was sitting in the layer's seat. The gun wheel sort of slowly rolled away and laid down, and I must have watched it fascinated. The next thing I knew was the Major on his feet shouting "It's every man for himself."

'We attended to our wounded and made them as comfortable as possible. In the meantime the enemy were occupying our positions. The nearest tank from us was about eight yards. I remember looking at it spellbound. I can see the number painted on its side today as I did then – 78. The tank commander spared us a glance, but the follow-up infantry took more interest. One of the German NCOs started giving us instructions or orders. None of us could speak German and he couldn't speak English. It was standstill until from out of the blue appeared a German officer who could speak reasonably good English. He said that the wounded would be attended to as soon as possible and that all those who could walk should evacuate themselves from the battle area immediately and pointed the direction in which we were to march. As best we could, with the walking wounded, we struggled our way through the German positions, infantry, anti-tank guns digging in, right down into the Cauldron itself. There appeared to be a German Brigade headquarters close by. In the distance was seen coming towards the HQ several German vehicles. They drew to a halt and as the dust cleared everyone around the HQ seemed to shoot up as if they had been given an injection. I took a close look at the person who was gripping the handrails of a half-track and leaning forward there could be no mistake, the cause of all our troubles, General Rommel himself. With him, was his staff, a half-track, a wireless truck, a couple of queer things like Volkswagen and an eight-wheeled armoured car. The commander of the brigade that we were close to gave the Nazi salute and Rommel returned it with a salute to the peak of his cap. Everyone looked at him as if he was God. He wasn't tall. He appeared to be squat and his uniform wasn't hard to describe. The German officer's cap and what appeared rather funny, a pair of British anti-gas goggles around the top. What we could see of him was covered with a leather overcoat and dangling from his neck what looked like a cross. He seemed to give his orders in a quick guttural voice and now and again a wave of his hand. In a few minutes it was all over. Heels clicked, salutes were given and Rommel and his staff were already in a cloud of dust. I think it dawned on us for the first time that we were POWs. I think we must have met it with mixed feelings; happy that we were still alive and for us the war was over.'

In fact Bombardier Blackmore's war was far from over. Some days later, after incredible adventures, he managed to escape back to the British lines.

TANK ATTACK IN THE DESERT

Such was the confidence of the Axis commanders in those heady days of June and July 1942, that Mussolini flew to Tripoli intending to lead the Victory Parade through Cairo and Alexandria mounted on a white stallion. It was a vain journey. The attacks of Panzerarmee Afrika were halted at a series of prepared defences called the Alamein Line. The pursuit battle had so exhausted the enemy forces that they would not be able to fight their way through the British positions until they had recouped their strength.

Throughout July Eighth Army attacked at various points along the Alamein Line and their assaults were met by Axis counter-attacks just as thrusts by the Italian/German units were repulsed by the British and Dominions Army. The fighting was to gain tactically important ridges and the tank battles which were a feature of the bitter struggles wore down the Axis strength. On 21 July 1942, the Afrika Korps, the core of Panzerarmee, had only 42 'runners' and the strength of the Italian tank force was 30 vehicles. Although there were a further one hundred German machines under repair, the Eighth Army had in 1st Armoured Division alone, no fewer than 170 'runners' and with the newly arrived 23rd Armoured Brigade there were another 150. The tide of battle was turning in favour of Auchinleck's army.

On one fateful day in July, that British advantage in numbers was reduced when the armour made a stupid blunder. Not that this particular instance was seen as anything new or exceptional by the infantry who felt that blunders were what the tank regiments seemed always to make. Mutual hostility existed between the armour and the Foot amounting almost to a hatred. R. Cooper, 50th (Tyne Tees) Division:

'There was a feeling among the infantry units of Eighth Army that whenever our tanks were needed they were never there. We felt let down by them. At the height of a battle our tanks would suddenly roar away leaving us defenceless against the Panzers. If we had known then, as we know now, that they were going to refuel or to load up with ammunition or that they were regrouping, we would have understood. As it was nobody told us anything and all we knew was that our tanks were dashing away trailing clouds of dust and that presently along would come Rommel's boys.'

John Bucknall, who had been in the desert since the first battles, was on duty on the day of the armoured blunder:

'Our tank people never seemed to learn. Time after time Rommel would entice the regiments on to a line of dug in 88s. Our tank commanders seemed unable to grasp this tactic. One thing was certain when fighting Jerry; one mistake and you were dead. On 22 or 23 July, I am not certain which day it was, I was on duty in Cairo HQ, when a staff officer came out of the Signals Office looking as white as a sheet. Really ghastly. The word soon spread. We had lost an entire armoured brigade in a couple of hours. Only later did I learn that the 23rd Armoured Brigade, fresh out of Blighty, had gone in at the charge to support the New Zealander's attack.'

The New Zealand Division had been ordered to take Ruweisat Ridge which lies about halfway between El Alamein station in the north and the impassable Qattara Depression in the south. Whoever held Ruweisat was in the dominant position. In the bitter fighting to take it, the New Zealand Division lost 700 men and it was during the battle that 23rd Armoured Brigade was committed to 'lift' the New Zealanders on to the objective. John Bucknall:

'The 23rd Brigade had been in the Middle East for only ten or so days. They hadn't had a chance to get their knees brown. Why that unit was ever chosen to make the attack, Heaven alone knows. I have heard it said that the Prime

Minister insisted they be put straight into battle. He didn't or wouldn't realize that it is not just the climate to which you have to become accustomed. You have to learn the desert, and the 23rd hadn't. They did not know about terrain or about the Jerries, and that inexperienced brigade was put in to support the Kiwis in a crucial operation. According to what I heard, and what I have read since confirms what I heard, the regiments charged, just as they would have made a cavalry attack. They had no idea of wireless procedures and because of that they couldn't be told that immediately ahead of them was an unswept minefield. Within minutes the charge had been brought to a halt as tanks blew up one after the other and as the tanks in the second line tried to pass those which had already been blown up, they too ran over mines and were destroyed. The leading regiments lost fourteen tanks in about as many minutes and not one of them had fired a shot because there was no enemy to be seen. The charge had halted in the middle of that minefield and nobody knew it, but the tanks were halted almost under the muzzles of a German anti-tank gun line. As usual, Jerry's positions were well sited, well dug-in and well camouflaged. His gunners had a sitting target. A whole brigade of Valentine tanks, more than a hundred of them, immobile, within range and bewildered by what happened.'

'Then the Jerry anti-tank guns opened up and while they were in action the 88s, which had been hidden behind a ridge, came forward and formed line. On either flank of the gun line the Panzers formed up and under that combined barrage the 23rd Brigade was cut to pieces. In post-battle reports, so I heard, the officers of the brigade complained that the Germans had fired on tank crews making their way to the rear after their vehicles had been knocked out. Those officers were still mentally on schemes on Salisbury Plain. The brigade had begun its "Charge of the Light Brigade" attack at about 8 in the morning. By midday it had been destroyed. It had advanced no farther than five miles. Only eleven Valentines got out from that shambles.'

In addition to the 99 tanks lost with 23rd Armoured Brigade, Eighth Army had suffered other casualties that day. A total of 131 machines; 40 per cent of its total strength had been wiped out. Truly could the planners at Eighth Army write on 27 July 1942, in an Appreciation of the situation in the Western Desert, 'None of the formations of Eighth Army is sufficiently well trained for offensive operations. The Army needs either a reinforcement of trained formations or a quiet period in which to train.' It got both when Montgomery took over Eighth Army. He insisted upon, and was given, reinforcements and time to train them. The result was the Battle of El Alamein; the last victory by an independent British Army during the war.

EL ALAMEIN: NOVEMBER 1942

The ex-soldier's view of the Battle of El Alamein is coloured by the arm of service to which he belonged. To the tankmen it was the charge by 9th Armoured Brigade across the Axis gun lines which broke the enemy. The infantry and the sappers consider their mine-lifting activities and attacks as the most important considerations. The gunners believe that it was the barrages they fired which destroyed the morale of the German and Italian troops. A. G. Bell, who served in an artillery regiment, gives lectures to local Territorial Army on his wartime service, part of which was spent in the desert.

'The build-up of troops, vehicles and equipment [in the summer of 1942] created a great air of expectancy and when Churchill made a surprise visit to the front we knew that great things were afoot. At last, on the morning of 23 October, my officer came around with General Montgomery's latest order of the day and said that in fact tonight was the night. He said that if we cared to go over to his dug-out, which was on higher ground, at about 9 o'clock that evening we should have a good view of the start of the battle. The full moon was up as I walked across to Captain Monk's dug-out. There was sporadic firing up and down the line so as to give Jerry the impression that this was just like any other night. By 9.30 p.m. there was total silence. We sat in deathly silence as the minutes ticked away and then at twenty to ten all hell was let loose. No less than 1,500 guns on that 10-mile front opened up simultaneously and continued pouring shells on selected targets for ten minutes. There was another ten minutes' silence to allow the guns to be re-layed. Then they spoke out again, this time in a creeping barrage behind which the infantry were to advance. All the details were explained to us so that we could appreciate what was going on. Clouds of dust were expected which might cause confusion, so for the artillery a number of searchlights were switched on pointing vertically to act as aiming-points. For the infantry who might lose direction the Bofors guns were to fire a burst of tracer shells every five minutes on fixed bearings. Gaps were to be created in the minefields by flail tanks which would be followed by Engineers with mine-detectors and behind them more Engineers with iron posts and white tape to mark the cleared routes. In due course the infantry advanced and on the Highland Division's sector the troops were led in by regimental pipers.'

IN THE MOUNTAINS OF TUNISIA, 1942-3

The Anglo-American landings in French North Africa brought their forces behind Rommel's desert army. It is true that in November 1942, the Allied formations in Algeria and Tunisia were few in number and more than a thousand miles from the desert. But the Anglo-American forces would grow in strength and would then begin to drive down upon the Axis hosts. Between the Allies in Tunisia and Eighth Army in the desert, the German/Italian Panzerarmee would be destroyed. Hitler's response was to rush in troops, principally airborne detachments, who created and held a bridgehead perimeter. The story of the war in Tunisia from November 1942 until May 1943, is of German attempts to hold that bridgehead and of Allied attempts to smash it and, thereby, to bottle-up the Axis forces. The German troops who landed at Tunis airport on 9 November flung out fighting patrols which raced for and seized the dominant high ground to the west of Tunis. Medjez el Bab was the key to the campaign, but just outside that little town rose a high and isolated mountain peak which the British knew as 'Longstop'. The Germans called it 'Christmas Mountain' because of the battle which is described by E. W. Fitness, of 2nd Battalion, Coldstream Guards.

'In the last week of December 1942, we felt that something big was afoot. The Company Commander's conference ended our speculation. We were to attack after nightfall on 23 December. The enemy was to be cleared from the hill that had faced us so grimly since we had moved into Medjez el Bab two weeks earlier. When we had achieved this a tank thrust was to be made towards Tunis. That hill was known as "Longstop". The battle plan was simple. The Guards were to take Longstop and on the morning of 24 December they were to be relieved by American troops. Tanks could then thrust forward towards Tebourba and Tunis with supporting infantry. Reports on the opposition were sketchy, but it seemed that the German troops were well dug-in and were receiving reinforcements. Our Company's [2nd Company] line of advance was by way of a thin strip of woodland running parallel to a railway line. Our objective, The Halt, was a stopping-place on this line just beyond the enemy-held reverse slopes of Longstop. The 23rd December was not unlike the previous days – cold, wet and miserable. The Company moved off with our Platoon [No. 11] last of all. We were all carrying a heavy weight of extra ammunition and rations and progress was slow. The moon cast eerie shadows as we passed burnt-out vehicles, evidence of a previous battle. Occasional bursts of machine-gun fire came from Longstop. We made our approach, waiting for our artillery barrage which was to open up just before the attack. It started and we hoped that the whining shells, passing overhead, were pinpointing their targets. It was not long before the Germans began to reply, and the angry snarl of their Spandau machine-guns told us that our forward companies were meeting stiff opposition. Very lights illuminated the scene and mortar shells began to land nearby. The woodland was thinning out, giving only minimum cover, but our platoon was ordered to push through the two leading platoons and get to The Halt as soon as possible.

'Ironic comments were made as we advanced. "Don't let the train go," and "You won't need a ticket," mingled with cries for stretcher-bearers. Our platoon was now reaching the end of the woodland, using what little cover the few remaining trees and undergrowth offered. In the distance, we could see our objective, a small building at the side of the railway line. We were heartened to see figures silhouetted on the skyline immediately to our left, as we knew these must be the forward platoons of our other companies. Our platoon was still intact as we reached the last fifty yards of the woodland. We edged forward; only a few yards separated us from The Halt. Violent explosions suddenly tore the ground. Flashes of blue light blinded us and the air was full of pieces of metal. Explosion followed explosion. It was impossible to tell what had happened. We hugged the ground as the explosions continued. Machine-gun fire pinpointed us. Through it there were cries for help. Most of the platoon had been hit. Again the ground was wrenched by explosions. At last we understood. We had walked into a minefield. The Germans, masters as they were at defensive tactics, had anticipated that the woodland could be used by an attacking force under cover of darkness. Their plan had worked well. By calling to each other we knew there were a few man capable of carrying on to the objective, but it was unnerving to realize that after only a few seconds most of our platoon were no longer in the battle. The remainder pressed forward, our Bren-guns sounding sluggish in reply to the rapid fire of the Spandaus. We reached The Halt. Then, together with the other two platoons, fought on to a point about fifty yards beyond The Halt and started the difficult task of digging-in before dawn. Fire from machine-guns enveloped us from our flank and front. Tracer bullets carved a pattern in the sky. The noise of vehicles to the rear of the German positions indicated that they were receiving reinforcements. Some of these were seen on the skyline, but quick bursts from our Brens dispersed them. We each managed to scoop out some form of slit-trench. Camouflage was out of the question. Roughly five yards apart we were positioned between the railway line and Longstop. The small building behind us made it easy for effective range-finding by the enemy mortars. We began to wonder if the Americans could relieve us. If we were not relieved our numbers were too few to last long against counter-attack. Our ammunition was low and our position would be ruthlessly exposed at the break of dawn.

'Enemy machine-gun fire became intense. Mortar bombs fell amongst us and the Germans were able to gauge our position. We fired back endeavouring at the same time to conserve our dwindling ammunition. A few of the enemy managed to creep to within a short distance of our position, but they were quickly dealt with by hand-grenades and rifle fire. Then the increased volume of fire sweeping over us confirmed that the enemy had been reinforced and had succeeded in working round our flanks. Mortar bombs fell around us and we were pinned down in our exposed positions. The incessant croaking of bullfrogs played on our nerves. Then dawn began to break and we realized that we could not expect to be relieved. No troops could advance over the flat, open country behind us without running the gauntlet of murderous machine-gun fire and concentrated mortar barrages. Suddenly it became quieter on Longstop. We hoped that this meant the exchange had in fact taken place and that the Americans were firmly established. Our own position seemed hopeless. Further casualties had reduced our numbers and we were no longer in contact with the battalion. A runner managed to get close to The Halt and shouted to us to move to the woodland as soon as possible.'

Although E. Fitness's account does not mention it, a US formation had in fact relieved the 2nd Coldstream Guards. The platoons of No. 2 Company had been so isolated that they could not be relieved by the incoming Americans. Meanwhile, the men of his platoon were looking for a way to reach the woodland in accordance with orders.

'Our one hope of doing this seemed by way of the railway cutting running from The Halt into the German lines. This was pitted with mortar holes and covered with severed telegraph wires and smashed telegraph poles. It did offer some cover if we could first cross the open ground. The Germans had anticipated this and were using a machine-gun on fixed lines to sweep the cutting. Daylight came. Our position was desperate. We were outnumbered by the enemy who was firing on us from three sides while at our backs was the minefield. A number of us reached the bottom of the railway cutting. The Germans had seen us and their gunfire was intense, tearing into the earth around us. Heavy rain added to our discomfort. We hugged the ground moving slowly, inch by inch. A few of us reached The Halt, our movements being impeded by wiring. Again we hugged the ground, moving slowly, intending to skirt the area of the minefield. One of our number was trapped in the German wire entanglements which were strewn in front of us. It took us some time to free him and then, slowly, still harried by the fire of the machine-guns, we made what we hoped would be a safe deviation around the minefield. Our chief need at this stage was to get one of our survivors to the nearest Field Dressing Station. He was suffering intensely as the result of bullet wounds and severe shock. After what seemed an eternity, we arrived at the FDS, feeling very tired, dirty and dazed. We handed over our colleague and were then informed that the battalion was reforming at a farm some distance away. Wearily we set off to rejoin it. We were soon halted. Two German aircraft were doing a strafing run. We dived off the rough track into some stunted bushes, escaping a hail of machine-gun bullets. A shot from a nearby Bofors AA gun scored a hit and to our delight one plane came down in an adjoining field.

'We were too tired to talk, although our minds were full of thoughts of comrades whom we knew would fight no more battles. We wondered how the remainder of the battalion had fared. The rain stopped and the sky became clearer. Eventually we reached the farm. Exhausted, we sank down on the side of a small stream waiting for blankets to arrive. The rain started again. Very heavily this time. Our blankets arrived – wet and soggy. A flurry of activity around the Company Commander's area made us wonder what was to happen next. The news was not long in coming. The position on Longstop had deteriorated rapidly and we were to return immediately to make a counter-attack.'

The Americans who had relieved the Coldstreams had been struck by a German counter-attack before they had settled in and had been flung back.

'Considerable ground had been lost and every effort was to be made to wrest the lost territory back from the enemy. We were too tired to think objectively of what this meant. We left our wet blankets, collected fresh ammunition and started off again. We reached Chassart, roughly a mile from Longstop and formed up. Three Companies were to make a frontal attack and the remaining platoons were to be responsible for carrying ammunition and other supplies. For the second time in less than twenty-four hours we set off towards Longstop. The heavy rain had soaked well into the ground and every step taken through the heavily churned-up mud was a demanding physical effort. We reached the American defence line. Very little was said as we passed through, apart from repeated comments that it was "Hell up there". Heavy rain and mist obscured most of the hated Longstop. Machine-gun fire crackled as our companies split into formation and worked towards the top. Soon the air was filled with bullets, mortar bombs and shells. The Germans had recaptured the crest of the mountain and were fully prepared for our coming. Fighting continued, sometimes at close quarters as we struggled upwards. Casualties were heavy as we sought to move from one exposed spot to another, all the time trying to gain a few more yards. Darkness fell and the all-revealing Very lights illuminated the bitter scene. We began again the feverish efforts to dig-in and to hold the ground we had regained. Throughout the night vehicles were heard behind the enemy lines. Once more they had pushed up reinforcements. The whine of German mortar bombs continued as our positions were bombarded frequently. An uneasy daylight began to break through and the enemy's fire stepped-up in intensity. What appeared to be armoured cars had worked up part of the slope on our right flank and added the weight of their fire power to that which raked us from above. This was war. The infantryman's war. No glamour, just simply a grim, deadly battle where boys quickly became veterans. Many would die. We scrambled from boulder to boulder in our efforts to escape the withering fire of the Spandaus. At the same time we inched towards the mist-shrouded crest, becoming fewer in number as the enemy's efforts took toll of our decimated but proud battalion. This was a Christmas we would never forget. "Peace on earth, goodwill to all men," seemed a long way off on Christmas Day, 1942.'

East of Medjez el Bab, in the spring of 1943, the 4th British Division went into action for the first time in Africa. The aim of the offensive was to drive the German paratroops from hills they occupied around Peter's Corner on the Medjez–Tunis road. With those positions in British hands the final offensive could begin. It was due to open on 23 April 1943, but the strong and experienced Fallschirmjaeger launched a pre-emptive attack. Their operation struck the 2nd Duke of Cornwall's Light Infantry. A very dear friend, the late Joe Harris, described that action:

'We were very unlucky in that it was our first major action in Tunisia. From the time that we moved towards the front, we had always occupied positions won by other units, being in a sense, follow-up troops. The intention was plain. We were being quietly broken to active service life so we had the usual stand-tos, patrols and small wiring-parties. Around our company positions there were several unburied dogs stinking like hell and crawling with maggots. Quite nasty. Some of us were detailed to cover the dead animals with earth. This was not an easy task as the soil was only a few inches deep. Below that were huge rocks and boulders. Still, we did manage finally to cover the smelly carcasses.

'We were relieved in those positions by a unit from the 1st Division and then we moved to a place between Medjez el Bab and Peter's Corner. The positions we were now holding were called "The Basin" because the area was a number of low hills surrounding a low-lying piece of ground. At 'O' Group our Platoon Commander told us that Jerry was just over two miles away to the east and holding some low features around Peter's Corner. He also told us that the Jerries were all fanatical Nazi paratroops from the Hermann Goering Division. They must have known that we were fresh in the line, having just relieved the Loyals. I think it might have been the Arabs that told them we were new troops. They passed between our lines and the Germans as freely as anything. The first night we were in the line, 20 April, we stood-to as usual at last light but were not ordered to stand down. Instead our Section Corporal told us that the Hermann Goerings were expected to attack us that night. So far as I remember it was just before midnight when the firing started. Out in the dark open ground in front of our positions there was a lot of Spandau fire and explosions. There were carrier-parties from the RA out in front of our positions, out there dumping shells for the big attack. Those carrier-parties were being guarded by sections from one of our platoons. From that firing it was obvious that those out in no man's land were being attacked by Jerry fighting patrols. From the volume of fire it was clear that our men were fighting back with a will. Then, quite suddenly, it was all quiet on the plain. Then a lot of flashes were seen from the enemy area and crash, crash, crash; his stonk started.

'Under that stonk the Hermann Goerings attacked us. Even though shells were falling all around us we did not duck below the parapet of our slit-trenches, but remained with our rifles or Bren-guns pressed into our shoulders waiting for the order to fire. In between the intervals in the barrage we could hear the sound of tank engines and I learned later that one of the platoons was attacked by flame-throwing tanks or by a flame-thrower – I can't remember which. It was a strange night. There were bursts of fire all round us; some close at hand and others farther away. This firing would start quite suddenly, continue for some minutes and then stop. Then it would begin somewhere else. And all the time Jerry was stonking us with mortars as well as with artillery shells. Those mortars were deadly. You couldn't hear them coming like you could hear a shell. The first thing you knew was a blinding flash of light and then an explosion. Jerry's Spandaus seemed to be all around us making us feel that we were surrounded on all sides. Our battalion was supposed to have Vickers machine-guns in support, but I don't remember hearing them firing. As we lay there with our elbows on the trench parapet looking out into the dark, I thought several times that I could see shapes but without the order to fire, you didn't dare open up. Once the order was given we would fire fifteen rounds rapid for a couple of minutes. This brought a quick response from the Germans. Their mortars would switch target and would drop their bombs on our trench line. They were ranging and aiming at the flashes from our rifles and from the Bren. It went on like that all through the night. At one time we seemed to be running out of ammunition, but the A Echelon men came up with fresh bandoliers so that we could carry on firing. I also remember the different coloured flares that Jerry fired. Red and green mostly, but also white ones. When these white ones burst high up in the sky it was like daylight for a couple of minutes. One of them lit up a German group as it was trudging up the hill towards the Company on our left. We caught that group in enfilade fire, but the light died before we could get them all.

'In this, our first fight in North Africa, we lost over a hundred men; killed, wounded or missing. Not all of them were killed during the German attack. Some, who had been on escort to the artillery carrying-parties, were caught in a minefield by a Jerry battle patrol. Our battalion had been unlucky. We lay right in the path of the German attack and its whole weight fell on us. They had wanted to take the high ground from us, but had not succeeded and had retreated back to Peter's Corner.'

John Mitton, formerly of the RTR, described the anecdote he sent in as amusing, for he had tried to impart that, 'We were at the time green and naïve civilians playing at being soldiers' when he was first 'shot over'. His story continues:

'After three years' training in England without hearing a shot fired in anger, the powers that be had finally decided that we were required abroad and, fresh from Blighty, here we were in Tunisia. So far the war had passed us by and as we were carried by tank transporters towards the front it was just like being on an exercise back in England. We just sat and enjoyed the February sun as we were carried along. Leaving Le Kef, we proceeded on tracks towards El Arrousa over ground that was very reminiscent of our last training area, the South Downs, just behind Worthing. On this particular morning after a long night drive, the sun was now up, the road lay straight ahead, when the order came to disperse off the road, camouflage, maintainance, etc. The tank commander took me off the road to the right into a natural hollow some 100 yards from the Troop Leader who, for some reason best known to himself, had remained where he had stopped on the roadside verge. He stood out uncamouflaged and silhouetted. The rest of the squadron had gone to ground and were not visible.

'Having duly camouflaged, maintenance was next. During the night's run both tracks had stretched and had to be tightened, so with Mick the gunner, who was also the crew's aircraft recognition expert, we were working away under the cam net between the horns at the front of the tank. As we both worked on the bolts of the idler wheel, I saw out of the corner of my eye a movement to the right up and over the road. Two planes in tandem, engines throttled back, were cruising just above the road coming across our front. As they came nearer I said to Mick, more out of curiosity than anything else, "What are they, Mick?" He took a long look and said "Spitfires." I said, "What, with black crosses?" The two Messerschmitt 109s, with their black crosses prominently displayed on the fuselage, passed over the Troop Leader's tank and continuing down the road, climbed and turned in the distance. Now they were coming back on full throttle just above the road. Mick and I watched in silence. The first bore down on its target; a burst of black smoke from the underbelly then a split second later the noise of a long machine-gun burst and the scream of the engines which was repeated as the second plane came in to repeat the exercise. We ran. Fearing the worst, not knowing what to expect, mentally stunned by what we had seen, the whole episode could not have been more than a couple of minutes' duration. We both rounded the rear of the vehicle, fearing the worst only to find the crew sat at breakfast a couple of yards from the tank side. And there between them and the vehicle was a deep rutted gulley of ground, churned up by both planes' gunfire which had passed between them. No one hit, tank untouched, but a very shocked crew. The war had finally found us. Up till now playing soldiers had been enjoyable, but when the other side started using live ammunition it was not funny any more. They could have killed us. By the end of the month all of us would have been blooded in action and learning the hard way.'

War in Sicily and Italy

Sicily is remembered by many of my correspondents as being a Europeanized version of Italy's North African provinces. The one difference was that in Sicily there were no Arabs, more white women – most of whom were unapproachable – and a feeling that we were now, at long last, beginning to win the war. The general theme of most accounts of Sicily is the failure of American pilots to put down our airborne troops over the correct targets, the tenacity of the German defence around the Primasole bridge and the battle for Centuripe. From correspondence it is clear that in many ways the Eighth Army was still, mentally, in Africa.

The peculiarities of dress which had marked out the Eighth Army soldiers were retained in Sicily and by the time the army was in Italy the oddities of dress had become eccentric as if to emphasize that the wearer was one of the 'originals' of Eighth Army. R. G. Bell was kind enough to supply me with an extract from 7th Medium Regiment's History:

'In the matter of dress, the campaigns in the desert and in North Africa had created a very casual attitude among most units of the Eighth Army towards personal turnout. Officers offended with their corduroys and coloured scarves, other ranks largely by their stage of undress. It was fashionable to serve the guns stripped to the waist, and quite properly in such a climate, but the habit grew even away from the guns and in Sicily it included such additional unconventional items as "captured" civilian straw hats, cloth caps or "toppers". On one occasion, it must be recorded, a somewhat amusing incident (which caused mild repercussions) happened to a certain Troop of 27/28 Battery. The Troop, led by the GPO in his truck, was advancing to a forward position in action; the four guns towed by the 7th Medium special brand of Matadors with their sawn-off tops, open to the sky, containing the usual loads of ammunition, gun stores, etc., the odd chicken or other livestock, with the gun detachments lying around on top of all, almost naked and wearing a varied type of headgear, none of which had come from the Quartermaster's Store! Down the road towards the Troop drove the Corps Commander's car with the Corps Commander (General Sir Oliver Leese) and the CCRA, who had been up visiting one of the OPs. General Leese, recognizing the regimental sign, which was very well known to him, must have been rather surprised (or was he?) on approaching the leading Matador to see it driven by a bronzed body, naked to the waist, wearing a bowler hat of civilian pattern and with pipe in mouth. However, the General raised his own peaked cap in civilian fashion to the driver, who responded by removing his pipe and lifting his bowler in salute. It is hoped that honour was satisfied on both sides, but in closing this record it must be added that a letter (NOT from the General) was received by RHQ within 24 hours, stressing the point that as the Regiment was now fighting in a civilized country, the matter of dress . . . etc., etc., etc.'

The Eighth Army had, of course, been in the desert for years and that time 'up the Blue' had had its effect. In a country where much of the fighting took place in open desert, there had been no need to worry about damage to cultural buildings and the few civilians living in the area managed to remove themselves from the battlefield well in advance, so that the concern about non-military casualties did not arise. Under such conditions it was hardly surprising that there was non-military influence most of which manifested itself in the matter of dress. The Eighth had fought for years in the desert. By comparison, its sister army, the First, entered and completed its service in Africa within six months. It had had no time to become eccentric in the way that Eighth Army had, and when the two armies met it was a shock to them both. The First wondered just who were these scruffy gypsies while the Eighth were astonished at the military formality which was still very evident and which its own units had abandoned years earlier.

A photograph taken at the conclusion of the campaign in Sicily shows Montgomery standing on a headland looking towards Italy. That country would be the next objective. Sicily had been only a stepping-stone to the invasion of Europe. The invasion of Europe would only be accomplished when the first Allied soldiers debarked on the shores of Italy. At the highest levels of command in Britain and America, it had been anticipated that two Allied armies, the US Fifth and the British Eighth, would advance quickly up the length of the Italian peninsula. The intention of opening this Second Front in Europe would be to draw German forces away from Russia; the First Front. A second consideration would be to gain airfields from which Allied bombers could raid the oilfields of Roumania as well as other economic targets in the Balkans. The third advantage which would be gained would be the political one – the liberation of Rome, making the cradle of Christianity the first European capital to be freed from the Germans. As the first units of US Fifth Army headed towards the invasion beaches of Salerno the news was broadcast that the Italians had surrendered. As Ron Bullen wrote in his history of 2/7th Battalion, The Queen's Royal Regiment:

'It might have been armistice night. The Italians had capitulated and, somehow, the news had spread like lightning. The Brigade Commander records: "I had a nasty moment when I heard on the evening of D minus 1 that Italy had signed an armistice, because I thought the troops might think they were on an easy wicket and run into a packet of trouble. I had a personal signal made to all ships to the effect that it was the Boche we were fighting anyhow and not the Italians." '

Other units did not have so wise a commander. H. Rawlinson, an infantryman:

'You can well imagine what effect such an announcement had on us. As far as we were concerned half the war was over. The Jerries would surely follow the Italian lead and pack it in. Then there would be only the Japs to finish off. When we touched down near Battipaglia [9 September] the reception we got from the Germans surprised us. Some of our lads thought that the German units could not have heard the news that the war was over, but then when the 88s came in and the Tiger tanks started attacking, as they did several days later, it was plain that the Jerries had no intention of packing it in at all, but that they were fighting like hell to drive us into the sea.'

CASSINO

The staunch German resistance at Salerno was an indication of how determined the enemy was to hold Italy. It was evident that the intention was to delay – if possible to halt indefinitely – the Allied northward advance at every river line and every mountain range, and the Germans built defences to strengthen positions already naturally strong. One such area was at Cassino, a small town to the south of Rome. At that place lies the Liri river valley, a narrow strip of land between the mountains and the sea. No advance could be made towards Rome without passing through the valley and to reach its mouth the town of Cassino had first to be taken. That town lay at the foot of Monte Cassino on whose summit stood the world-famous Benedictine abbey. In order to reach the town of Cassino Fifth Army would have to advance over a wide and open plain under the eyes of German observers on the mountains behind Cassino town. The attacking troops would have to cross the fast flowing River Rapido, capture the town and force the Liri valley, before they could debouch out of the hills and advance upon Rome. It is the fighting to achieve these objectives which makes up the story of the four battles for Cassino.

The first of these offensives opened on 17 January, with a thrust across the River Garigliano by a British Corps which formed part of Fifth Army. Then two US divisions were committed in an operation so badly planned and so incompetently handled that a disastrous outcome was inevitable. Later in January, in an attempt to strike into the back of the German divisions holding Cassino and to split the defence there, the Allies made an unsuccessful amphibious assault at Anzio/Nettuno. The American infantry losses in the first battle of Cassino were shocking, but the attacks were ordered to be continued. To support the US forces, three divisions of Eighth Army were brought across the width of the Italian peninsula and put into the fight. Their attacks, which opened on 12 February 1944, mark the opening of the second battle – made notorious by the bombing of the monastery on 18 February, which was carried out because it was believed the Germans were using the building as an observation post. Another aerial bombardment was made on 15 March, and was followed by an artillery barrage, during which nearly 200,000 shells were fired into the town. The Eighth Army infantry and armour who fought in this, the third battle of Cassino, had as little success as had the earlier offensives. The fourth and final battle opened on 11 May, with a barrage fired by 1,600 guns. Six days later and the troops of the French Expeditionary Corps had reached a point in the mountains behind the German positions. The defenders of Cassino, chiefly the paratroop battalions of the Luftwaffe's 1st Airborne Division, had been outflanked and would have to withdraw. On 18 May, Polish troops raised their national flag over the ruins of the Abbey. The town fell to British divisions, chiefly 4th and 78th Infantry, whose accompanying armour smashed through the Liri valley and on to the flat ground leading towards Rome. At Anzio/Nettuno, the beachhead had been contained by German troops that included 4th Para Division. The British forces that had captured Cassino linked hands with the Anglo/US forces striking out of the Anzio beachhead and the drive upon the Italian capital began.

On 5 June 1944, the first troops of the Allied armies entered the Eternal City. The first major political objective of the campaign had been achieved. By a bitter twist the importance of the first climacteric of the Italian campaign was eclipsed within a single day, when on 6 June, the Allies landed in Normandy. The sacrifice of the four battles of Cassino was ignored in favour of the news from France, but those losses had been heavy and nearly 350,000 men of the Anglo-American forces had been killed, wounded or were missing. Among the battles of the Second World War, there were few in which the infantry suffered as grievously as their forefathers had in the trenches of the Great War. Stalingrad and Cassino were two battles in which it was not unusual for soldiers of the opposing sides to share the ruins of the same house. The fighting in Cassino was often hand to hand and bodies lay unburied, rotting in the rain of the Italian winter. On the German side the units detailed to carry out the terrible task of bringing in the dead had to tie scarves soaked in eau de Cologne round their faces and around the nostrils of the horses carrying the dead against the stench of decay and decomposition. One of the most bizarre sights to be seen in Cassino was the pair of German Army jackboots which stood on the platform of the railway station. Out of the tops of those boots projected glistening white shin bones. This may have been the most bizarre sight, but to Fred Majdalaney the most poignant one was the row of little boots sticking out from under British Army blankets. These marked the Gurkha dead for the Gurkhas being small in stature, had small feet. The rows of little boots was a sight which moved Majdalaney, a hard-bitten journalist and veteran of the Tunisian campaign, to unashamed tears. Cassino was an infantryman's Calvary – a bloody and bitter agony. George Webb served there with the 3rd Battalion, The Grenadier Guards, and although he concludes his story by saying it was a quiet sector, the reader can judge for himself what this meant.

'No. 9 Section of No. 3 Platoon, No. 1 Company, relieved some regiment, I forget which one, and we took over a cellar of a house on the south side of Cassino. The house had been razed to the ground. We were separated from the Germans of General Heidrich's 1st Parachute Division, by a river bank and our positions were some 400/500 yards apart. We observed German movements by telescope, similar to submarine periscopes, and I suppose the Germans did the same when observing our positions. One afternoon we had the order to remove all tracer rounds from the Bren-gun magazines and that at about 11pm that night we were to fire on a certain target on a fixed line. Half a dozen blankets were soaked in water so as to diminish any muzzle flash from the Bren. In our Section we had a very good soldier, but he was a little on the dim side. I was a lance-corporal and second-in-command of a Section, with a sergeant as the section commander. When the order to fire was given – in a count-down from Company headquarters – a blaze of tracer was fired from our Bren-gun. It was thought that the man responsible was the dim-witted one. Seconds after the incident the Company Commander came on the field telephone and the air was blue. I am sure the sergeant would have been relieved of his stripes had that been possible at the time. Among the other things our Company Commander said was that we were sure to be shelled because the tracer would have given our position away. Sure enough, within three minutes or so we had a hell of a stonk. After it had finished I suddenly thought of the two sentries who were positioned in an abri outside the cellar. When I reached them, one Guardsman just sat there with his rifle between his knees like a waxwork model in Madame Tussaud's. The other Guardsman seemed too numb to say anything. When we examined the first sentry some time later it was found that a piece of shrapnel, no bigger than a little fingernail, had pierced his great coat and had gone straight through his body. You could hardly see where the shrapnel had penetrated. The next thing was to get him back to the RAP at first light. Now the Germans were not very particular about the Red Cross flag and had been known to fire on stretcher-bearer parties, even though these were displaying the Red Cross flag. So consequently, I had a devil of a job getting a volunteer to accompany me to carry the stretcher bearing Nobby's body to the RAP, which was some 400/500 yards away. I did eventually get a volunteer and we ran and walked with the stretcher. We were not fired on and the MO pronounced Nobby as being dead. It subsequently transpired that the barrage that had fallen on us after the tracer bullets incident had not been German retaliation but by a quirk of fate it was some American 4.5 howitzers whose shells were falling short. According to our regimental history " . . . the battalion was not called up to attack nor to resist attack nor even to patrol . . . " What was unnerving was the fact that smoke shells by day and by night were fired by the RA and at night when the empty canisters fell on to the rubble outside our cellar it seemed as if someone was advancing on our positions. This resulted at times in our standing-to for long periods with our fingers on the triggers, so to speak. We were also in Cassino when the American Fortresses bombed the abbey. This was as terrifying for us as it was for the Germans.'

Nearly every unit of Fifth and Eighth Armies was involved in the struggle for Cassino. It was one of the few battles involving the Western Allies in which conditions were similar to those that had obtained in France and Flanders during the First World War. Conditions in the stricken city were so appalling that battalions had to be rotated frequently. In the late spring of 1944, 4th British Division, which had been all but broken-up after the campaign in Tunisia, was reinforced, reactivated, brought to Italy and in time entered the battle for Cassino. Danny Exley was an NCO in one of the infantry battalions of 12th Brigade:

'For the fourth and final battle of Cassino we were put in the picture properly. We would be in the big push which was to be carried out by US Fifth Army and British Eighth Army, of which our division, 4th Infantry, was a part. Eighth Army was given the task of attacking and capturing the town of Cassino and Monastery Hill. Once that hill was taken the battle would be over because it dominated the whole battle area. Every move made by the Allied armies was watched by the eyes of the enemy on Monastery Hill. We were told that the battle would commence at 11pm, with the greatest barrage since Alamein. Two thousand guns would be used to smash into the German lines and God help those who were on the receiving end. At Zero Hour all hell broke loose as the massed guns of Eighth Army opened up. It shook us with fear and fright and we were behind the gun lines. God knows how Jerry felt. Was he ready for this lot and would he stand and fight? Until it was our turn to enter the battle all we could do was to sit down and wait. At dawn we moved forward to the assembly area just behind the forward gun line. After a few hours, information began to filter through; nothing definite, mostly rumour, but things did not seem to be going so well. A slight bridgehead had been established and the only way to get to the weak forces in that bridgehead was to get a Bailey Bridge erected as quickly as possible. So far the work of the REs had been held up by heavy enemy shellfire and sniping and their casualties had been quite heavy. But the bridge had to be erected at all costs. As the day passed it was clear that the Germans were standing their ground and had not started falling back on our sector. Still we had no bridge across the river although the Sappers were working under extreme conditions. God help the men in the bridgehead. We knew they must be looking over their shoulders, sweating and cursing and saying, "Where are those 12 Brigade bastards who are to relieve us?" They had been holding the bridgehead for nearly 24 hours and must have become desperate by this time. By the following morning the bridge had been built for the cost of fifteen Sappers killed in action and 57 wounded.

'The first armour to cross Amazon bridge was 17/21st Lancers following behind the infantry who had crossed over into the bridgehead. The 12th Brigade was now moving fast. The Black Watch and the Royal Fusiliers were soon over and Jerry began to leave his positions and fall back. By noon it was our turn to cross which we were to do mounted on tanks. I was on the lead tank with our platoon officer. After ten minutes' drive we could see that the bridge was still under fire. As we came close to it ready to turn on to it we came under fire from a Jerry machine-gunner. The tank stopped for some reason making us a sitting target. Our platoon officer was hit right across his legs. He fell off and crawled to a crater, gave me the thumbs-up signal and made himself comfortable to await the stretcher-bearers. We never saw him again. He had joined us only that morning as a replacement. We never even knew his name. We jumped off the tanks and raced across the bridge dodging the fire as best we could. The bridge was littered with dead and wounded. Men were lying on stretchers waiting to be evacuated. Some wounded men were attending to the more seriously wounded. Bodies wrapped in blankets were being removed for burial. The bridge was also littered with vehicles, some of which were burning. Once the rifle Companies were clear of the bridge they advanced towards their objectives. On our way we had to move up a track. We had to keep to one side to let the walking wounded pass on their way to the rear area. We pushed on and got the better of the snipers. Some were killed, but most of them had a field day, picking off our comrades all day. When they had no more ammunition they just broke their cover and put their hands up. Some were shot down where they stood. They had fought like soldiers. Now they died like soldiers. We took our objective. Jerry was well dug-in and his positions were well sited. We winkled him out and took over his trenches ready to receive the shelling and mortar fire which would come in once his troops were clear of the position. Within an hour we got it alright and it lasted on and off over a period of a couple of hours. First he tried his heavy mortars, then he sent over his airbursts; the ones which did most damage. These shells explode above the target and shrapnel rains down into the trenches and positions.

'After the barrage stopped, Sherman tanks arrived to give us protection in case we got counter-attacked. Then Vickers guns came up, again to give strength to our position. By the evening we were well entrenched and ready to resist any attack. The bridgehead was small but reinforcements were pouring over the bridge and every hour we were getting a stronger hold of the ground we had taken. It became dark and it seemed to us we would not be moving tonight. Our only orders were to watch our front and be ready to hold and to fight off any attack the enemy might make. It was a long night and although we were all tired we could only snatch a few minutes sleep. As it began to get light we received orders to advance and take another objective. We moved forward at 5.00am and a mist came down. We took no notice of it at first, but after a while we could not see a few yards in front of us. The tanks stopped but we were ordered to keep going forward on a compass bearing. The tanks started to crawl forward again. We had the worry of them crushing us. In the end we let them get in front with a couple of our men in front of them to guide them while the rest of us followed up behind – following the noise. There was no contact with anybody on the left or right. All of a sudden the mist began to clear and the Monastery came into view towering over us. The German OPs would have a field-day. We were caught out in the open. We spread out as quick as we could and moved forward. It was then that Jerry put in his counter-attack. We hit the ground and started to fight him off. We were surrounded and our Company Commander shouted to us to kill as many Jerries as we could. This was the moment we had been waiting for. We had a real battle but we could not move forward and had to start digging-in. Jerry was holding us. When the enemy infantry stopped firing, over came his heavy mortar fire followed up by shellfire. Then we got the airbursts. Things quietened a bit. He must have fell back on to another prepared position. At six that evening we received orders to cut the road which was his only escape route out of Cassino. This task was to take another four days of hard and bitter fighting and reports that "everything was going to plan" did not seem true to us. We did not seem to be moving. Our casualties were very heavy indeed and the shelling and mortaring seemed to increase.

'As we left our slit-trenches to form up in extended order, some of our comrades never moved. They were the aftermath of the heavy shelling and mortaring which had been belting down for the best part of eight hours. Those sights never did us any good even if the dead soldiers were German. Us who survived knew that any second we could be like them if your luck runs out. We spread out and faced our front. We were to advance on a battalion front. We were waiting for the RAF fighters to strafe the enemy positions and then our guns were to soften up the opposition with a barrage. Some of the shells from the barrage dropped short, killing and wounding officers and men waiting to advance. We moved forward cautiously with fixed bayonets. Jerry was not far away. Ahead we could see a road which we had to capture and cross. We had advanced about a thousand yards with no contact when all of a sudden two or three machine-guns opened up just 50 yards away. It was too late to take cover. Men fell like ninepins. We destroyed the machine-gun posts, crossed the road and carried the advance into open country. By now Jerry opposition in some places was beginning to crack, but on our sector the enemy made us fight for every bit of ground. Then it was clear that the fighting for Cassino was ending and on the morning of 18 May the Monastery and town fell to Eighth Army. On 20 May we turned our backs on Cassino. It was over, but none of us could forget the bloodshed and it still remains imprinted in our thoughts.'

THE GOTHIC LINE

With the fall of Cassino the liberation of Rome followed quickly and on 4 June the Allies entered the city. This splendid piece of news was eclipsed two days later by the announcement that a successful invasion of Normandy had been accomplished. Thereafter, the campaign in Italy took a secondary place in the minds of the British public. North of Rome the Allied armies took up their former formation, with Fifth Army on the Tyrrhenian side and Eighth Army on the Adriatic, and pushed their way forward. During September they struck the German defences of the Gothic Line. The troops of British 56th Division were told that the timetable for the offensive was "Two days to reach Bologna, four days to reach Venice and a week to reach Vienna.' They were also told, according to Thomas Weller, that the Germans had three divisions facing Eighth Army:

'Those three divisions were short of everything. One had only a limited supply of ammunition for its three machine-guns, a second had no rations to issue and the third German division had only one gun and that was drawn by oxen. There were some Eighth Army soldiers who believed it all. We had with us gunners from LAA regiments who had been guarding Alex and Cairo since 1941. Their units were broken up and they were posted lock, stock and barrel into infantry regiments. They believed the rubbish that the IO told them. Mind you, he was only repeating what he had been told at Brigade or Division and was duty-bound to pass it on. Well if Jerry had only one gun and that was drawn by oxen, then we reckon that poor bastard animal must have been mated with a greyhound because that so-called one gun was firing along a battle front that reached from Rimini and well into the mountains.'

Donald Featherstone served with 51st RTR in Italy:

'Some of the unit's toughest fighting (including eleven assault river-crossings in three weeks) took place in the Gothic Line on the Adriatic coast of Italy in the autumn of 1944, although it began on a note of comedy. To conceal the movement of armour from the Florence front, the unit's tanks went by transporters by night while the men were driven across in trucks, their tell-tale black berets hidden in packs and each man wearing some form of wide-brimmed soft-felt hat from a hat factory captured at Montevarchi. Although a chrono-logical blur, the Gothic Line still paints a vivid picture in the writer's mind of slit-trenches dug in the shelter of lines of vines where grapes could be had by merely stretching out the hand, at least until we learned painfully that this same salubrious vegetation could set off the proximity fuzes of the 88mm shells fired at us on a flat trajectory, converting them into airbursts. Our camp site below Gemmano or was it Coriano Ridge was soon vacated because of the stench of Canadian dead unable to be moved from the minefield. It was here that I acquired the moon-shaped scar that still adorns my right elbow, when a sudden mortar stonk caused a general dive into slit-trenches. Mine was already occupied by a snake so, turning in midair like an Olympic diver, I flew into Sergeant Stan Saville's trench and his steel-tipped boot heel caught my arm and opened it up.

'We lost a lot of good men. One of our drivers could not escape from his Sherman because the depressed barrel of the 75mm gun would not allow the lid of the escape hatch to be opened to its full extent. And Lieutenant Neale's Churchill, knocked out in midstream when crossing the River Ronco, blocking the crossing, was later drawn by war artist Eric Kennington and for many years was commemorated annually as an In Memoriam notice in the *Daily Telegraph*. In the incessant rain of that time we took our chance outside the slit-trenches which quickly became ponds. And the mountain village of Camerino from which the ground dropped away to leave the world stretching before the eye, echoed flatly with artillery fire that flickered colourfully at night. It was here that the RSM was doing a line with a black-garbed widow, a poor, fat lady, who rarely spoke, but gazed uncomprehendingly at these loud-talking, guffawing men from another planet. Then there was the mad dawn dash by the tanks across Forli airfield. When the town was entered it was said that the departing Germans left an Italian partisan hanging from each of the tall lamp-posts in the town square. One of them was a woman. At least that's what I seem to recall, but it was 45 years ago, wasn't it.'

John Mitton, MM, describes an incident in November 1944, as Eighth Army advanced towards Forli:

'In typical British Army fashion, after I returned to the regiment, from a six-weeks' driving and maintenance instructors' course, my OC told me he had a job for me. Radio Op in the regiment's Tactical HQ, driving a scout car and maintaining liaison between the tanks and the infantry. Talk about a round peg in a square hole. One morning we crossed over a river. A few hundred yards in from the crossing-point, our B Echelon vehicles were under fire from Spandaus on fixed lines. We turned left into a farmyard where TAC HQ was located. The infantry FDL was about half a mile from us. There was a brooding, uncanny silence even though there was a great deal of activity and excitement, particularly when the Spandaus fired. Stupidly, we selected as bed spaces in TAC HQ's farmhouse, that part of the room which was in the direct line of fire of those guns. They opened up from time to time, the bursts ricocheting off the wall by the door and then whining away through the trees. It was quite indiscriminate fire. If we wanted to go out we had to wait until the burst had stopped, then open the door, run like hell and hope he didn't fire again until you had made the corner. Sometimes you were lucky – sometimes not. The heavy rain flooded the rivers and swept the bridges away. We of A Squadron and the infantry ahead of us were cut off. One dark night I was detailed to go up to Casa Bordi and deliver a message to the OC. The driver of the infantry Bren carrier drove flat out into the wall of darkness. Half a mile on we were stopped and challenged by a vague figure who suddenly materialized from nowhere. To the left I could make out

Casa Bordi. The rain had stopped and an occasional coloured German flare rose into the sky and lines of Spandau fire lanced across the fields. We drove across a second field; finally the farm building loomed up ahead, there was a low challenge and then we went inside the house. The building was full of infantry who were sat against the walls resting, looking dirty, tired and in need of rest. Outside was a Sherman with a neat hole punched through the gear box, put there by a German fighting patrol with a *Panzerfaust*. There was another unexploded Panzerfaust stuck in the upstairs curtain frill. Shortly before we arrived the house had been attacked but this had been beaten off and three prisoners taken. Because I would be going back to TAC HQ I was told to take them with me. The prisoners looked very young, about 15 years old, frightened, dejected and a little ludicrous with their long field-grey overcoats down to their ankles. What had happened, I wondered, to the great German Army; the ones who had been in the Afrika Korps; big, blond and arrogant? I don't know who was the most scared, I or the prisoners.

'But before I could take them back I had to deliver the message to the OC. To the right there was the faint silhouette of a Churchill, closed down, engine switched off but with a faint light coming from the turret whose cupola was open. I climbed up the outside and looked down inside the turret. The Commander was standing on the floor of the turret looking at his maps when I tapped him on the head. I thought at that moment I had given him heart failure. With headphones on, intent on reading his map, to be tapped on the head when you least expect it, especially when surrounded by the enemy isn't exactly good for the nerves. Tearing his headphones off Major Powditch asked what the ********** hell was I doing there and to clear off as it wasn't safe. I felt safer than he did as he was in a steel box, blind, hearing over the 19 Set of Tigers in the immediate area and unable to do anything but sit there in the turret, cold and with the rain trickling down his neck. I passed my message, made my way back to the infantry carrier, met up with the SSM and the prisoners and then away we roared, down the road and into the farmyard of TAC HQ. It was only then that we found the SSM had been left behind at the FDL. He was not amused and said so in no uncertain terms when he finally arrived back on foot. The rest is history. The bridges were rebuilt, Forli airfield was attacked and taken and we moved into the centre of the town, where on the first morning, after a good night's sleep in the Post Office, we were blown out of bed by a German SP gun.'

The speedy reaction of the German High Command in Italy brought sufficient German divisions into the line to hold Eighth Army. The British hope of driving up the old Roman road from Rimini to Bologna and then via Venice through the Lubljana gap into Austria and on to Vienna, died when heavy fighting for the first objectives of the offensive upset the timetable of the offensive. The hope of reaching Bologna within two days faded and it was not until 6 months later that the city finally fell. As in all offensives there were accusations of cowardice. The 1st Armoured Division was hated because one of its regiments refused to go in at Tavoleto in support of the Gurkhas. It was a disgrace that was never lived down. Later in the offensive and deeper into the mountains, George Webb of the Grenadier Guards sent an account of a reconnaissance patrol at Imola. The sober narrative conceals the strain and danger of such a mission:

'After a bout of leave [left out of battle] I was summoned by the Commander of No. 2 Company and told I was to take a reconnaissance patrol to recce a position held by the Germans and about two miles or so in front of our positions. The Major told me that he had already sent three or four patrols out, but these had returned with no worthwhile information. He took me on to a mountain peak and we observed the German positions through binoculars. I was given instructions that by no means were we to engage the enemy, but to try and ascertain the strength of their forces in that particular area. I was told to choose my men, preferably those who would volunteer, but only to take two. I had no difficulty in obtaining the services of one Guardsman – a cheeky Cockney. The other man I asked was a lance-corporal and he too volunteered. On reporting to the Major I was told that I could not take the lance-corporal as the Company was short of NCOs. I then made the choice of a young Guardsman, who had recently been transferred from the Brigade Intelligence unit and who could speak German. I told him that he would be in the middle of the patrol, so it was up to him to identify any Germans that we might bump into and to tell me what they were saying. I took a compass bearing on the German positions and we set off about 21.00hrs, through atrocious mountain shrubbery. After about 20 minutes we crossed a mountain stream and as we were crossing I slipped and dropped the compass. I retrieved it but it was muddy and not of much use. Casually I asked the men, "What shall we do now?" wondering whether or not they would like to carry on and not march on a possibly faulty bearing. I was given a blunt reply of, "You are the Sergeant. It's up to you." "Right," I said, "You wait here. I will go back to the start-line and get a new compass bearing. Then we will go on from there."

'This I did. In the course of events we had to rest frequently, because it was almost like going on all fours as we made our way up the mountain. On one particular occasion, after a short rest, as I rose from my sitting position I saw a form rise up in front of me, and only about three or four yards away. My Tommy-gun was pointing downwards and I thought for all the world that my time had come. But instead, nothing happened. It was a mountain goat or sheep, but the silhouette appeared to be that much like a human being. I was quite sure it was a German but vastly relieved when the form ran away.

'On we went and I was overjoyed when I came to the actual spot where we believed the Germans to be. No one seemed to be about and it was in my mind to see if I could locate an Italian farm and see if there was anything that we could scrounge. All of a sudden I heard a voice – "Is that you, Tommy?" Immediately I thought that we had hit the wrong place and that British troops were occupying the place. The next thought was that it might have been one of my Guardsmen speaking to the other, because the Cockney was called Tommy. Before I could react all hell let loose. Schmeissers, and either grenades or mortar bombs exploded all around us. We were under orders not to engage the enemy, so I called the men together and was about to beat a hasty retreat when one of the two – the lad who could speak German – shouted out, "Get down! get down!" and dropped to his knees. I said, "No, we are getting out," but he wouldn't budge. I pulled him by the shirt collar six or seven yards and he yelled, "Leave me, leave me!" Unfortunately, that is what I did, because of the intensity of the German fire. As we made our way back to the battalion positions I heard that poor lad crying out something like "Mercy! Mercy!" It was clear to me that he had been hit by a grenade or something and the more he shouted the more the Germans poured their fire upon him. When I reported to the Major that I had lost one man and that there was at least a "Platoon strength" of Germans on that position, he said, "You will have to report to the commanding officer." When I saw the CO and told him how sorry I was to have lost a man, I can remember his exact words. He said to me "Sergeant Webb, this is war." I am led to believe that nothing was ever heard of the man we lost, from that day to this. He was listed as missing and having died of wounds. He is not buried anywhere, but his name appears on a plinth in the Commonwealth War Graves cemetery at Cassino.'

'Monte Battaglia is more than 2,000 feet high. It stands, an isolated feature, high up in the mountain heights south of Bologna. It is not many miles from Firenzuola and nearer still is a little town called Castel del Rio. It is unlikely that you will find it on any maps available in England. Yet it is one of those places which the last war will make unforgettable to some men; and those men are the Grenadiers of 3rd Battalion, and the Welsh Guards. The battalions took over the area from the Americans late in October 1944. Four miles away from the ruined castle which surmounts the hill, all mechanical transport had to be left and from that point everything was brought forward on mule back. In places one could only reach the summit by clinging to ropes. The clay slopes were as slippery as a glacier. Our positions formed a salient projecting into the German positions and were under observation from three sides. Monte Battaglia was a key point which the Germans were trying hard to recapture. For days while the Guards were on this height it rained incessantly. On other days the mountains were shrouded in thick mist. Life in the slit-trenches, half filled with water and lashed by driving rain can well be imagined. Add to this the incessant shell and mortar fire, day and night, filth, excrement and the stench of unburied corpses of German and American dead, and you get a picture of a virtual hell on earth. Our positions lay at the junction of a long earthern causeway, only wide enough to carry a single track and pin-pointed by enemy mortars. That track was used by 150 mules and 100 men of the ration-parties, night after night. The surface soon became knee-deep mud and a stretcher party needed about 3½ hours to reach the nearest point from where a jeep could drive.

'In the worst spot they had known since Cassino, the Guardsmen hung on grimly. Then, one dark night, doubtless judging that days of continuous bombardment must have shattered the defenders, the Germans attacked in force. The Guardsmen let them come in. There was confusion as the first Germans fell over the trip-wires and then all hell broke loose. For men who for six days or more had been pinned in their slit-trenches there was no need to cry "Up Guards and at 'em!" They were in and among the enemy before the Germans realized just what a hornets' nest they had struck. When the battle was over the Guardsmen had taken nearly one hundred prisoners and the remaining Germans who had launched the attack were lying dead on the hillside. They did not attack the position again.'

F. Richmond:

'The onset of winter – "whoever called it sunny Italy had never been there" – first reduced and then halted full-scale military operations by both the US Fifth and British Eighth Armies although aggressive patrolling continued. Rivers barring the Allied advances were in full spate; there was a lot of snow, almost incessant rain and a great deal of misery. It had been a long and wearing campaign. We began it wildly optimistic [at Salerno on 9 September] believing that the war was over. After D-Day in France, Italy became a backwater and so few reinforcements were coming from home that units had to be broken up. They broke up one of the brigades of my division [56th London] and replaced it with a Gurkha brigade. It had been a long slog up the length of Italy and against the grain of the country. Now we faced our second winter – our second Christmas in Italy. Speaking for myself I remember only two highspots in the last months of 1944. One was seeing Dave and Joe O'Gorman – the comedians. The second, and nicer memory, was when Gabrielle Brun (I think I've spelt her name right) came to a transit camp where I was and put on an impromptu show for the blokes who were confined to camp awaiting transport up the line. I shall never forget seeing that lovely girl, standing on a table and belting out a whole succession of songs and all without a band or even a piano. She was marvellous.'

THE LAST PUSH AND INTO AUSTRIA

Nineteen months after the Allied armies had landed in Italy, to begin what had been anticipated would be a rapid advance up the peninsula, they were at last approaching the River Po. There remained only a few more mountains to take and then the Allies would be on the flat Lombardy plain. How often had the Allied infantry been given the reassurance, "This is the last ridge", when they received orders for an attack. Those who looked at maps realized that the oft-repeated promise might at last be true for beyond the last peaks really did lie a plain. But they saw, too, and with despair, that once they had crossed the Po and had thrust across the plain of Lombardy, there lay before them the Alps, into whose protection German Army Group 'C', defending Italy, would withdraw to defend the Fatherland. To fight a war in the Alps against the men who had turned Monte Cassino into a hell, was a chilling prospect. The 78th Division was one of the few formations that did not lose its fighting edge. Perhaps because it lost so many men and had to receive so many replacements, that its combat units always contained 'fresh' men led by experienced commanders. One of those new men, the fresh blood to infuse the 78th, was Robert Hayward. He joined 5th Buffs in time for the final battle in Italy and fought his first action with that battalion.

'We finally arrived at a camp near Forli, just behind the front, close enough to hear the guns and to realize you weren't dreaming. It was on the evening of 8 April 1945, as we were queuing with our mess-tins for the evening meal, that the guns opened up and kept up the barrage all that night. We knew that the attack across the River Senio and on to the Po was on. That night we were driven up to a small village and joined our battalion. My mate and I were posted to a platoon which had taken over a house with the occupants living upstairs. The men in the platoon had fought all through the North African campaign and up into Italy. They looked at us and asked if we had come straight from school, how old we were and what was our demob group number? When we said "60" they laughed. They were in "24," "25" and "26" groups for release. Next morning, after being issued with two bandoliers of ammunition, two grenades, an entrenching tool and hardtack rations, we boarded troop transport lorries and crossed the Senio over a small bridge. We headed towards the front. It was a lovely spring day, the sun was shining and we arrived at a point where the trucks could go no farther. Looking out of the truck we saw our first dead British soldier. He was dressed exactly the way I was, which gave me a scarey feeling in the pit of my stomach. We grouped behind the guns that were still pounding away at the enemy positions. Some time during the afternoon our platoon officer told us to gather round and with a map in front of him explained what our objective was. We were brigaded with the Argylls and the West Kents. It worked out that two battalions were in the Line and one was held in reserve. That night we passed through the Argylls and I shall always remember the Jocks saying "good luck" to us as we passed them. We marched in single file along the road, passing by dead horses lying stiff on the ground. Fire and tracer bullets seemed to be coming from all directions. We had a Churchill tank to keep us company and at one stage my mate and I had to crawl round the side of the vehicle so that it was between us and the gunfire. There was firing everywhere and German prisoners with their hands on their heads were being marched to a place behind the line.

'This went on all night and my mate, Sid Allen, and I could have dropped on the spot and gone sound to sleep where we were. Our platoon officer kept paying us a visit to see how we were. Also the platoon sergeant who was really concerned about us. I remember he kept singing *Melancholy Baby* most of the time. We never did reach our objective that night. This was a small bridge. Instead we finished up in some sort of orchard. At dawn we were told where to dig our slit-trenches. Ours was in the front line of trenches and there was another line behind us. We managed to hide our Churchill tank. Sid Allen and I got the names "Digger One" and "Digger Two" because we finished our trench the fastest of the lot. By the time we had finished digging it was daylight and the sun was shining. We were told to keep quiet so as not to give our position away. We took turns in looking out of our trench and things were reasonably quiet. On one occasion we saw a German patrol and I remember that one of them wore a shiny black steel helmet. About noon we opened a tin of M & V stew and ate that between us with some hardtack biscuits, which almost broke your teeth biting through them. The Germans were in position half a mile in front of us in a wood and during the afternoon our CO ordered rocket-firing Typhoons to blast their positions. The few houses that were about all had big white sheets hanging from their windows.

'Not until 6 in the evening were we relieved by a Canadian tank unit which came amongst us and opened up with everything they had before moving forward towards the enemy line. We got out of our trenches for the first time since dawn and it was nice to get the circulation back. I never knew how many Germans were in front of us until I saw them coming back with the Canadians. I nearly had a fit.

Some were even riding on the tanks. It wasn't until we found a place in a field to sleep that we were informed we had been cut off throughout the whole day. Hence the reason we were ordered to keep quiet and to let the German patrol pass by without firing on it. I couldn't have slept more soundly if anyone had given me a Mickey Finn. The next morning our Section was given the job of carrying out a daylight patrol, led by Corporal Barnett. We hugged the woods that had been alive with Jerries the previous day and except for meeting some Italian partisans wearing red scarves, and some Italian people trying to get back to their homes, plus a few false alarms, things were pretty quiet. I was really pleased to get back to our platoon and to see my mate again.

'During the rest of the day the rocket-firing Typhoons were really giving the Jerries a pasting. It was hard for us greenhorns to relax. We were all tense and excited, whereas the old soldiers were resting and even having a nap. However, we paid for it that night because we could hardly keep our eyes open. That night was almost a repeat of the previous one; advancing along the road. This time we could see the German slit-trenches and our troops fired into them although they appeared empty. The Germans had marked these trenches with a pole sticking up with a lump of straw or grass tied around the top, which I found very strange. This time, before dawn, we dug-in at the side of a country lane and seemed to be on our own. I was pleased when the platoon officer crept up to us to tell us that there would be a "stonk" in a few moments and to keep our heads down because it was ours and there were some Jerries nearby who needed to be cleared out. When the stonk happened it was too close for comfort and we were praying that no shells would fall short. Among the loud bangs you could hear the Italians in their houses screaming all the time and we were glad when the guns ceased. That morning I received a letter – the first one – as I sat on the side of my trench I was amazed that the army knew where I was. We rested that day and had a hot meal. Afterwards, a mobile bath lorry arrived. This had about twelve shower heads. At the entrance you took off all your clothes, discarded your dirty underwear and walked in. If you got one of the first six units you had a good shower. But gradually the water would peter out and at the end [shower head] you would be lucky to get a few drips. Then out of the other end to put on clean fresh clothes.

'About this time Jerry had left a lot of propaganda leaflets behind. One sticks in my mind. It was about seven inches long by four inches wide and on the front was an attractive Italian signorina carrying a basket of flowers and fruit with the River Po in the background. On the reverse side was a skeleton holding in one hand an American steel helmet and in the other a British one with the words "We are waiting for you". It also showed the details of how fast the river flowed, the widest and narrowest parts and the best places to cross, etc. I had this fear of crossing the river because I was not a swimmer and with all the gear we had to carry the situation didn't seem all that rosy. Lorries brought up little, collapsible boats made from wood and canvas. You stood inside them and pulled up the sides, wedging them with wooden struts. We rested for a few days and then one afternoon we lined up for rations and ammunition. We knew we were going back in. You could see the look on the faces of the men, knowing that the war was nearly over. Some had seen years of action. They didn't want to cop it now. As we lined up to march out that night one of the boys who carried a radio pack overheard that the Jerries had surrendered in Italy. The date was 2 May 1945; four days earlier than in Germany. What a relief.

'We crossed the Po on a pontoon bridge then, in convoy, made our way towards the Alps. The chalk and dust that came off the roads made us all look like ghosts. Our platoon stopped at a little railway track and that night we lit a huge bonfire, like a beacon, so that the Germans could come marching in to surrender. It was funny hearing them marching towards us knowing that a day or so earlier you were killing each other. They were unable to surrender during the day because the Italian partisans were stopping them doing so. Trips were made to places where the Germans were, to rescue them from the partisans. There were weapons everywhere, discarded by the surrendering Germans.

'A day or so later we were again loaded on to lorries and made our way to the Austrian border. It was a long and tiring journey and the road twisted up and around the sides of mountains seeming to go on forever. Then we started the descent which took us over the frontier. We took over the first village (Mauthen), and occupied the only hotel. This had previously been in the hands of the Germans. We cleared out all the clothes they had left in the wardrobes and took great pleasure in taking a photo of Adolf Hitler off the wall and putting it on a fire. It was great to have a roof over our head and a good bed to sleep in. It took a while for the villagers to come out of their houses because we were the first enemy troops they had seen. We had orders not to fraternize with them. The first few days were spent cleaning up the hotel, smartening ourselves up, blancoing our gear white and spit and polishing our boots. The officers put their pips back on and sergeants and corporals put up their stripes. The war in Europe was now over. The occupying forces had a mammoth task of sorting out thousands of displaced persons. I wish I could have finished my army service there, but in September I was posted to Greece.'

War in the Far East

THE FIRST CAMPAIGN IN BURMA AND MALAYA

In December 1941, the Empire of Japan opened a war against America and Great Britain. In a swift blaze of conquest Japan flung back both opponents and by February 1942 the British Army in Burma and Malaya was being forced to retreat by an enemy who, striking through the jungles, had caught it off-balance.

British Far Eastern defence plans had been predicated upon an enemy seaborne assault upon the large cities of Britain's far eastern Empire. It had been considered militarily impossible for large bodies of enemy troops to move through the jungle which covered Burma and Malaya. Although the Japanese were as unfamiliar with the jungle as were our own soldiers, they quickly learned to live in the conditions encountered there. They did not see the jungle as a barrier between them and Britain's Asian cities, but rather as a covered approach towards those objectives. Consequently they moved large bodies of troops through the jungle by splitting them into small parties, using whatever transport was available. Not being dependant for supplies upon a long and tortuous line of communication, the Japanese troops advanced quickly and came up behind the British prepared positions defending the coastal towns.

The Japanese strategic plan against Britain was to capture India through Ceylon and/or Burma. The Ceylon thrust was not developed; the campaign in Burma depended upon the struggle by both sides; the Japanese to enter the sub-continent through the 'gateways,' Imphal and Kohima, and the British to prevent this. The high-tide of Japanese Imperial effort turned at those two small villages and once these offensives had been foiled, Slim's Fourteenth Army – the forgotten Army – began to force the Japanese Army out of Burma and then to go on to reconquer the territories which had been lost in the first flush of Nipponese Imperialism. When the full force of the Japanese assault fell upon the British Army in Burma, forces were brought from other theatres of operation to hold back the enemy thrusts. One unit rushed from the desert fighting was 7th Armoured Brigade. At first it was ordered to help defend Singapore, but by the time the brigade arrived in the Far East the city had fallen. The following account of armoured actions around Rangoon is taken from *The Tank*, with kind permission of the Editor:

'The Brigade numbered 114 Stuarts; 10 in Brigade Headquarters and 52 each in the 7th Queen's Own Hussars and 2nd Battalion Royal Tank Regiment.

On 21 February 1942, it began to unload at Rangoon and spent the first few days in Burma preparing itself for the battles to come. Meantime the Japs were driving west from Thailand and the Burma Corps was already hard pressed on the Sittang River, east of Rangoon. The 2nd Royal Tanks were the first to be blooded and standing patrols found the oncoming Japs at intervals along the west bank of the Sittang. The Burma Corps came streaming back and soon the 2nd RTR was fighting a very confused and bitter action. One tank was knocked out by a Jap mortar when it was running at 30mph on a tarmac road. Japs were nowhere to be seen, yet the tanks were fired on from all directions. The Browning machine-guns took their toll and later many Japs were killed as they came unsuspectingly upon the standing patrols. Meantime 7th Hussars had accounted for five Jap tanks, which were all knocked out by the 37mm guns, at a range of 400 yards. The 37mm shot went through them all very easily taking with them pieces of Japanese. The only other tanks which were encountered were Stuarts which had been captured earlier. The Armoured Brigade was ordered to delay the Japanese drive on Rangoon, but those instructions were countermanded by General Alexander who based the defence around Mandalay – a move which gave Field Marshal Wavell time to organize the defence of India. There followed a series of actions against Japanese infiltration parties as the Burma Army retreated slowly northwards. At Prome, the largest roadblock of all, 7th Hussars lost 10 Stuarts after 48 hours' fighting. Many of the crews who had to bale out were not seen again because the Japs were waiting for them with bayonets. There were scores of Japs killed here and many snipers hung dead in the palm tree tops where they had tied themselves. One officer's tank was knocked out and he was captured by the Japanese during the night. Tied hand and foot to a roadblock, he managed to escape when the British 25pdrs opened up on it.

'The Japanese infiltration parties detailed to make roadblocks were generally armed with either light mortars or automatic rifles. They used petrol bombs against the tanks. Quick to seize the initiative, they would creep up close enough to the tanks to lob in hand-grenades and to fire at the visors. During all this time the tanks had little respite and drivers would leave the leaguers at first light knowing that a long day's fighting lay ahead and that through the night they would have to withdraw to the next stand. But the worst stroke of fortune was yet to come. Whereas the road from India met the Chindwin River at Kalevo, the road from Burma met the Chindwin six miles farther south. Thus, when the tank crews arrived at the river they had to destroy all the equipment they had so carefully maintained throughout the campaign. The Brigade was ordered to march out and reach the Indian frontier as best they could. In some cases the men marched for over a week and their fitness was proved since not a single man was lost during the retreat on foot.'

John Wyatt of 2nd Battalion, The East Surrey Regiment, was one of those who had been fighting against the Japanese from the first days of the war:

'Ourselves, that is the East Surreys, the Leicestershires and the Argylls, were the first white troops in action against a superior enemy. Our first battle was at Jitra which the Japs had no difficulty in taking as we had very little air support and no tanks . . . We fell back withdrawing and fighting and put up a stiff resistance at Gurun which stopped the Japs for about three days. We had been in action for two weeks and found ourselves at Gurun. At about 4 one morning we heard the Jap [tank] column. We were told by the officer in charge, "Last man, last round." We smoked our last cigarettes and said goodbye to each other. Dawn was just breaking when the Japs broke through. All hell let loose. Three aircraft came over and there were bombs all around us. All we could do as we crouched there was to wait for one to hit us. The planes flew off and four tanks rumbled up the road and gave our positions hell. They flung everything at us. All of a sudden we heard a shout, "Run for it lads!" and we ran and that was the last I saw of the officer. I shall never forget him as we ran past him, pistol in hand, holding off the advancing Japs while we got away. We also left another East Surrey propped against a tree. He had been hit in the ankle, a water-bottle and rifle was left by his side. I dread to think what the Japs did to him when they found him. He must have had a lonely death. We waded through about a mile of paddyfields, reached the safety of the jungle and then set out to find the British lines. We tramped about twenty miles, or so it seemed, and reached safety about 5 o'clock that night. Then for sleep, food, clean clothes and a shave, for we had lost everything. Most of the battalion reached safety, but a lot of chaps are still missing – some of my friends, too.

'We marched to Johore where we were cut off and where a miniature Dunkirk took place. There were about 400 of us, now known as the British Battalion because the casualties had been so heavy to the East Surreys and Leicesters that we had had to be amalgamated. We were taken off right under the noses of the searching Jap troops by two gunboats, the *Dragonfly* and *Firefly*. They took us to Singapore. After a brief rest we went into action when the Japs crossed the causeway. I was hit in the shoulder by Jap mortar fire at Bukit Timah racecourse, rescued by Chinese guerrillas and taken to Alexandra hospital where I survived the massacre by Japs who had gone beserk and so passed into captivity.'

The confusion of those first days is reflected in Sidney Sheldrick's account, which described the convoy in which he sailed as containing:

'The most unlucky bunch of soldiers in World War 2. The large convoy had sailed from the UK on the very day that the Japs bombed Pearl Harbor and we became the convoy that nobody wanted and what was more terrible, we were the convoy that nobody knew what to do with. Winston Churchill decided that as a token gesture to the Dutch we would be landed on Java. Sadly our 8,000-odd total of soldiers contained no infantry or tank units. All the soldiers were either RAOC, RASC, light or heavy anti-aircraft regiments. Few had seen action at all.'

Gunner Evans, whom we first met at Dunkirk, then went on to Far Eastern service with his anti-aircraft regiment which set up its guns on the golf course at Kuala Lumpur.

'The day before the fall of Singapore we were ordered to the docks to try to get away in two boats. We loaded the guns on board; half on one boat, half on the other. The Japs were knocking the hell out of the docks. My wife's name saved my life. We were going up the gangplank on one ship when Jock Liddle stopped dead nearly causing me to fall off into the briny. "Digger," he said, "Look there." On top of the funnel of the second ship was my wife's name, *Iris*. "Come on," said Jock. "She'll look after us." The reason why we left Singapore was to protect a secret aerodrome in Sumatra. We landed in Palembang, then moved inland into the jungle. The next morning there was a trial run on the guns. Then about half-past nine the chap on spotting duty shouted, "Planes approaching!" The chap on the UB2 shouted, "They're dropping parashooters!" So we loaded shrapnel and fired on them. You could see them doubling up as the shrapnel pierced their bodies. When it quietened down the lads wanted their breakfast. You had to go to an open piece of ground, so the lads volunteered me to go. Off I went, made some buckets of tea and started the bacon. When I looked up there were three painted soldiers, just like the doll ones you buy in a box. They were Jap paratroops. So I just dived [into the river] and swam to the gun pits. We fired into the jungle where I last saw them. We decided to go and see what damage the shrapnel had done. Tommie Gill put the only Bren-gun we had on to my shoulder and fired it from there. Two lads with the only two rifles we had fired at the first lot of bushes. One chap said, there's something a back of this bush. He kept poking about with his rifle. Then he fired. A Jap squealed and died. We went farther into the jungle but all we saw was Jap paras hanging in the trees.

'The pilots of the secret fighter drome were doomed. We had orders to destroy our gun as we had no more ammunition and get across the Palembang River. A lorry took some of our group halfway to the river and then went back for the remainder. They passed us heading towards the river, but *en route* the lorry was ambushed and they were killed. We lost four more going to their aid. One of our gun lorry drivers, Allen, a Geordie lad, took the Bren-gun from the officer, placed it on his hip like a gangster and went in. He was stunned for a bit by a hand-grenade, but he got up shouting "You yellow bastards!" and wiped out the four remaining paratroops. We found a steam train, but had no driver until out of the blue came two British sailors. Their boat had been sunk by the Japs. They told me, "Tell your mates to get mounted. We'll drive it." We were well on our way when the train stopped and an officer came along. The Japs had dropped a second batch of paras on an Australian bomber drome and he wanted volunteers. I was detailed to go, but would have volunteered anyroad, because we were like a close-knit family. I still think back how artillery lads, not trained in jungle warfare, took on the finest jungle fighters in the world. Some of our lads were Glasgow tram drivers, Irish lorry drivers, Geordie dock workers, Welsh and Yorkshire coal miners and office workers, also two butchers. I'd go through hell with them. They joked about everything and if we were moving from one place to another the Welsh lads would start them all singing. We set off towards the aerodrome; one rifle between eleven men, hoping to be armed by the Australian air force. When we got there all the bombers were on fire. We set up guards while the rest of us washed our feet. We had not had our boots off for days. What a shock I had when I took my sock down. My feet were all blue. I thought of gangrene. One of my mates said, "It's allright, Digger, its the dye out of your boots through going through the swamps." Next morning we tried to get in touch with the Aussies. We found a few of them tied to trees. When we were resting one of the lads came running up to the officer telling him that some more Japanese paras had been seen in an open clearing. The officer told me to sort them out. No rifle, no arms at all. Off I went. Orders are orders.

'I got to the clearing and stood there with my arms crossed fascinated as I watched a dozen Jap paras moving towards the bomber drome which was all ablaze. They just ignored me. Whether they thought I was a native or whether they were trained to go for their target, I do not know. I could see their eyes looking at me. What I can't understand is why I was not frightened. We boarded the train again and finished up at a sea port, Osthaaven, facing Java. Our Major volunteered us for anti-paratroop fighters for the Dutch in Java. So we sailed across to Batavia. We went by train to the other end of Java. We didn't have much food so some of the lads went hunting. They brought in mountain goats – like donkeys with twisted horns. It took Arthur Barnet, a skilled butcher, twenty minutes to kill them. They were really tough. One morning I woke up and there were Mongolian guards. So I told the lads, be careful as we were surrounded. They took us to a prison camp just outside Batavia which was already occupied by Americans, Aussies and Indians. We were prisoners-of-war of the Japanese.'

THE FIGHTING IN SINGAPORE

Impressions of conditions in Singapore and the fighting for the city were given by a great many former soldiers, and from their accounts I have selected that of C. W. Carpenter of the Norfolks, to describe the confusion of the fighting and the bewilderment of surrender. What follows is only part of his much longer typescript.

'December 29th, 1941. We sailed from Mombassa and as the shore faded from view we were told our ultimate destination; Singapore!! Well we wanted action, by golly we had got ourselves a real beauty. The latest news was bad; the situation was really serious. The Yellow Peril was advancing rapidly on all fronts sweeping away all opposition. Murdering, raping, looting as they advanced and worst of all taking no prisoners of war. We were told that an officer and a sergeant from the Intelligence Corps were to give us a lecture on what they had learned from behind the Japanese lines and show us some of the arms and equipment they had captured. The officer told us that we should have not trouble in pushing the Japs right back where they had come from. He said the Japs were terribly short of modern arms, equipment and supplies. The sergeant was backing up the officer's statements by showing us the various guns and equipment. Some of it must have been issued in the Boer War. He went on to say that the Japs were shortsighted and were so scared of darkness that they would not move at night. The lecture finished on a happy note. We were confident that in no time at all we should have pushed the Japs back to where they belonged and taught them a lesson. January 16th, 1942. The sound of smallarms fire was heard in the distance. The enemy was not far away. Runners came back from the forward Companies to say that one of our scouting patrols had run into a heavy force of Japs and had suffered heavy casualties. Men were coming back wounded and bewildered. From the reports they gave we realized that we were up against a very cunning enemy. Our men were being shot down and our lads could see nothing to fire back at. During the night large parties of Japs had got in behind us. They had used boats to land behind us and as we had not got even a rowing-boat they had no trouble at all. The Japs were fanatics. Death was an honour to them. I have seen one of our light machine-gun sections, consisting of about four Bren-guns, firing their guns until they were literally too hot to handle, surrounded by piles of dead Japs and still they have come forward shouting their blood-curdling scream of *Banzai!* and overrun the gun position.

'January 29th, 1942. A conference was called for all senior officers. The news our CO gave us was grave. Japanese forces were only twenty miles away and were overrunning our defences. It had been decided to withdraw from Malaya and make a stand at Singapore. So the battle for Malaya was over, but the Japs had had a taste of British stubbornness and fighting qualities. All our forward troops had been in constant action for the past four to five weeks against the cream of the Imperial Japanese Guard. The withdrawal began and our troops came through our lines. Tired men, disillusioned men, but not beaten men. The withdrawal from the mainland of all the Allied troops was now complete. Australian troops on the island gave the rearguard troops covering fire. The rearguard action was fought by one of the toughest and bravest regiments in the British Army, the Argyll and Sutherland Highlanders. With bagpipes playing, kilts swinging, one would have thought that they were on a drill square somewhere in Blighty. What a glorious sight they were. The won not only the respect of us all on the island but the enemy as well. An Australian Major [whose infantry unit Carpenter joined] told us the situation on the island was desperate, water was so short it was being rationed. The death rate was high, disease was spreading, bodies of the dead and carcasses of animals were rotting everywhere. There would be no question of surrender; evacuation was impossible. The Japanese Army Commander was still demanding an unconditional surrender. Our Army Commander was still adamant. "No surrender at any price." The whole Commonwealth force was behind him to a man. After the last round had been fired it would be hand-to-hand fighting with fixed bayonets. Saturday, February 14th, 1942. The light was beginning to fade. We all wondered what would happen tomorrow. While our guns were firing we were still active. I know that if it had been left to the troops we should never have surrendered. The streets would have been piled high with our dead and wounded. The end came abruptly when the civilian authorities approached the military commander and pleaded for a surrender.'

The rapid advance of the Japanese Army into Burma and Malaya struck and split the hastily formed British front and forced the defenders back. The confusion that existed in the British colonial territories in those early days of the Far Eastern campaign has been recalled by many correspondents and is shown here in the experiences of Arnold Watson. He was a Private soldier in the RASC, who reached Singapore on 28 November 1941. War with Japan had not yet broken out. Nine days after Watson's arrival the Japanese struck at Pearl Harbor. In the fury of the enemy assault, Kuala Lumpur fell and Arnold Watson's unit, which was in the city, was split up. He moved to Malacca where he joined another RASC detachment until that city fell, in its turn. His letter touches upon the highlights of those days.

'We went down-country from Malacca to Johore and at Baharu we helped to take the wounded from hospital to a waiting Red Cross ship in Singapore. We worked until the Japanese air raids stopped us. The ship, packed with wounded, left the port during an air raid. Back in the city some hospitals still had wounded men and, of course, casualties were coming in the whole time. There were no more hospital ships to take them away. The nursing sisters and doctors refused to leave the wounded men and stayed with them until the Japanese Army arrived. We RASC men reported to a camp at Bukit Timah Road and were sent to a naval base in search of food. Our first foray succeeded, but when we went a second time we could not reach the depot. Japanese tanks barred the way. It was very clear that the city must soon fall. The order was given that all equipment which could be used by the enemy was to be destroyed. This meant all arms and all forms of transport. Lorries and motor cycles were the obvious ones and we set about making them useless. One sad task at this time was to have to shoot the horses on the Singapore race track, so that the Japanese could not use them.

'By this time the evacuation of British women and children was in full swing and our unit helped to embark Service wives and families. This was a terrible time. The Japanese air force had command of the air and bombed transports just outside the harbour, sinking most of them, with a great loss of life. The general deterioration of the military situation meant that while some formations were arriving in the dying city others had been ordered to leave it. Those fragments of units that had been smashed during the retreat were evacuated while fresh units were coming in from the liner *Empress of Asia*. Those "unblooded" units were too few to halt the Japanese drive and when the city fell some battalions marched almost from the ship and into prison camp.

'When Singapore city was surrendered some of us went to Blakang Mati island, so small that you could virtually walk round it. We found out that the Japs had already landed there, so one night about twenty of us left in a small boat. The intention was to sail to some British-held point. Nobody wanted to become a prisoner of the Japanese. During our short voyage we picked a couple of airmen out of the water. They were lying exhausted in a dinghy and when we found them they were very far gone. Neither of them had the energy to speak and both died the next morning. Our sense of humour did not leave us during this very hazardous trip. I was sitting as look-out in the front of our dinghy looking through a pair of binoculars. I saw a boat and asked what flag it was flying. I pretended not to know that a white flag with a red circle on it was, of course, the Japanese flag. It was flying on an enemy gunboat which was checking the river traffic. We would not have been able to pass the control-point in our dinghy so we beached it and headed inland. We were lucky enough to find an old bus which took us down-country. When we next came to the sea there was a British ship the *Danie* on which we sailed to Java. Even there we were not safe and a group of ninety of us, led by Captain Johnson of the RASC, who had led us in our first invasion, took over the *Uchang*. This was a flat-bottomed, wooden river boat and in that craft we sailed out and straight into a naval battle. While we were sailing through the fighting a Japanese submarine surfaced alongside us. We were lucky. We had two flags with us; our own White Ensign and the Japanese one. We flew the Jap flag when their submarine surfaced and it submerged again without checking us. For the duration of the three-weeks' voyage I was the cook, serving up chiefly rice and bully beef. Eventually we landed in Ceylon and for a short time I was with an Indian Base Ordnance workshops in Colombo.'

When HMSS *Prince of Wales* and *Repulse* were sunk, the possibility of a Japanese strike through Ceylon became a probability. To counter that threat, reinforcements were rushed from India and among them was the 114th Field Regiment Royal Artillery. Don Harding:

'The Japanese invation did not take place, but tragedy struck the regiment. They took away our beloved 25pdrs and gave us 3inch mortars. We were now the 114th Jungle Field Regiment – RA with peashooters. After our training period in Ceylon we went to a place called Ranchi in Assam, where the 20th Indian Division was formed. We moved to the railhead at Dimapur, thence by road to Imphal and on to the Manipur–Burma border. There we were in various areas supporting infantry units and the regiment was now split into three batteries. Each battery consisted of a further two troops. So you can see that whereas before we were more or less together as a regiment, now we were spread through the division in small groups and it was only during the few rest periods that we were together again.'

Don Harding was sent on a course and his letter recalling his return to the unit at Witok begins in a way that will be familiar to most soldiers:

'I had hardly unpacked my kit before I was assigned as OP wireless op on a detachment of mortars in support of 4/10 Gurkhas on Hilltop 2007, overlooking the River Chindwin. My particular unit or Troop was of two mortar sections each of four mortars. Each section would support an infantry Company from within that Company's perimeter. The mortar fire was directed from an OP by an officer supported by a specialist and a signaller (me) who was in contact with the mortar position by line telephone and/or radio. We came under heavy attack from the Japs but held the position. It was during this action that Ron Biggs was killed and Jack Price wounded by a mortar bomb which exploded on the parapet of the slit-trench they were manning. We were eventually relieved by another section, but they had to pull back sharply on a night evacuation. The Japs were, by now, attacking on all fronts and we returned to Witok and another Jap attack. Then came the withdrawal along the Tamu road to Palel and then to a position which we had to hold to stop the Japs advancing on Imphal. That was a place that the Japs had to take if their "march on India was to succeed". By this time Kohima was under siege and our main supply line to India, the Manipur road, was cut. Our positions were known as "Crete", "Scraggy", "Malta" and "Gibraltar". There we took the brunt of the heavy Japanese night assaults to take Imphal. Endless nights of shelling by Jap 105mms, until about 1am, then wave after wave of infantry attacks. Our mortars had a devastating effect on those attacks, but still the Jap infantry came forward. Our men would blaze away from their slit-trenches and so it would go on until just before dawn when their attacks would cease. There would then be a brief respite during the daylight hours, except for spasmodic sniping. Then the same all over again the next night, and so on, night after night. One night, after the shelling stopped, everything went deadly quiet. Then we heard the ominous rour of tank engines approaching "Scraggy". We thought it was our lot until the lead tank was hit by shellfire. It blocked the road and stopped any further tank advance.

'The Jap offensive was finally broken. Their supply lines, always over-extended, ceased to function and the final blow, the start of the monsoon season, helped to halt their operations. We were able to take a well-earned leave and enjoy a period of rest in Calcutta. At Wenjong we got our 25pdrs back; at last becoming proper Gunners again. We fought our way to the Irrawaddy River, crossing the mile-wide stream on makeshift rafts at dead of night. On the road to Meiktila we received an Intelligence report that a Japanese division was pushing south on the west bank of the Irrawaddy, but that some units had crossed over and were coming down a road on the east bank, running parallel to the river. An ambush was set up by an Indian unit (Frontier Force Rifles) with our 25pdrs and 5in Medium batteries in support. Our OP party was a shallow slit-trench on the forward perimeter right next to the road. The guns were ranged in on the road and then it was a case of waiting. Night fell and for a few hours all was quiet. Suddenly out of the darkness thundered a truck. It smashed right through the ambush, but the second one was halted by smallarms fire and grenades. It stopped in the middle of the position. The convoy of lorries behind it halted and the guns opened up, bang on target. Then came the biggest fireworks display I have ever seen. The trucks were carrying ammunition. Shells were exploding and smallarms ammunition was crackling away like jumping jacks and the whole place was lit up. I was trying to contact the OP on the radio, but the static interference was too bad to make contact. At the same time we were trying to keep our heads down and also keep our eyes peeled for wandering Japs. Suddenly out of the smoke a figure appeared. Bill Bridger let rip with his Sten and killed a Jap practically on top of us. The rest of the night was spent waiting to see if the Japs would attack. But all was quiet in that respect. When dawn broke we were able to see the havoc wrought by our guns. The convoy had been destroyed and about a hundred Japs were killed. From Mandalay we pushed south towards Rangoon with skirmishes all the way. The Japanese were in retreat, but far from beaten. Every soldier fought to the death and few prisoners were taken. I was taken sick before we reached Rangoon and, much to my disappointment, by the time I had recovered the war was over.'

VICTORY IN THE FAR EAST

The last days of the reconquest of Burma were recalled by Tony Pellet, who had served in the same artillery regiment as Don Harding:

'It was July, we were well into the monsoons which meant that a great deal of time it was raining "cats and dogs". For us the war had now passed by, except for one Troop of guns which had been sent to Pegu to assist in dealing with the Japs who were trying to get out. The talk now was of going home to "Blighty" – repatriation had started for those who had been overseas 3½ years or thereabouts and all those who had come out with the Regiment in 1942 (which was most) qualified for this. The talk was true, but the Regiment had to stay and go on to French Indo-China (now Vietnam). We, the old hands, could not go until our

replacements turned up. They did and were all much younger than us. A lot had
come from the 12th Army Group and had been in the invasion of Europe. They
were not very happy about the prospect of fighting the Japs, having had to deal
with the Nazis, but there it was. Someone had to do it. We old hands were told to
get our kit ready and hand our weapons in, then be prepared to move out. We
were leaving to be transferred to a holding-unit known as 12th FRU. After all
these years the name still registers, still with dismal memories. One of the places
best forgotten, but somehow never quite. It turned out to be a collection of tents
in the middle of nowhere just outside Rangoon. We arrived to be met by some
Infantry NCOs who did not seem to be expecting us. They certainly knew
nothing about a horde of Gunners asking when was the boat going to be ready to
take them home. The Infantry NCOs started to treat us as though we were newly
arrived white-kneed rookies, ready to go into action. This did not amuse us and I
think secretly we were a little scared. Was it possible that if we didn't do
something positive we might find ourselves going through the sausage-machine
and posted to some Infantry mob bound for Singapore, or worse still left to rot in
Burma? It was worrying. Feelings got worse when we were segregated from our
own senior NCOs, and the infantry's main preoccupation was to make the camp
safe against Burmese dacoits. We were very amused. It was hardly likely that
having met the Japs we were concerned about a few Burmans who might have
bows and arrows. In the end a state of mutiny existed, something that shot and
shell, rain, half-rations and no beer had never reduced us to before. One day
nearly all the Gunners were put on a charge for some trifling reason. They
dropped that because there were too many to deal with. We felt like breaking out,
but somehow we didn't. I suppose the remains of our self-discipline prevailed
and in any case there was nowhere to go. Somehow our senior NCOs got to hear
of this and they managed to get through the red tape and make a complaint to the
CO of the camp. The result was that we were moved to another part of the camp
and our own NCOs took charge. Of course, we responded and there were no
problems or misunderstandings.

'It was while we were here that the "Bomb" was dropped and the war ended.
We were stuck in this camp with one bottle of beer to celebrate a victory to which
we had contributed in no small way. As far as the "Bomb" was concerned most of
us did not moralize over it. At the time it was considered by many that it no
doubt saved thousands of Allied lives. Those, for example, who had to retake
Malaya and occupy Japan and all those who were living under wretched
conditions as POWs. It is probably true that their lives were saved. At about this
time there was a spot of unrest among the British troops in Rangoon, the bulk of
whom were awaiting repatriation. But it seemed to be going very slow,
somewhere the pipeline was getting blocked. We were told it was a shortage of
shipping. The result was that the lads were getting upset and in one or two cases,
though it wasn't mutiny, things happened that were very close to it. Lord Louis
Mountbatten and General Bill Slim came back to Rangoon to sort things out and
the steam was taken out of the situation. There is no mention of this in the
Official History of the War in South-East Asia – but it did happen.

'At last came the day to leave; as usual, at the crack of dawn we piled into
trucks to take us down to the docks [and] the ship *Felix Rousell*, lying in the

Rangoon River. We boarded. No one smiled, no one cheered. All looked somewhat dazed as though it was not true. We were actually getting on a ship and going home to Blighty. The war, a way of life for six years, was over – or nearly over – for us. We could not take it in.

'One morning it was very foggy and apart from the cries of the sea birds all was quiet. We were hove-to off the Liverpool Bar, at the entrance to the River Mersey, waiting to go into Liverpool. The tale going round the ship was that there might be delays. There was a strike in the docks at Liverpool and we might not get off that day. The troops were not amused. We had lads with us who had been POWs under the Japs. What a welcome home for them! We went down the river and waited for the dockyard hands to tie us up. Meanwhile there was much shouting from the troops and caustic remarks directed at the dockers. We only wanted to be tied up and to get ashore. We didn't need their help. All our belongings were carried on our backs. After a long-winded discussion the dockers agreed to do whatever they had to do and the gangplanks were lowered. A band was playing; someone made a speech (we didn't take much notice of) and then we started going ashore, the POWs leading off, which I expect was only fair . . . Then slowly the Hastings train (from Charing Cross) backed in and we got in. In two hours we would all be home again. Hastings where it had started for us on Friday 1 September 1939. We were on our way home. The Great Adventure was all over and we could start being normal human beings again.'

The Rewards of Soldiering

DEATH

The first dead men seen on the battlefield did not bring the violent shock that is portrayed in films. Death in many forms was not unfamiliar to the working-class man of the Second World War. Infant mortality and a catalogue of fatal illnesses took away relatives, friends and neighbours and it was the custom for the corpse to be laid out in a coffin in the house. Dead bodies – in civvie street, better arranged and presented, but nevertheless dead bodies, were a normal feature of life. The dead on battlefields often bore no disfiguring wounds so that they appeared to be asleep.

'In one attack we passed over ground which another Company had already crossed. Lying flat on his back with a knee drawn up was one of my mates – "Pop". We called him that because to us 19-year-olds he seemed so old. He was probably about 30. He looked so natural. The only thing missing was his ground sheet. Pop never lay on the grass without one. He was paler than usual, but he lay there quite peacefully with only the blood on his chest and stomach to show where he had been hit. All those things I registered in two or three paces. I felt no terrible sadness at that time, although now, forty years on, I still remember him and can see him on that Italian hillside on a warm, autumn morning.'

The fresh-killed dead were one thing. Those that lay unburied and open to the elements were frightening in their grotesque, inflated obscenity as the following accounts show. F. Shaw:

'We were advancing along a road. It had been raining for days and the ditches were filled with water. My Section Corporal and I were leading the platoon. We both saw this movement in a ditch on the right side of the road and both realized it was a Jerry crouched down with his back towards us. We both fired and hit him. When we reached him it was clear he had been dead for days and had been crouched in that water-filled ditch for all that time. He was blue-green in colour, horribly bloated and his scalp was peeling off in one place. I don't know how the Corporal felt, but I was ashamed that I had fired at a man already dead. He was the worst sight I ever saw during the war.'

J. Cartwright, RTR:

'On a ridge outside San Savino, near Rimini, there was a Jerry spreadeagled on the road, with another sprawled backwards in a hedge. The one on the road was absolutely flat. Tanks had run over him and his squashed body was like something you see in cartoon films. Clouds of bluebottles were all over him – not many on the man in the hedge and they flew off when the officer and I went through his pockets for documents. I could not read German, but the officer told me that the man in the hedge came from Sudetenland in Czechoslovakia and the entries in his Army book confirmed that he was in the 29th Panzer Grenadier Division.'

Robert Fleming, RAMC:

'One of the worst duties I had was to take the bodies out of tanks which had been recovered from the battlefields. The "brewed-up" ones were worst. We usually tied scarves around our mouths and noses, more to stop germs than anything else. It was no easy task getting the bodies out. They fell apart. Some had been incinerated down to their boots. The things we were looking for were identity discs. They were almost indestructible. It was a rotten job sifting through the rubbish on the bottom of a tank searching for a couple of identity tags, but it was necessary and someone had to do it."

Henry Saunders, Infantry:

'The worst parade in the war was the roll-call after an attack. If you have had a pasting you are still a bit jumpy. The roll-call brought back all that you had been through. It was usually held on the morning after you came out of the line. We would then be paraded and once you were all together you realized how many had gone. The CSM would call us to attention for the officer and then he would read out the roll. Those on parade would respond to their names. When there was no response the questions would begin. "Did anyone see him fall? Was he wounded? Where and how badly? Was he killed? How? Where?" The Company clerk would take down the details and so the parade would go on until everybody was accounted for. Sometimes parties of us would be detailed to walk across the attack area looking for any mates that were missing and who couldn't be accounted for on the roll-call parade. We also had to help the Pioneer platoon collect any arms and equipment in our attack sector. There was always piles of it.'

Paradoxically, the longer the time spent on active service, the more upsetting were the battlefield sights; the fallen and the wounded. One did not become more accustomed to them. The opposite was true – they affected the soldier more. It was, perhaps, the realization that his luck was draining away. There was an awful inevitability at the back of every fighting soldier's mind. He had only to look round the circle of his comrades to see how few there remained of those who had sailed out with the unit for overseas service. Each day of battle cost men. Each group of men who became casualties would include a veteran. It was, thus, only a question of time before one's own turn came and one would feature in that heart-breaking roll-call parade described above.

MUTILATION

To be wounded was not the dramatic affair seen on TV or in the films. Many did not realize at first they had been hit. Others, unaware of the seriousness of their wounding, tried to carry on with their duty. One such was the late Bunny Warren, a Regular soldier. He had excelled at most sports, particularly swimming. He went to France with the BEF in 1939. On the fighting retreat to

Dunkirk he was hit in the side by a tank shell and sustained wounds that might have finished a less fit man. He recovered consciousness on the open beach and realized that he would have to make arrangements of his own if he was to avoid being left behind. Warren walked into the sea and began to swim. In later years he recalled that he knew no more until he woke up in Mount Vernon hospital, eight days later. Declared medically unfit for service, his pension amounted to a few shillings each week; a derisory amount which was only increased some forty-five years after his wounding. Another man who overcame the pain of his wounds was ex-Sergeant Frank Lovett, MM. He was wounded in an attack upon Stoppiace in Italy. George Webb, from whom I received the story, wrote that Sergeant Lovett was badly wounded in the stomach. According to eyewitnesses half of it was shot away. The Sergeant reached for his small pack, removed his face towel and placed it over his wounds, waiting calmly until the stretcher-bearers came and carried him to the RAP.

George Webb was wounded on Monte Battaglia in October 1944.

'I can well remember there were the ruins of a castle at the top of Battaglia. When we passed by to get to our positions we had literally to walk over the dead American soldiers who lay adjacent to the ruins. The stench was quite unbelievable. The Americans had not dug-in like the British Tommies. All they had done was to scrape out foxholes which were totally inadequate against the relentless and accurate German shelling. No. 3 Company was moving forward and one of my men stepped on a mine. I didn't know at the time that it was a mine. We were in the last section of the Company and my first thought was that we had been ambushed by Germans. I can remember seeing, out of the corner of my eye, a white, blue and red flame. I turned round with my Tommy-gun at the ready. The Nos. 1 and 2 on the Bren in my section had been blown to pieces. Another chap was shouting for help. He had a leg blown off and the rest of the section had dispersed. I learned later that the man who had lost his leg was the one who had set off the mine. I looked down at my denims and saw that the left side was all torn. I put my hand inside the hole where the gaiters had held the denims in place. It was as if I had dipped my hand into a bowl of hot creamy custard. When I got back to the RAP a piece of my thigh was also missing. It looked to me as if someone had come along with an axe and had put a U-shaped cut into my thigh. What worried me at the time was that I did not have a lance-corporal as 2 i/c of the section. I had to delegate a senior Guardsman who, unfortunately, was a bit bomb-happy.'

F. Farmborough was wounded several times, twice while undergoing training:

'In 1941 I left the infantry after volunteering for the Commandos. After intensive training I was posted to No. 4 Commando. Often we would go out on practice exercises, nearly always using live ammunition. Before the green beret was introduced we used to wear cap-comforters and on a number of times I had mine taken off by shrapnel from the mortars. As you can imagine I was known as "shrapnel". In 1942, I got a chunk through my right knee and in 1943, another chunk through my right elbow. In 1944, we were on our way to Normandy and one of the lads was trying to run a book on who would get it first. But as we pointed out, whoever did get it first wouldn't collect. So instead we had a kitty and cut the cards. Sure enough, I won and my mates weren't surprised. I collected a fist-full of occupation money which I promptly lost at cards. But I fooled them really, because although I did cop it on D-Day, it wasn't by shrapnel. I copped a couple of bullets instead.'

John Logue of the RASC:

'The first time I was wounded was in Sicily. When we were taking the DUKWs out and in from the supply ships we usually had a Pioneer Corps bloke with us to hold the DUKW steady against the ship while they were lowering the stuff into it. Anyway, we were on our way back to the beach when this bloke says to me, "Paddy, there's water coming in." I knew I could get down into the bottom of the DUKW and get the pump fixed to get the water pumped out, but your man couldn't drive the DUKW. So I had to show him how to keep it on a steady course; it had a steering wheel just like a lorry. When he was settled behind the wheel I got down into the bilges. I don't know how long I was there, it was ages anyway, but the first thing I knew was the thump as the DUKW hit what I thought first of all was a rock but which turned out to be a spike on the beach; one of those big anti-invasion spikes. There was a big hole torn in her so we had to get out and start walking up the beach. We could see nobody, but I thought we were bound to be close to our own people. Then I heard a strange sound and I knew he had stepped on a mine. I tried to push him out of the way but it was too late; the mine had popped up and exploded. He was hurt; there was a lot of blood and I started to carry him. After a while I saw an officer, one of the beach landing organization blokes. He asked us how we had got there and I told him. I told him the Pioneer Corps lad was pretty badly hurt. The officer said, "You are hurt, too," and when I said no, he told me I had a wound in my thigh. We had walked through a minefield, he said, and it was a miracle we hadn't been killed! About an hour later I knew I had been hurt when my leg started to stiffen up. I was evacuated back to North Africa and by the time I came back to my unit we were ready for Salerno. I was wounded a second time at Anzio. We had gone in on 22 January, and had a couple of our blokes killed on the way in by mines. These were Italian mines in a wooden box and the detectors couldn't pick them up so the Engineers had to prod the beach with bayonets to find them. It was on 9 March that I was wounded. I had just finished my shift and parked up my DUKW. My relief said to me, "Paddy, you've got a puncture." I told him I'd give him a hand to repair it and as I climbed up the ribs on the side of the DUKW a shell burst above me and something hit me in the leg. I just dropped down off the DUKW. After a while an ambulance arrived and I was put on a stretcher and was slid into the ambulance, just like sliding a drawer into one of the old bread vans. So there I was lying with my head up towards the driver's cab when the ambulance was hit by a shell. It landed at the front and the next thing we knew the vehicle was on fire. I thought to myself, "Paddy, this is it," for the driver was on his own and he was running round the back of the ambulance screaming for help, but there were three of us inside who couldn't even help ourselves, let alone him. I was put in a hospital on the beachhead. The beachhead wasn't very big and everywhere in it was being shelled, including the hospital. It was hit while I was there and I thought, "Paddy, Hitler's out to get you." On the way down to Naples on a hospital ship one of the nurses came over and turned me on my side and told me to look out of the porthole. There was Vesuvius blowing its top all this smoke and flame and ash flying everywhere. I can tell you I was certain that somebody was out to get me and if it wasn't Hitler, then it was a great big volcano.'

CAPTIVITY

Another possible consequence of war was captivity. Much has been written of the horror of being taken prisoner by the Japanese and those who served in the Far East recall their determination not to be taken alive. As Don Harding wrote:

'Our main fear was to be captured by them as the only outcome would be a slow and painful death after interrogation. So even in the most critical situation surrender wasn't even considered.'

This chapter includes accounts of some of the brutalities, humiliations and degradations suffered by just a few of those thousands of British soldiers who became slaves in the Far East. The intention to murder them all in the event of a Japanese reverse was only prevented by dropping the atomic bomb which took Japan out of the war and thereby saved the lives of other British soldiers who would have been killed fighting on the soil of mainland Japan.

In respect of the Germans and Italians it was believed that if the newly taken British prisoner survived the first five minutes of captivity he could expect to reach a prison camp. The condition in which he arrived might vary, but arrive he would. Jeffrey Holland was captured during the battle of Leros in November 1943 and taken by ship to Pireaus.

'Upon our arrival the British column was marched through Athens, watched by a sympathetic crowd of Athenians. The intrepid Captain Olivey, LRDG, stepped out of the line of march and merged into the crowd; for the rest of us two weeks in a transit prison. At the railroad station lines of boxcars, festooned with barbed wire stood ready, doors open, into which were herded groups of forty prisoners. Each man was provided with a three-day ration; a hunk of grey bread. The doors were slammed shut and bolted from the outside. The train pulled out. For fifteen days and nights the prison train clanked its way through Greece, Yugoslavia, Bulgaria and Hungary. Arriving at the station in Budapest, after a journey of twelve days, the troops received one half-inch of potato soup in their mess-tins. The journey resumed. Three days later a ring of lights – Stalag VIIA, Moosburg, Germany. The doors to the boxcars were flung open and the lice-ridden, emaciated troops merged from a month of hunger and privation and staggered into the cold dawn. It was Christmas Eve, 1943.'

That there were exceptions to the thesis that to survive the first five minutes of captivity ensured arrival in a prison camp we have seen from the tragedy of the Norfolks in France in 1940. Much depended upon the unit making the capture and its morale. Generally, the better the regiment the better the treatment. Inevitably, each German who spoke English would say at some point, "For you the war is over," and this could lead into a dialogue during which he would claim that we Anglo-Saxons had no business to be fighting each other: "What do you want with Latins or Slavs?" It is very likely that the Jerries had variants of that line to tell their French, American and Russian prisoners.

For you the war is over, did not really apply to British office prisoners who were expected to make escape attempts. Other ranks worked and could be employed in a great variety of jobs. Very few were on the land. There was no 'peasant' tradition in Britain and most prisoners were given duties in factories, down mines and on the railways. In whatever field the soldiers were employed it gave them a chance to carry on, as one correspondent put it, 'buggering up the German war effort'. The extent to which one carried out small acts of disruption was determined by the attitude of the German employers and guards towards the prisoners. A good employer might only be given a very minor go-slow operation. Those who were brutal were given the full disruptive treatment. Jeffrey Holland recalls:

'We were quite Bolshie by 1943. By 1944 we could get away with murder – given the right circumstances. We knew that they were going to lose the war and they knew it too."

It is true that a lot depended upon the period of the war. In the first years of their conquest some Germans were often brutal and arrogant. As the military situation deteriorated British soldiers took more and more chances to sabotage the enemy war effort. Escape was seldom possible for other ranks for they lacked the skilled committees which ran the officers' efforts, but some did get away. There is one man who, so it is said, having escaped from a camp at Wolfsburg in Austria, gave himself up voluntarily. He had intended to reach Yugoslavia – only a handful of miles away – but had stopped to talk to some Russian women who had been recruited by the Germans to work on the land. Those ladies had had no sexual comforting for some time, and what began for him as a short sexual interlude became a terror from which he only escaped by surrendering to the local gendarmerie. Truly life as a POW was no picnic!

Tishy Parker's account of life as a prisoner was philosophical in tone:

'Very few people indeed would realize the implications of becoming a prisoner-of-war. Those who have gone through such an experience fully understand what goes through one's mind, especially during the first few days of captivity. The whole basis of finding yourself behind barbed wire, often happening through circumstances beyond your control, makes you think at that time, "Why me?" Then after a few days it registers. It means being cut off from home, friends, family, relatives. No more meeting people you know, or celebrating birthdays or anniversaries. You can't even make plans for the future. If you were in a normal prison for some crime you would have a certain sentence with a chance of remission. But a POW does not know when, or even if, he will be released. I suppose, in some respects, it was just as well you don't know, as the possibility of existing for five years behind barbed wire could mean you losing your reason – which many did. Just think what it is like. Every step you take from the time you get up off the straw bed, to when you return, you are followed everywhere. Endless roll-calls. No baths. No sanitation. Lice, fleas, sores, boils. You name it; we had it. We worked out in all weathers: rain, sleet, snow, freezing winds as only Poland and east Prussia could serve up. Working on roads, railways, canals, farms; all part of our day-to-day jobs. It was sometimes possible to remain in the main camps, but I preferred to go out on working-parties rather than stagnate by walking round the wire all day long. I suppose that we [the British] were lucky inasmuch that we were covered by the Geneva Convention, which gave us protection, up to a point. That did not mean that you wouldn't be shot, or receive a donation from the butt end of a guard's rifle. More so, if he was in a bad mood, or he had had news from home that his town had been bombed the previous day.

'Having worked alongside Russian POWs in east Prussia, I do admit that they had a far harder time than we did, with no Red Cross parcels or anything from home. In fact they were entirely disowned by their government. Our position was governed by events. If everything was going smoothly for Jerry you got what you were entitled to. If it wasn't that was your hard luck. You got no Red Cross parcels. This may seem no hardship, but to work an eleven hour day on 'Jerries' Menu' was cutting it a bit fine and was pretty grim. We were allowed one-fifth of a loaf per day, which was equivalent to about a 1½-inch thick slice from a small Hovis, together with a litre of soup. As the bulk of German food was ersatz, you never really knew what you were eating. People might wonder how we did survive for five years. You had no idea how long the war would last so you took it day by day and at every opportunity made the guards' lives as awkward as possible. As you may know, most Germans are very methodical in their habits, so we set about upsetting their routines and putting them out of their stride. If we were working on the railways, at the end of the day's work we would manage to put some pick-axes, shovels and crow-bars on the lines which meant they were chopped in half. When we were working on a building site with Polish workmen, when any excavation was made we would fling in anything (tools or equipment) we could lay our hands on and with split-second timing the Poles would follow up with barrow-loads of wet concrete.

'It would take some considerable time to relate every incident and happening over a period of five years; some tragic, some laughable. But to get through five long years as a POW you needed to have a strong sense of humour.'

The long-term effects of POW life are evident in the attitudes and behaviour of many ex-prisoners. Compulsive hoarding is just one symptom and deep bouts of depression are another. Thomas Burden, who was taken during the 1940 campaign, is a victim to the latter.

'The first months as a prisoner-of-war were terrible and even now I still have days when I get depressed thinking about the years I lost out of my life. Once things settled down and the Red Cross parcels came through then the situation got a bit better. This was now late in 1940 and the Germans were cock-a-hoop. They had won the war. They said it was only a question of time before they invaded and Britain would be beaten. We suffered when London was bombed and the Jerries gloated over it. But we consoled ourselves with no news from home being good news. Mind you we sweated when the post came up and the handwriting on the envelope wasn't the one you were expecting. We were all afraid that bad news would come in a strange handwriting. Anyway, by the end of 1940, we had had enough cabbage soup to last a couple of lifetimes and did not want any more. With the Red Cross parcels arriving regularly we could have a change of diet. We knew we would not starve – but we wouldn't get very fat either. I was in a number of camps, mostly in Silesia and Poland. In some the camp staff were real swine. Sometimes, as a punishment, so they said, but really out of sheer spite and jealousy, they would open all the tins in the parcels so that the perishable contents had to be eaten before they went off. We soon got round that though. When it happened we would take the tins with us when we left to go on outside work. There was another POW camp alongside ours holding foreign soldiers. We would tell them to be alongside the wire at a certain time and then we would lob over our damaged tins into their compound. It drove the Germans mad but it helped to feed the other prisoners, some of whom were very badly off. The German treatment of the Russians was downright inhuman. Some of our work details passed close by the wire of the Russian laager. We would throw across to them things like German ration bread and hardtack. Those poor devils got nothing from home not even letters, but then I reckon that even if Stalin had allowed parcels to be sent the Germans would not have distributed them. They really hated the Russians.'

A great many former prisoners of the Japanese supplied anecdotes. Their stories of courage moved me so deeply that I found it hard not to include them all verbatim and unabridged. That, of course, was not possible, but from the catalogue of sad and bitter memories recalling degradation and almost daily beatings, I have selected extracts from several accounts. The first of these is the story of Bill Turner, a Regular soldier of 2nd Battalion, The East Surrey Regiment. This has been selected as representative of the daily life in a camp on the Burma railway:

'The working day started at 06.00hrs every morning and then when you got outside to line up for your first meal of the day the line was about 100 yards long. Try and imagine this. You are starving, it is raining cats and dogs, you are standing there with your tin plate or something and when you get to the front of the queue all you get is a little dried fish and milktin of rice. The morning is as black as Newgate's knocker and as soon as you get your little bit of eats you move over to form another queue in case any food is left over. You are standing there bareheaded, a little bit of rag tied around your vital parts and nothing on your feet. You have had no wash, but what you have got is a great big dirty beard, but hardly any hair on your head. Smothered in sores and racked with fever you can't stop going to the toilet. Lice- and crab-ridden, and all this just to start with and you still have to go out to work. The work on this part of the railway was pure murder and slavery at its highest. The Japanese guards and engineers were pure bred ✱✱✱✱✱✱✱✱✱. Absolute swine. On our first morning we were ordered to collect tools; a great big 14lb coke-hammer, cold chisels of all sizes, bamboo baskets and chunkels for digging. You had ten minutes for a break all day and when you got back to camp it was just as black as when you left it in the morning. Sometimes you worked 19 hours. In fact anything between 14 and 18 hours was quite normal. You worked until they told you to stop and that was it. To top it all, it was the monsoon season. One day I got detailed to go with another party up the line. We had to chop down bleeding great trees and then to carry them to a certain area. When we had brought them to the collecting-point the Japanese used elephants to drag them away. After two or three hours of carrying the trees your shoulder started to bleed. We were sent back to the main camp. When we arrived the place itself looked just like a graveyard. A stench was everywhere and I said to some bloke, "What's the smell?" and he said that cholera had broken out. One of my mates showed me where the cholera sick were. That was a sight I shall always remember because the lads in there didn't look human. The Japs were getting annoyed because the numbers on the working-party were getting smaller and smaller for the reason that illness in the camp was taking its toll. The death rate was about 70 per cent. We all had to work even if we were sick. If the Jap medical officer said you had to work then that was it. What our Medical Officer said didn't stand a chance. The outcome was that you had fellows with dysentery, malaria, beri-beri, ulcers, malnutrition, all working like slaves and actually dying trying to lift a hammer or trying to lift baskets full of wet earth, digging in the heat and humidity, plus hardly any food. So far as the Japs were concerned if you died lifting one basket of dirt they were satisfied.'

Many of the accounts I received told stories of men who carried out sabotage of Jap-baiting, knowing full well the risks they were taking. Arthur Penn, a Bombardier of the 5th Searchlight Regiment of the Royal Artillery, had a friend, Mac, with whom he was ordered to cut steps in a rocky ridge. As a result of one piece of baiting the guard charged at Mac, who side-stepped: "Foaming at the mouth the Nip started to bash Mac with his rifle butt. The defiant Scotsman could control himself no longer. He picked up the hammer and smashed the nip's rifle as it came towards him. There was a sickening thud as Mac brought the hammer down on the Nip's head. Shouting at the top of his voice Mac then charged at the nearest Nip and felled him with a blow to the throat before dropping dead, filled with rifle bullets."

At various times during the war in the Far East the Japanese shipped prisoners to the mainland in convoys which, towards the end of hostilities, had to run the gauntlet of US submarines. Walter G. Mole, of the RASC, had spent two years of hell on the notorious Thailand railway before he was returned to Singapore for onward trans-shipment.

'Late in 1944, I was told that I had been selected for a party destined for Japan. On arrival at the Singapore docks we were pushed up the ship gangways. I saw our quarters. Hundreds of men were being forced into the hold of the ship where tiers of platforms, just like shelves, had been fixed up. As I reached the entrance to go down the narrow steps, the stench from the perspiring human cargo below was unbearable. Despite the terrible conditions we had encountered during our POW days, we never lacked discipline and through previous experience we knew just how to get organized and did not give way to despair, whatever the odds.

'We discovered that there were twenty-odd ships in the convoy and our ship was one of the largest. We had been at sea for seven days and as dusk fell our convoy was attacked by Allied submarines. We were ordered below and the Nips stood guard at the entrance. As each depth-charge exploded it was like a clap of thunder echoing through the hold and each time it felt as though the ship had been struck. All through this terrible ordeal there was still an air of calmness and, true to British tradition, nobody panicked. For the next few nights we went through the same ordeal and the convoy was now reduced to five ships. We knew our turn was to come and dreaded the nights. When the guns above us started to fire again everyone's mind must have been on that narrow staircase; our only means of escape. Our lads queuing on the stairway to use the latrines gave us a report on the action taking place and when we were told that another ship was ablaze it was now received with mixed feelings. There was an uncanny silence. Each time the guns fired someone had the presence of mind to call out not to panic and order was maintained.'

The ship was hit while Private Mole was on deck on his way to the latrines:

'I soon realized the terrible position. There were hundreds of our men down below and they had to be got out without panic. An officer calmly called down the stairs and told them they could all come up and get some fresh air. Meanwhile me and some of the other lads were throwing batons and rafts overboard. I decided it was time for me to leave and one of my pals found a rope that was tied to the rail and hanging over the side. It was a very long drop and the rope was only about six feet long. As I hung there in midair I could feel my friend climbing over me (on his way down the rope), so I just let go. I swam like mad. I heard voices and thank God they were English. It was three of our chaps clinging to a raft about four feet square. After an hour or so our raft drifted into another that was much bigger, but crowded with POWs. About thirty yards from us was an upturned lifeboat crowded with Nip officers still with their swords and briefcases. A prettier sight I hadn't seen for years. Our boys were getting in good spirits now and some of the rude remarks that were shouted out to the Japs were nobody's business and to cheer them up we sang to them *Sons of the Sea* and *Rule Britannia!* Several hours later a tanker was spotted and as it sailed towards us suddenly it was a sheet of flame and when the smoke disappeared it had vanished. Some more smoke turned out to be a couple of Jap destroyers. They picked up all the Japanese survivors but some of our men who had swum alongside and tried to scale the rope-ladder were thrown back into the water. Two Nips with daggers started stabbing at our boys. We could hear firing and I was told that the Nips on a destroyer were shooting at us in the water. The shooting stopped and then the Nips invited us to come aboard, but knowing what bastards they were we were reluctant to do so. After about fifty of us had been crowded to the extreme front of the ship an alarm was given and the Nips all rushed to action stations and made off. All the food we had was a bucket of rice dished out in our greasy hands and when evening came we were so cold that we huddled together like a load of monkeys. The next morning we arrived at the port of Hainan.'

As the war situation deteriorated the Japanese seemed to become more brutal. American bombers were now raiding the mainland islands on a round-the-clock basis. Tom Evans, who was working in a pit, remembered the raid whose aftermath showed the high morale of the British prisoners:

'One night the raid was so bad that the new commandant asked our senior officer if his men would help save the camp. We agreed because we wanted to see if the bombers were making a good job. Our man who was acting as lookout shouted that the bombers had destroyed the mine. We all cheered as we thought, no more pit work. Next morning four prisoners and a guard were sent to collect the rice rations from down the village. We loaded our hand truck. Then we saw the women and children had no rice because the bombers had destroyed it. We felt sorry and dished ours out to them. When we got back to the camp and told the British officers and men, they agreed with what we had done. The Japs were spellbound. The commandant could speak perfect English paraded us and praised us for what we had done, putting women and children in front of ourselves and for saving the camp. The commandant said, I have always admired the British as a very brave people. As he was saying this a Japanese sergeant came on parade, all nice and clean. The commandant grabbed him and said, "Look at these Britishers, all black and tired through saving the camp. How is it you are so clean?" One day the US bombers came over dropping leaflets. We got one off one of the Japanese miners who translated it. It said "We have split the atom. If you don't surrender we shall drop the bombs!" A few days after this we came up from the [new] mine; and there it was – a miracle mushroom. The Jap guards said it [radiation sickness] was a disease. We agreed but we knowed different. One miner [Japanese] who had done soldiering and was a Christian came to us, put his arms around us and said, "War is finished. You have won." The villagers were round the camp like flies asking for food and cigarettes, offering their young daughters. The lads gave them food and cigs, feeling sorry for them and knowing we were going home. Eventually the camp was liberated and the prisoners sent telegrams home announcing that they were well and safe and *en route* back to the United Kingdom. A lot of the lads had received telegrams saying their wives had married again or had had babies by other men. You couldn't blame them as we were posted as missing believed killed for two years. I was one of the lucky ones. My wife had faith in my coming back. Its a good job she did because it took at least twelve years to get over it [being a prisoner of the Japanese].

As the war neared its end Walter Mole recalled:

'The Japs seemed to be getting more aggressive with us and found any excuse to give us a beating. This must have been around the time the atom bombs were dropped and some of the men were made to dig trenches around the camp and about five feet deep. Nobody knew why at the time. Soon afterwards we saw aircraft for the first time and the guards said that all POWs would be executed. Whether those trenches were to be our graves we never ever knew. They were never used as air raid shelters.'

That the Japanese intended to murder the prisoners in their hands was no idle rumour but was substantiated by documents at the war's end. It is the belief of the former prisoners that only the swift ending of the war by the dropping of the atomic bombs prevented a bloodbath.

The news that the war had ended was given to Bill Turner via the Thai driver of a steam-roller. That man had passed the information to some prisoners who then listened to the illegal wireless set that had been constructed in the camp out of odds and ends.

'I couldn't believe it and the first thing I heard was Ann Shelton singing. That night I couldn't sleep. In the morning we thought we would have to go to work but we had to go back to our huts. Then a British officer came in and said that the war was over. We had a church service out there in the open, just a Cross made out of an ordinary piece of wood. Your religion didn't matter. We were all one, Protestants, Catholics, Jews – they were all there. The British officer got us together and said that although the war was now over, we were not to go out as some Japs that had been coming down from Burma were just up the road and that they wouldn't hesitate to shoot the lot of us. We were also told to stay in our huts because aeroplanes were going to drop some containers with medical supplies and clothing. One fellow in his excitement dashed out to grab one of the containers and got hit straight on the head. What a way to go after all the terrible things he had gone through. One of the containers, when it was opened contained medical aids for use in brothels. It must have been a joke by some person with a great sense of humour. On the subject of brothels . . down the road there was a small village and one of the lads suggested to go down there and see what he could find. Our mate hadn't been in more than five minutes and out he came at the run and believe me I didn't stay there. When we stopped I asked him what all that was about and he said because he didn't have any money. I don't know where he got the strength from after all we had been through. The next day in strolled the fellow we had seen driving the steam-roller and he had the rank of Major plus the fact that he had with him about thirty Chinese women guerrillas, all with grenades and smallarms. He told us that we would soon be going home.'

When Walter Mole left Tokyo to go home he experienced one of the most emotional moments of his life.

'All the biggest battleships and aircraft carriers in the world were assembled there and as our ships passed, every craft from submarine to battleship had their crews manning the decks, sounding their sirens and giving three cheers as we passed. We cheered them back and some started to sing *Rule Britannia*. To me this was the end of the nightmare.'

List of Contributors

Jacky Allen
Malcolm Armstrong
H. J. Bagshaw
A. G. Bell
J. P. Blackmore
H. Braem
Jack Brewin
Martin Brice
T. Bridges
John Bucknall
Ronald Bullen
Thomas Burden
C. W. Carpenter
J. Cartwright
John Clark
Roy Cooke
Roger Cooper
John Donovan
William Donovan
R. A. Doyle
John Eardley
'Nobby' Esplin
Thomas Evans
Daniel Exley
R. Fairclough
F. Farmborough
Donald Featherstone
Harold Field
E. W. Fitness
Robert Fleming
Donald Harding

Joseph Harris
H. Hagley
Robert Hayward
Michael Henshaw
D. Hischier
Jeffrey Holland
Ronald Howard
Henry Jackson
Frederick James
Frederick Jarvis
A. Jenkins
Ronald Johnston
R. A. Joyce
Jack Kelly
Albert Kingston
John Logue
Frank Lovett
R. Maloney
Anthony Marshall
Trevor Marshall
J. Millet
John Mitton
Walter G. Mole
Charles Morrison
John Newark
Tishy Parker
Trevor Parnacott
T. Payne
Anthony Pellet
Arthur Pellet
Arthur Penn

H. Penrose
Arthur Pickford
William Priest
Joseph Ramsden
H. Rawlinson
F. Richmond
Charles Ridley
Thomas Rodney
Raymond Roys
J. Rowlands
H. Samuels
Henry Saunders
F. Shaw
Sidney Sheldrick
L. Smith
Samuel Staples
E. W. Stonard
R. Stuart Wilson
Albert Stubbings
William Summers
J. Talbot
Brian Thatcher
William Turner
Arnold Watson
George Webb
Thomas Weller
R. H. C. Wileman
A. Withey
John Wyatt

Index

A

Africa, 18, 83–103
Air attack, 102
Air supply, 31
Alamein, 86–7, 95–6
Aldershot, 12
Aldershot Tattoo, 11
Allen, Jacky, 12
Americans, 45–50, 54–5
Armoured Brigade, 7th, 119
Armoured Division, 79th, 77
Armstrong, Malcolm, 61
Artillery, 89–93
Artillery bombardment, 79, 84
Artillery, Royal:
    28th Field Regiment, 89
    114th Field Regiment, 126
    387th Heavy Anti-Aircraft Battery, 15
    7th Medium Regiment, 103
    5th Searchlight Regiment, 138
Artist's Rifles, 3
Austria, 115–18

B

Bagpipes, 24
Bagshaw, H. J., 79, 81
Battaglia, Monte, 114, 132
Bell, A. G., 88, 95, 103
Benevento, 39
'Bevin Boys', 7
Bir Hakim, 43
Black market, 39–40
Blackmore, J. P., 92
'Blue', 84
Bombay, 19, 21
Bovington, 4
'Boxes', 84–5
Brewin, Jack, 3, 69, 71
'Brew-up', 85–6
Brice, Martin, 36
Bridges, T., 78
Brooke, Field Marshal Viscount
    Alanbrooke, 82

Brothels, 33–4
Bucknall, John, 94
Bukit Timah Road, 125
'Bull', 31
Bullen, Ron, 104
Burden, Thomas, 4, 136
Burma, 127–9, 137–8
Burma railway, 137

C

Caen, 74
Canadians, 68–71
Capodimonte, 31–4
Captivity, *see* Prisoners of war
Carpenter, C. W., 123
Cartwright, J., 130
Cassino, 105–9
Casualties, *see* Death *and* Wounds
Catering Corps, 28
'Cauldron', 'Battle of the', 89
Chatham, 15
Churchill, Winston, 82, 96
Cigarettes, 39
Clark, John, 31
Collaborators, 44–5
Conscientious objectors, 40–1
Conscription, 6–7; *see also* Enlistment
Cooke, Roy, 24, 27, 61, 84, 86
Cooper, Roger, 40, 94

D

Danie, 125
Death, 130–1
De Gaulle, General Charles, 43
Dehydrated food, 29
Depot Company, 5–6
Desert, Western, 83–103
Desertion, 36–8
Dieppe, 68–71
Discipline and punishment, 14–17, 24–7,
    36–8
Donovan, John, 63
Donovan, W., 60

Dorset Regiment, 19
Doyle, R. A., 89
Drill, 9–10, 25
'Duckers and weavers', 36
DUKW, 133
Duke of Cornwall's Light Infantry, 100
Dunkirk, 65–8

E
Eardley, John, 17
East Surrey Regiment, 120, 137
Eighth Army, 83–102
Embarkation, 10–11
Empress of Asia, 125
Enlistment, 3–22
Esplin, 'Nobby', 18
Evans, Tom, 65, 121, 139
Exley, Danny, 107

F
Fairclough, R., 37
Farmborough, F., 73, 132
Featherstone, Donald, 4, 110
'Feet under the Table', 15
Felix Rousell, 128
Field, Harold, 28
Field Service Marching Order, 13–14
Fitness, E. W., 96
Fleming, Robert, 131
Food, 5, 8, 15, 28–31, 85
Forli, 111, 115
Fort Darland, 17
France, Battle of (1940), 60–5
'Fraternization', 35
French, 42–5, 55, 60
Funeral parade, 17–18
'Funnies', 47

G
Gazala, 83, 88–93
Geneifa camp, 26
George VI, 10
Germans, 55–7
Gothic Line, 110–14
Gough Barracks (Trimulgarry), 21
Goums, 44
Greeks, 54
Grenadier Guards, 14, 106, 112
'Gyppo Tummy', 86

H
Harding, Don, 19, 126, 134
Harris, Joe, 100
Hawick, 10
Hayward, Robert, 115
Henshaw, Michael, 51

'Herzog's Revenge', 30
Highland Division, 79–81
Holding Battalion, 9–10
Holland, Jeffrey, 134
Howard, Ron, 29

I
India, 18–22
Irrawaddy, River, 127
Italians, 57–8
Italy, 105–18

J
Jackson, Henry, 5
Jam, 29–30
James, Frederick, 39
'Jankers', 14, 27
Japanese, 58–9, 123–4
Jargon, 21–2
Jarvis, Fred, 11, 26
Jenkins, A., 78
Johnston, Ronald, 44, 54
Johore, 121
Joyce, R. A., 68

K
Kasserine, 47
Kelly, Jack, 19
King's Rules and Regulations, 20
Kingston, Albert, 75
Kuala Lumpur, 121

L
Laindon, 15
Lancastria, 68
Landing craft, 71–2
Latrines, 86
Leave, 10
Le Clerc, General Philippe, 43
Leese, General Sir Oliver, 103–4
Leros, 134
'Lion', 'Mr.', 10
Logue, John, 133
'Longstop' Hill, 47, 96–9
Lovett, Frank, 132
Loyalty, 23–4

M
'Mahommed', 'Whohoa', 23
Maidstone, 13
Malacca, 124–5
Malaya, 119–23
Maloney, R., 78
Marshall, Tony, 9
Marshall, Trevor, 19
M & V stew, 116

Medjez el Bab, 96, 99, 100
Millett, J., 32, 43
Misfire, 16
Mitton, John, 101, 111
Mole, Walter G., 138, 141
Montgomery, Field Marshal Sir Bernard,
   10, 24, 33, 42, 78, 95, 104
Morrison, Charles, 4

N
Naples, 31, 34, 37
Negro troops, 49
Nevasa, 20–1
Newmark, John, 3, 12, 20, 24
Norfolk Regiment, 123
Normandy, 71–7

O
OCTU, 4
O'Gorman, Dave and Joe, 115
Ordnance Corps, 25
Overseas service, 18–22

P
PAC centres, 33–4
Palembang, River, 122
Parades, 17
Parker, Tishy, 135
Parnacott, Trevor, 3
Payne, T., 31
Pegu, 127
Pellet, Tony, 127
Penn, Arthur, 138
Penrose, H., 18
PIAT mortar, 77
Pickford, Arthur, 12
Poles, 43
Pre-war soldiering, 13–14
Priest, Bill, 66
Prisoners of war, 24, 123
Proclamation Day Parade, 19–20
Punishment, *see* Discipline and
   punishment

Q
Queen Mary, 45
Queen's Own Royal West Kent Regiment,
   3, 10
Queen's Royal Regiment, 104

R
Ramsden, Joseph, 9, 25
Ranchi, 126
Rangoon, 120, 127–8
Rawlinson, H., 104
Regimental pride, 23–4

Regular soldiers, 25
Richmond, F., 115
Ridley, Charles, 9
Rhineland campaign, 78–82
Rodney, Thomas, 25
Rolls, Raymond, 77
Rommel, Field Marshal Erwin, 42, 83, 84,
   88–9, 93
Ronco, River, 111
Rotation, 48
Rowlands, J., 18
Royal Army Medical Corps, 131
Royal Army Service Corps, 133, 138
Royal Tank Regiment, 130
Rules and regulations, 14
Russians, 50–4

S
Salerno, 39, 47
Salzburg, 49
Samuels, H., 52
Saunders, Henry, 131
Seaforth Highlanders, 24, 27, 79
Sex, 31–5
Shaw, F., 130
Sheldrick, Sidney, 121
Shelton, Ann, 140
Shropshire Light Infantry, 24
Sicily, 103–4, 133
Siegfried Line, 78
Singapore, 123–6
Sittang, River, 120
'Soldier's Friend', 8
Soya link sausages, 29
Special Services Brigade, 73
Staples, Sam, 18
Stonard, E. W., 64
Stuart Wilson, R., 87
Stubbings, Bert, 13
Summers, William, 7

T
Talbot, J., 17
Tanks, infantry attitude towards, 94
Tank warfare, 88–9, 93–5, 101–2
Tattoos, 11–12
Territorial Army, 3–7
Thatcher, Brian, 67, 74
Traditions, regimental, 23–4
Training, 8–9, 14, 132
Transport by air, 31
'Trotter's Union', 36; *see also* Desertion
Tunisia, 46–7, 96–102
Turner, Bill, 137, 140
Tyneside Scottish Regiment, 60–1

U
Uniform, 5, 103–4

V
'Varsity', Operation, 82
Venereal disease, 33–4
Villers-Bocage, 75–6

W
Warren, Bunny, 131
Warwickshire Regiment, 24
Watson, Arnold, 124
Weather, 115

Webb, George, 14, 106, 112, 132
Weller, Thomas, 110
'Whohoa Mahommed', 23
Wileman, R. H. C., 15
Withey, A., 11
Wolfsburg, 135
Wounds, 130–4; self-inflicted, 38–9
Wyatt, John, 120

Y
Ypres, 45
Yugoslavs, 54